The
Garland Library
of
War and Peace

The
Garland Library
of
War and Peace

Under the General Editorship of

Blanche Wiesen Cook, *John Jay College, C.U.N.Y.*

Sandi E. Cooper, *Richmond College, C.U.N.Y.*

Charles Chatfield, *Wittenberg University*

Towards An Enduring Peace

A Symposium of Peace Proposals and Programs 1914-1916

compiled by
Randolph S. Bourne

with an introduction by
Franklin H. Giddings

with a new introduction
for the Garland Edition by
Blanche Wiesen Cook

Garland Publishing, Inc., New York & London
1971

Library of Congress Cataloging in Publication Data

Bourne, Randolph Silliman, 1886-1918, comp.
 Towards an enduring peace.

 (The Garland library of war and peace)
 Reprint of the 1916 ed.
 Bibliography: p.
 1. Peace. 2. European war, 1914-1918--Peace.
I. Title. II. Series.
JX1952.B7 1972   327'.172   73-147574
ISBN 0-8240-0340-3

Printed in the United States of America

Introduction

World War I radicalized many American reformers and intellectuals. For Randolph Bourne the transformation was stunning. Generally unaware of international politics only several months before the war, he wrote whimsical letters from the capitals of Europe proclaiming the beauty and tension-free spirit of places and people. In an article for the Columbia University Quarterly, *"Impressions of Europe, 1913-1914," there is no mention of the approaching crisis. Indeed, he acknowledged later that nobody "was more innocent than I of the impending horror." Yet, by 1915 he was one of the leading American critics of the economic, political, and social institutions which, he believed, made war inevitable and revolution likely.*

People as disparate as Vernon Parrington and John Erskine have written that Randolph Bourne was the most articulate and the "most important critic of America" as well as the most dramatic leader of "a kind of youth movement." Known as a "literary radical," which he defined as a "virile artist . . . deeply involved in social problems," he was primarily concerned about the relationship between the individual and the state. Fearful that freedom and liberty would be destroyed by the increasing militari-

5

*zation of America, he announced that "War is the
health of the state." War made the state all-powerful,
leaving no room for individual growth or liberty. War
and militarism, Bourne wrote in a 1914 article "The
Tradition of War," created bloated state institutions
which only benefitted "the aristocratic classes" and
always worked against social reform. He was absolute
in his opposition to the war and believed it not only
would halt social progress but would diminish permanently the very fabric of the American nation.
"War or America," he wrote, "one must choose. One
cannot be interested in both."*

*In "War and the Intellectuals" Bourne noted that
the election of 1916 was a vote by millions of
farmers, small businessmen and workingmen to keep
America out of war. Consequently, he blamed the
"college professors, new-republicans" and intellectuals for "riveting . . . the war-mind on a hundred
million more of the world's people." It was a "war
made deliberately by the intellectuals," and carried to
its outer limits by the lying propaganda of George
Creel's Committee of Public Information. Creel, for
example, insisted that the war was a crusade "not
merely to re-win the tomb of Christ, but to bring
back to earth the rule of right, the peace, goodwill to
men and gentleness He taught." Such statements
made it seem to Bourne that in wartime there was
"no other end but war." War, he insisted, destroyed
everything around it and all the fine intellectual
notions that drove governments to battle were in-*

6

INTRODUCTION

evitably smashed by the devastation it wrought.
There never was and could not be, Bourne concluded,
any kind of "democratic or antiseptic war;" it "must
in the end brutalize." Above all, Bourne believed that
war made inevitable what we now call totalitarianism.
In wartime the state becomes what "in peacetime it
has vainly struggled to become — the inexorable
arbiter and determinant of men's businesses and
attitudes and opinions." Then, loyalty becomes
synonomous with "orthodoxy" and dissent is con-
sidered the highest treason.

In addition to the articles he wrote and the
speeches he gave condemning the war, Randolph
Bourne organized the Committee for Democratic
Control with Amos Pinchot, Max Eastman, and
Winthrop D. Lane. Convinced that the people did not
want war, the Committee lobbied for the democratic
control of foreign policy and demanded that some
kind of referendum precede a declaration of war.
Bourne also worked for the American Association for
International Conciliation which published several
books he edited, including Towards An Enduring
Peace.[1]

Hunchbacked, dwarfed and never in the best of
health, Randolph Bourne died at thirty-one during
the raging flu epidemic of 1918. Many of his essays
originally published in the New Republic, The Dial,

[1] *Other books published by the American Association for
International Conciliation and edited by Bourne were:* Arbitration and
International Politics *(#70) and* The Tradition of War *(#79).*

7

INTRODUCTION

Seven Arts *and* The Masses *have been reprinted and are once again available. And now* Towards An Enduring Peace, *the collection of ideas he and so many others believed would finally lead the world toward international cooperation and progressive social and economic relations is also available.*

Excerpted from books, journal articles, manifestoes and organizational program notes, the selections in this book reflect the idealism of the most significant workers for peace and internationalism. Represented are the programs of the most significant peace organizations founded during the war: the Woman's Peace Party, *the* American Union Against Militarism, *Britain's* Union of Democratic Control, *Holland's* Anti-Oorlog Raad *(the Dutch Anti-War Council) and Germany's Peace Committee, the* Deutsche Friedensgesellschaft. *The individual statements included indicate the great variety of thought on peace and war. Selections by Jane Addams, Norman Angell, Arnold Toynbee, and Romain Rolland are among those presented. It is a valuable collection filled with facts about the origins of the war and warnings about secret treaties which would prevent permanent peace if enacted.*

Despite the factual revelations, Towards An Enduring Peace *is an optimistic collection of essays. For example, the German internationalist Rudolf Eucken believed that World War I might be "the starting-point of a new epoch" of peace and world stability. And why not optimism? As the Columbia University*

INTRODUCTION

professor of sociology Franklin Giddings pointed out
in his introduction, the nineteenth century had ended
"in a blaze of scientific glory ... The struggle for
existence had become a mighty enterprise of progress." Was it so unlikely that man's ability might
now be used to rebuild a reasonable, progressive and
peaceful world? The internationalists of World War I
thought it very likely and presented the programs
included in this book to show the way. They provide
for us today, among other things, an index to how
little on the road toward peace and stability we have
travelled since 1914.

Given Randolph Bourne's vigorous radical posture
and his reputation as a leader of a youth movement,
it is strange that Towards An Enduring Peace should
include such a traditional spokesman for international
arbitration and a League to Enforce Peace by
collective military force as Nicholas Murray Butler.
Stranger still that William English Walling, a socialist
supporter of the war effort who criticized those who
opposed it, should be the one American socialist
represented in the anthology. In his own writings
Bourne had treated these very men with derision.

Perhaps more striking, the optimism of many of
the selections was inconsistent with Bourne's frequently angry despair about the future of man in a
world created by war. It is a great misfortune that the
collection did not include commentary by its editor.
In its present form, this anthology stands in counter-
point to Bourne's other writings. Cherishing reason

and beauty, his mind was torn between despair over their destruction in war and hope for their regeneration in an enduring peace.

Blanche Wiesen Cook
Department of History
John Jay College, C.U.N.Y.

TOWARDS AN
ENDURING PEACE

A SYMPOSIUM OF PEACE
PROPOSALS AND PROGRAMS
1914-1916

COMPILED BY
RANDOLPH S. BOURNE

WITH AN INTRODUCTION BY
FRANKLIN H. GIDDINGS

AMERICAN ASSOCIATION FOR
INTERNATIONAL CONCILIATION
NEW YORK

VAIL - BALLOU COMPANY
BINGHAMTON AND NEW YORK

CONTENTS

iii

PART III. TOWARDS THE FUTURE

APPENDIX: PEACE PROPOSALS AND PROBLEMS

INTRODUCTION

When the storm has gone by and the skies after clearing have softened, we may discover that a corrected perspective is the result of the war that we are most conscious of. Familiar presumptions will appear foreshortened, and new distances of fact and possibility will lie before us.

Before the fateful midsummer of 1914 the most thoughtful part of mankind confidently held a lot of agreeable presumptions which undoubtedly influenced individual and collective conduct. The more intangible of them were grouped under such name symbols as "idealism," "humanitarian impulse," "human brotherhood," "Christian civilization." The workaday ones were pigeonholed under the rubric: "enlightened economic interest." Between the practical and the aspirational were distributed all the excellent Aristotelian middle course presumptions of the "rule of reason" order.

And why not? The nineteenth century had closed in a blaze of scientific glory. By patient inductive research the human mind had found out nature's way on earth and in the heavens, and with daring invention had turned knowledge to immediate practical account. The struggle for existence had become a mighty enterprise of progress. Steam and electricity had brought the utmost parts of the world together. Upon substantial material foundations the twentieth century would build a world republic, wherein justice should apportion abundance.

Upon presumption we reared the tower of expectation.

Yet on the horizon we might have seen—some of us did see—a thickening haze and warning thunderheads. Not much was said about them, but to some it seemed that the world behaved as if it felt the tension of a rising storm. With nervous eagerness the nations pushed their way into the domains of the backward peoples. They sought concessions, opportunities for investment, command of resources, exclusive trade, spheres of influence. Private negotiations were backed by diplomacy, and year after year diplomacy was backed by an ever more impressive show of naval and military power.

But we did not believe that the Great War impended. There would still be restricted wars here and there of course, but more and more they could be prevented. The human mind that had mastered nature's way could master and control the ways of man. Economic interest would bring its resistless strength to bear against the mad makers of the wastes of war. A sensitive conscience would revolt against the cruelties of war. Reason, which had invented rules and agencies to keep the peace within the state, would devise tribunals and procedures to substitute a rational adjustment of differences for the arbitrament of war between states.

The world has recovered from disaster before now, it will recover again. Presumptions that disappointed have been reëxamined and brought into truer drawing. Expectation has been more broadly built, it will be more broadly built again.

There is conscience in mankind, and the war has sublimely revealed it, as it has revealed also undreamed of survivals of faithlessness and cruelty. The presumption of rational control in human affairs has been foreshortened, but not painted out. In the background stand forth as grim realities, forces of fear, distrust, envy, ignorance, and hate that we had thought were ghosts. Conscience is as strong and as sensitive as we believed it to be; reason is as effective as we presumed; but the forces arrayed against them we now see are mightier than we knew. So now we ask, By what power shall conscience and reason be reinforced, and the surviving forces of barbarism be driven back?

There is but one answer left, all others have been shot to pieces. Conscience and reason are effective when they organize material energies, not when they dissipate themselves in dreams. Conscience and reason must assemble, coördinate, and bring to bear the economic resources and the physical energies of the civilized world to narrow the area and to diminish the frequency of war.

But how? General presumptions will not do this time. There must be a specific plan, concrete and practical; a specific preparedness, a specific method. And what is more, plan, preparedness, method must be drawn forth from the situation as the war makes and leaves it, not imposed upon it. They must be a composition of forces now in operation.

There were academic plans aplenty for the creation of pacific internationalism before the war began. The bankers had invented theirs; the socialists, the conciliationists, and the international lawyers respectively had invented theirs. The free traders, first in the field, had not lost hope.

It would be foolish to let ourselves think in discouragement that all these efforts to organize "the international mind" were idle. They were not ineffective. They did not organize the international mind adequately, much less did they reform its habits, but they quickened it; they organized it in part, they pulled it together enough to make it powerful for the work yet to be done.

What we have to face, then, is not the extinction or abandonment of internationalism, but the fact that the ideal, the all-embracing and thoroughly rational internationalism lies far in the future, and that before it can be attained we must have that partial internationalism which is practically the same thing as the widening of nationalism that is achieved when nations coöperate in leagues or combine in federations. The league of peace may be academic or it may soon stand forth as a tremendous piece of realism, we do not know which, but the forces that are holding many of the nations together in military coöperation now are present realities, and they will be realities after the military war is over. There will still be tariffs, but the areas within which tariff barriers will no longer be maintained will be immensely widened. Beyond these areas will be, as now, various arrangements of reciprocity. In like manner, there will be a determination on the part of the coöperating nations to stand together for the enforcement of international agreements and to discipline a law-breaking state that would needlessly resort to arms. The internationalism of commerce, of travel, of communication, of intellectual exchange and moral endeavor will continue to grow throughout the world, but in addition there will be the more definite, the more concrete internationalism of

x

the nations that agree in making common cause for the attainment of specific ends.

Within this relatively restricted internationalism there will be, there is now, a certain yet more definite aggregation of peoples, interests, and traditions upon which rests a great and peculiar moral responsibility. The English-speaking people of the world are together the largest body of human beings among whom a nearly complete intellectual and moral understanding is already achieved. They have reached high attainments in science and the arts, in education, in social order, in justice. They are highly organized, they cherish the traditions of their common history. To permit anything to endanger the moral solidarity of this nucleus of a perfected internationalism would be a crime unspeakable. To strengthen it, to make it one of the supreme forces working for peace and humanity is a supreme obligation.

FRANKLIN H. GIDDINGS.

CONCERNING THE AUTHORS QUOTED

Jane Addams has been head resident at Hull House in Chicago for many years. She is widely known for her leadership in the social movement, and particularly for her connection with the International Congress of Women at The Hague.

Norman Angell is the author of "The Great Illusion," and one of the most brilliant of the workers in the cause of peace. He is also the author of "International Polity," "Arms and Industry," and "The World's Highway."

Ed. Bernstein is one of the leaders of the German Social Democracy of the revisionist wing.

H. N. Brailsford is a prominent English traveler, correspondent, and essayist, and one of the most illuminating writers on world-problems. His books include "The War of Steel and Gold," "Shelley, Godwin and their Circle."

Nicholas Murray Butler is President of Columbia University, Acting Director of the Division of Intercourse and Education of the Carnegie Endowment for International Peace and Chairman of the American Association for International Conciliation.

Charles Roden Buxton is a prominent English Liberal, and member of the Union for Democratic Control.

John Bates Clark is Director of the Division of Economics and History of the Carnegie Endowment for International Peace and Professor of Political Economy at Columbia University.

Bernhard Dernburg is the German ex-Minister of Colonies, who spent some time in America at the beginning of the war as semi-official spokesman for German opinion.

Charles W. Eliot is President Emeritus of Harvard University, and a leader in the peace movement.

Rudolf Eucken is one of the most widely-known of living German philosophers. He visited America in 1913.

G. Lowes Dickinson of Cambridge University, England, is author of "Letters of a Chinese Official," "Justice and Liberty," "A Modern Symposium," etc.

Franklin H. Giddings is Professor of Sociology at Columbia University.

John A. Hobson is one of the best-known English economists, the author of "The Rise of Modern Capitalism," "The Science of Wealth," "The Industrial System," "Towards International Government," etc.

Hamilton Holt is managing editor of *The Independent*.

Paul U. Kellogg is an editor of the *Survey* in New York.

Walter Lippmann is one of the most brilliant of the younger American publicists, an editor of the *New Republic,* and author of "A Preface to Politics," "Drift and Mastery," and "The Stakes of Diplomacy."

A. Lawrence Lowell is President of Harvard University.

Romain Rolland is the author of "Jean-Christophe." His attitude on the war has forced his exile from France to Geneva. His eloquent book "Above the Battle" expresses the emotion of a cosmopolitan soul confronted with the madness of a world-war.

Prof. L. Quidde was one of the leading German pacifists before the war.

A. A. Tenney is assistant Professor of Sociology at Columbia University.

Arnold J. Toynbee is the son-in-law of Prof. Gilbert Murray, and the author of "Nationality and the War," and "Greek Policy Since 1882." He is one of the most brilliant students of problems of nationality.

Lillian Wald is head-worker at the Henry Street Settlement in New York City.

William English Walling is a prominent American Socialist, editor of the *New Review,* and author of "Socialists and the War," etc.

Alfred E. Zimmern is in the English Education service, and is author of "The Greek Commonwealth."

PREFACE

The aim of this book is to present a discussion of some of the most hopeful and constructive suggestions for the settlement of the war on terms that would make for a lasting peace. The selections are taken from books, magazines, manifestoes, programs, etc., that have appeared since the beginning of the war. Part I contains a discussion of the general principles of a settlement, economic and political. Part II contains the more concrete suggestions for the constitution of a definite League of Peace. Part III presents some of the reconstructive ideals—"Towards the Future"—as voiced by writers in the different countries. In the Appendix are collected definite programs for peace put forward by associations and individuals, international organizations, etc., in this country, Great Britain, Germany, France, Holland, Denmark and Sweden, and Switzerland.

The books quoted form, it is believed, an indispensable library for the understanding of international questions:

"Nationality and the War," by Arnold J. Toynbee. New York: E. P. Dutton and Co.

"Towards International Government," by John A. Hobson.

"The Stakes of Diplomacy," by Walter Lippmann. New York: Henry Holt and Co.

"The Road Toward Peace," by Charles W. Eliot. Boston: Houghton Mifflin Co.

"The War of Steel and Gold," by H. N. Brailsford. New York: Macmillan.

"The War and Democracy," by A. E. Zimmern and others. New York: Macmillan.

"The World's Highway," by Norman Angell. New York: Geo. H. Doran & Co.

PART I

PRINCIPLES OF THE SETTLEMENT

PART I. PRINCIPLES OF THE SETTLEMENT: ECONOMIC

PROBLEMS OF ECONOMIC OPPORTUNITY

The growing dependence of modern civilized and thickly populated countries for the necessaries of life and industry, for commercial profits, and for gainful investments of capital upon free access to other countries, especially to countries differing from themselves in climate, natural resources, and degree of economic development, is of necessity a consideration of increasing weight in the foreign policy of to-day. Every active industrial or commercial nation is therefore fain to watch and guard its existing opportunities for foreign trade and investment, and to plan ahead for enlarged opportunities to meet the anticipated future needs of an expanding trade and a growing population. It views with fear, suspicion, and jealousy every attempt of a foreign country to curtail its liberty of access to other countries and its equal opportunities for advantageous trade or exploitation. The chief substance of the treaties, conventions, and agreements between modern nations in recent times has consisted in arrangements about commercial and financial opportunities, mostly in countries outside the acknowledged control of the negotiating parties. The real origins of most quarrels between such nations have related to tariffs, railway, banking, commercial, and financial operations in lands belonging to

Most international quarrels have economic origin.

3

one or other of the parties, or in lands where some
sphere of special interest was claimed. Egypt, Morocco,
Persia, Asia Minor, China, Congo, Mexico, are the most
sensitive spots affecting international relations outside
of Europe, testifying to the predominance of economic
considerations in foreign policy. The stress laid upon
such countries hinges in the last resort upon the need of
"open doors" or upon the desire to close doors to other
countries. These keenly felt desires to safeguard existing foreign markets for goods and capital, to obtain by
diplomatic pressure or by force new markets, and in
other cases to monopolize markets, have everywhere been
the chief directing influences in foreign policy, the chief
causes of competing armaments, and the permanent underlying menaces to peace. The present war, when regard
is had to the real directing pressure behind all diplomatic
acts and superficial political ferments, is in the main a
product of these economic antagonisms. This point of
view is concisely and effectively expressed in a striking
memorandum presented by the Reform Club of New
York to President Wilson:—

> Consider the situation of the present belligerents.
> Serbia wants a window on the sea, and is shut out by Aus-
> trian influence.
> Austria wants an outlet in the East, Constantinople or
> Salonica.
> Russia wants ice-free ports on the Baltic and Pacific,
> Constantinople, and a free outlet from the Black Sea into
> the Mediterranean.
> Germany claims to be hemmed in by a ring of steel, and
> needs the facilities of Antwerp and Rotterdam for her Rhine
> Valley commerce, security against being shut out from the
> East by commercial restrictions on the overland route, and
> freedom of the seas for her foreign commerce.
> England must receive uninterrupted supplies of food and
> raw materials, and her oversea communications must be
> maintained.

4

This is true also of France, Germany, Belgium, and other European countries. Desire for commercial privilege is the primary cause of war.

Japan, like Germany, must have opportunity for her expanding population, industries, and commerce.

The foreign policies of the nations still at peace are also determined by trade relations. Our own country desires the open door in the East.

South and North American States and Scandinavia are already protesting against the war's interference with their ocean trade.

All nations that are not in possession of satisfactory harbors on the sea demand outlets, and cannot and ought not to be contented till they get them.

Nations desiring to extend their colonial enterprises entertain those ambitions for commercial reasons, either to possess markets from which they cannot be excluded, or to develop such markets for themselves and be able to exclude others from them when they so determine.

The generalization from these statements of fact is expressed in the formula, "The desire for commercial privilege and for freedom from commercial restraint is the primary cause of war."

Now, that the foreign policies of nations are, in fact, determined mainly by these commercial and financial considerations, and that the desire to secure economic privilege and to escape economic restraints is a chief cause of war, are indisputable propositions. So long as these motives are left free to work in the future as in the past there will be constant friction among the commercially developed nations, giving rise to dangerous quarrels that will strain, perhaps to the breaking-point, any arrangements for arbitration that may be made. . . .

Disputes arising from these economic causes are even deeper seated and more dangerous than those connected with the claims of nationality and autonomy. Indeed, political autonomy is shorn of most of its value unless

5

it is accompanied by a large measure of economic liberty
as regards commercial relations with the outside world.
The case of Serbia, liable at any moment to be denied
access to the sea, or to be cut off by Austria from her
chief land markets, is a case in point. Or once again,
would the autonomy of such a country as Hungary, Bohemia, or Poland, however valid its political guarantees,
satisfy the legitimate aspirations of its population if
high tariff-walls encompassed it on every frontier?
Such instances make it evident that no settlement of
"the map of Europe" on lines of nationality can suffice
to establish peace. The effective liberty of every people
demands freedom of commercial intercourse with other
peoples. A refusal or a hindrance of such intercourse
deprives a people of its fair share of the common fruits
of the earth, and deprives the other peoples of the world
of any special fruits which it is able to contribute to the
common stock.

If any international Government existed, representing
the commonwealth of nations, it would seek to remove
all commercial restrictions which impair the freedom of
economic intercourse between nations.

These restrictions are placed by the Reform Club
Memorandum under the four following categories:—

First. There is the restriction of tariffs imposed by nations.

Second. There are restrictions upon the best uses of
International commerce, of the terminal and land transfer
facilities of the great trade routes and seaports of the world.
A few such ports command entrance to and exit from vast
continental hinterlands. It is vital to these interior regions
that their natural communications with the outside world
should be kept widely open, and this is equally vital to the
rest of the world. Obstructive control of such ports and
routes to the detriment of the world's commerce cannot and
should not be tolerated by states whose interests are ad-

versely affected. But routes and ports are needed for use, not government; and port rivalries constantly tend towards offering the best and equal facilities to all. The swelling tides of commerce are clearing their own channels, and mutual interests will more and more prompt the states through which the principal trade routes pass to facilitate the movement of commerce.

Third. There are restrictions upon opportunities to trade with territories ruled as colonies or being exploited within spheres of influence. This is what now remains of the old mercantile system which flourished before our Revolutionary War, and which has been weakening ever since. Great Britain claims no preference for herself in her colonies. Other states have been less liberal. The fear of such restrictions being applied against them is to-day the main motive for a policy of colonial oversea possessions. If industrial states could be assured of the application of the open-door policy, no state would envy another its colonies. Colonies should be the world's.

Fourth. There are restrictions in the free use of the sea. Unlike land routes, ocean routes are offered practically without cost to all, whithersoever the sea runs. Over these, however, until modern times commerce has been subject to pillage by regular warships as well as by pirates. The claims of commerce have been more slowly recognized on the sea than on the land; and, to an extent now unthinkable on land, warring states still feel free to interfere with neutral traders. . . .

Another factor of increasing importance in the recent conflict of nations has been the competition between groups of financiers and concessionaires, organized upon a "national" basis, to obtain exclusive or preferential control in the undeveloped countries for the profitable use of exported capital. Closely related to commercial competition, this competition for lucrative investments has played an even greater part in producing dangerous international situations. For these financial and commercial interests have sought to use the political and the forcible resources of their respective Governments to enable them to obtain the concessions and other privileges they require for the security and profitable application of their capital. The control of foreign policy thus wielded has been fraught with two perils to world-peace. It has brought the Governments of the competing financial groups into constant friction, and it has been the most fruitful direct source of expeditionary forces and territorial aggressions in the coveted areas. As the struggle for lucrative overseas investments has come to occupy a more important part than the struggle for ordinary markets, the economic oppositions between European Governments have become more and more the determinant factors in foreign policy, and in the competition of armaments, upon which Governments rely to support and to achieve the aims their economic masters impose upon them.

John A. Hobson, "Towards International Government," pp. 128–139.

8

TRADE AS A CAUSE OF WAR

Decent men in the belligerent countries feel a natural Idealism hides real causes of war. repugnance in time of war to any discussion of the economic bearings of the struggle. If nations are to fight with clear consciences and single hearts, they must fight on in the belief that any objects which concern their statesmen beyond the objects of defense and national security are purely idealistic. We are all pragmatists in wartime; we believe what will conduce to victory. Cool observers see clearly the widening out of an immense range of colonial, imperial, and economic issues which will confront us at the settlement and after it. But these things are not debated as we debate the issues of nationality in this war. One might suppose from a study of our press that we are much more vitally interested in the fate of the Slovenes than we are in the trade of China.

This idealism is absolutely sincere, and a natural consequence of the exaltation of emotion which belongs to any war of nations. We can endure the thought that our young men are falling in many thousands for the liberties of little peoples. That brief statement of our aims would end in bathos if we were to add to it the subjection of China to Japanese suzerainty, the partition of Turkey into spheres of influence, the acquisition by the Allies of the German colonies, and the setting up of a Russian customs house at Constantinople. The mischief of this obsession is that the very field which stands

9

Our need is
organization
to make
international
change with-
out war.

most in need of illumination from critical yet idealistic thinking is left in a half light of semi-secrecy, and the will of democracies hardly dreams of intervening in the clash of the interests which divide it. Public opinion and the fortunes of war will govern the settlement of Belgium and Alsace, but in our present temper it is only too probable that all the colonial and economic issues involved in it will be left to the diplomatists with only the interests behind them.

The penetrating memorandum addressed by the New York Reform Club to President Wilson has sketched broadly but with sure insight the commercial and colonial questions which helped to lead up to this war. None of these issues appeared in the negotiations which preceded the war, but most of them were latent in the consciousness of the statesmen and even of the peoples. The curse of our unorganized Europe has been that fundamental change has rarely been possible save as a sequel of war. Diplomacy was always busied with a pathetic conservatism in bolstering up the *status quo,* or in arranging those little readjustments which might just avail to stave off war. We shall not banish war from Europe until we are civilized enough to create an organization that can make and impose fundamental changes without war. The best we can do in the meantime is to prepare to avail ourselves of the brief moment of settlement during which the structure of Europe will still be fluid under the shock of war, to bring our idealistic and democratic forces to bear upon these larger issues.

The Reform Club's memorandum deals with three of these questions: the abolition of capture at sea in wartime, the freedom of the world's straits and highways in time of war, and the exploitation of colonies under a system of protection. The system of legalized piracy

10

which permits navies to prey on commerce in wartime is Free trade would remove incentive for colonies— undoubtedly the most potent incentive to swollen armaments at sea. So long as it survives, the opinion of the mercantile classes will never effectively back the demand for economy in armaments, for it is bound to regard navies as an insurance. The question of the ownership of straits stands high among the many competing causes of bloodshed. It explains the German struggle for Calais no less than the Allied expedition to the Dardanelles. One may doubt, however, whether a proposal to neutralize any of the more vital of these straits—the Straits of Dover or Gibraltar, for example—would stand a chance of calm consideration on the morrow of such a war as this. It will be feasible when war is no longer an ever-present terror; and when that day comes it will have lost its importance. Far more central in our problem is the general question of colonialism. It is a commonplace to say that modern industrial peoples desire colonies almost solely for economic reasons, and that one of the chief motives for this expansion would disappear with any approach to free trade. If the British colonies had not granted a preference to the mother country, and if French colonies were not hedged about with an impenetrable tariff wall, the feeling among German industrialists that their expansion was "hemmed in" would have been less acute, and the pressure for "places in the sun" would have been less powerful.

But it is doubtful whether the question of markets is as potent a cause of armaments and war as the competition to secure concessions, monopolies, and spheres of influence. The export of capital means much more for the modern politics of imperialism than the export of manufactured goods. The *conquistador* of to-day is the financier who acquires mining rights in Morocco, loan privileges in Turkey, or railway concessions in

China. The foreign policy of Great Britain and our
place in the European system has been governed for a
generation by the occupation of Egypt, whither we went
in the wake of the bond-holders. It explains our long
bickerings with France; it helped to fling an isolated
France into the arms of Russia; it brought us finally
into the disastrous bargain over Morocco which underlay
our feud with Germany. The competition of national
financial groups for concessions in Turkey or China is
not the competition of the market-place at home. Behind the financier stands the diplomatist, and behind
the diplomatist is his navy. There is a clash of armor-
plates when these competitors jostle. The struggle for
a Balance of Power in Europe has often seemed little
more than a race for the force and prestige which would
enable the dominant Power or group of Powers to secure
the concessions of the monopoly spheres which it coveted
in the half-developed regions of the earth. No modern
nation would openly make war to secure such ends as
these, for no democracy would support it. Even the
half-evolved democracy of Russia recoiled from the
Manchurian War. But every nation, by pursuing these
ends, makes the armed peace and the unstable equilibrium which prepares our wars.

The remedy is so simple that only a very clever man
could sophisticate himself into missing it, and it is as
old as Cobden. It is not necessary to establish universal
free trade to stop the rivalry to monopolize colonial markets; it would suffice to declare free trade in the colonies,
or even in those which are not self-governing. To deal
with the evil of ''concessions'' all that is required is a
general understanding that financiers must win their
own way, by merit or push or bribes, and that the doors
of the embassies will be banged in their faces when they
seek support. These sentences are easily written, but

12

they would involve the democratization of diplomacy everywhere, the overthrow of the colonial group in France, and the confounding of the national economists in Germany. Colonial free trade must be declared by international agreement, The force which might work such miracles is nowhere mobilized, for, with all their will to peace, the democracies nowhere understand the bearings of these colonial and commercial issues on war and armaments. It requires some imagination to understand that when two embassies compete in Peking for a railway concession, the issue may be determined by the balance of naval power in the North Sea. It requires some habit of observation to realize that because this may happen in Peking, the investing and governing classes are bound to keep up the balance in the North Sea. The nexus is none the less simple and clear, and it will hold as long as diplomacy continues to engage in this disguised imperial trading, so long as capital possesses nationality and regards the flag as an asset.

There are none the less ways of escape which are neither Utopian nor heroic. It ought not to be utterly beyond the statesmanship of Europe to decree some limited form of colonial free trade by general agreement —to apply it, for example, to Africa. France would oppose it, but what if Alsace were to be restored on this condition? To open a great colonial market to Hamburg, while ending the dream of *revanche,* would be to remove the two chief causes of war in western Europe. American statesmanship may ere long have the power to propose such a bargain as this. For the plague of concession-hunting the best expedient would probably be to impose on all the competing national groups in each area the duty of amalgamating in a permanently international syndicate. If one such syndicate controlled all the railways and another all the mines of China and Turkey, a vast cause of national rivalry would be re-

13

and the
export of
capital inter-
nationalized. moved. The interests of China and Turkey might be
secured by interposing a disinterested council or arbitrator between them and the syndicate to adjust their
respective interests. Short of creating a world state or
a European federation, the chief constructive work for
peace is to establish colonial free trade and internationalize the export of capital.

*H. N. Brailsford, "Trade as a Cause of War," The
New Republic, May 8, 1915.*

14

ECONOMIC IMPERIALISM

The evils of an unrestricted competition for conces- sions and monopolies between rival financial groups backed by their Governments, are so notorious that diplomacy has found several typical formulæ for bringing them to an end. The obvious method of resolving such conflicts is the demarcation of spheres of "influences," "interest" or "penetration" within which each of the competing Powers enjoys a monopoly respected by the others. This method is open to two grave objections. In the first place, it is rarely adopted before a ruinous conflict has exhausted the competitors. For years or decades they carry on a trial of strength which affects not merely their local relationship, but their attitude to one another in Europe, and is measured year by year in their military and naval estimates. If we were to take the sum by which British and German armaments have increased in the present century, it would be possible to allocate the increase, roughly, somewhat as follows: 50 per cent. or less for the settlement of the question, Who shall exploit Morocco?; 25 per cent. or more for the privilege of building a railway to Bagdad and beyond it; 25 per cent. or more for the future eventualities which remain unsettled—the fate of the Portuguese colonies in Africa, and the destinies of China. In the second place, the delimitation of spheres of interest is almost inevitably fatal to the national existence of the country partitioned, and as inevitably adds a vast burden to the commitments of the Imperial Power. Persia

15

furnishes the obvious illustration. Sir Edward Grey is
clearly resolved that he will not allow himself by the
march of events to be drawn into the assumption of any
direct responsibility for the administration of the British sphere. It is a laudable resolve, but Russia may at
any moment frustrate it. She deals with her own
sphere on the opposite principle, and her sphere happens
to include the seat of the central government. That
government is already a puppet of Russian policy, en-
joying only a simulacrum of independence. How much
longer can a government which is not a government continue to rule the southern sphere? Sooner or later a
choice must be made. Either Russia must withdraw, or
some separate government under British protection must
be created for the south. Turkey is drifting rapidly
towards a dissolution in which the spheres which the
Great Powers already claim will be formally delimited.
It is easy to predict what that will mean. There will
be first provincial loans, then provincial advisers, and
finally a military control, under which each of these
"spheres" will become what Egypt already is, a depen-
dency of a European Power.

The method of avoiding financial competition by
marking off zones of monopoly, is clearly the worst
which can be pursued. There are alternatives. Let us
consider what methods might be followed if the Powers
were sage enough to shrink from the terrific conflict
which may one day overtake them for the partition of
China. China is so thickly peopled that crude conquest
presents few attractions. Even Japan could not settle
her surplus population in a country where every hill is
terraced and every field subjected to intensive cultiva-
tion. But there is here a field which capital is already
eager to exploit, and every year diminishes the resistance
of prejudice and inertia to its ambitions. The attempts

16

to mark out spheres of influence have so far been tenta- tive and unsuccessful. Our own claim to the lion's share, the Yangtse Valley, is admitted by no other Power, and it is doubtful whether the Foreign Office still maintains it. There are several principles which might be adopted if the Powers desired to avoid the jealous and dangerous struggle for concessions. In the first place, the simplest plan and the best would be the adoption of a self-denying ordinance by all the chief competitors. Let it be understood that British, French, and German banks may compete among themselves for railways and loans, but that none of them shall receive any aid or countenance whatever from the embassies or consulates of their respective countries. If that could be decided, the allotment of concessions would be set- tled either by the merits of the competitors or more prob- ably by their skill and audacity in bribing Chinese offi- cials. One may doubt, however, whether any of the Powers has sufficient faith in the honor of its competi- tors to enter on such an undertaking. A second and more hopeful plan might be borrowed from the under- taking negotiated by France and Germany over Morocco. They agreed to promote cooperation among their sub- jects, who were to share in agreed percentages in the coveted opportunities for public works. A vast ''pool'' or syndicate in which all the rival financial groups were represented, might be left to internationalize all the op- portunities of monopoly in China on a plan which would give to each its allotted share in the risks and profits. The scheme worked badly in Morocco, and indeed created the friction which led to the Agadir incident. Some- thing of the kind existed in China while the alliance of the banks of the Six Powers subsisted, and it eventually broke down. By this method friction may be avoided among the Great Powers, but China would be subjected

17

to an intolerable financial dictation, which would be
none the less oppressive because it was cosmopolitan.
There exists, however, in the Ottoman Public Debt, a
model which might be followed elsewhere. Its council
represents all the bondholders of every nationality, and
usually maintains good relations with the Porte. If the
railways of Turkey, China, and Persia could be amalgamated, each in a single system under a cosmopolitan
administration, the risk of partition and all the danger
to peace, which this risk entails, might be removed. The
obvious step is to confer on these syndicates of capitalists an international legal personality, which would enable them to sue or be sued before the Hague Tribunal.
Some disinterested council nominated by The Hague
should be interposed between the syndicate and the State
in which it operates, so that the intervention of diplomacy may be as far as possible eliminated.

The problems raised by the export of capital have
been considered in this chapter mainly from the standpoint of the creditor State, which sees its diplomacy involved in the process. We have found, so far, no solution which is satisfactory from the standpoint of the
debtor nation. The inroad of foreign capital always
means for it some loss of independence, and it has nothing to gain by agreements among competing Empires.
It may, indeed, keep its independence by playing on
their rivalries. Its shadowy autonomy vanishes when
they come to terms. The pacifist and the nationalist
are here divided in their sympathies. The former,
thinking only of European peace, rejoices when Russia
and Britain end their differences by the partition of
Persia. The latter, seeing only that a nation has been
destroyed, regards the agreement as a peculiarly evil
development of Imperialism. Both are right, and both
are wrong. The ideal expedient would preserve Euro-

18

pean peace without destroying the victim nationality. The Drago Doctrine.
To propose that expedient requires an excursion into
the realms of Utopian construction. We can propose
nothing which seems feasible to-day, but a solution is
conceivable which requires only an easy step in the
organization of the civilized world for peace. The motives for the partition of Persia were rather political
than financial. The object-lesson of Egypt, where the
occupation had its origin in debt, is a more typical instance of modern processes. It happens that the Hague
Conference has laid down a principle which is capable
of fruitful extension for dealing with such cases as these.
The Drago Doctrine, put forward by Señor Drago, a
jurist and statesman of the Argentine Republic, supported by the United States and eventually adopted by
all the Powers, provides that no creditor State may
use arms to enforce a liability upon a debtor State, unless a decision of the Hague Tribunal has recognized
the liability and prescribed the method of payment.
This doctrine, even as it stands, is of immense value to
minor but civilized States like the South American republics, Portugal and Greece, which may find themselves
obliged to defer payment of an external debt. The
Hague Tribunal would in such a case, if it realized its
opportunities, act as a good County Court Judge would
do at home—refuse to admit a merely usurious claim,
and lay down terms and dates of payment which would
admit of the debtor's recovery from any temporary difficulty.

But to defeat the more unscrupulous methods of the
international usurer, this idea requires some amplifica-
tion. It may be necessary for a debtor State, some
grades below the level of Portugal and Greece in civilization, to mortgage some part of its revenues, and to
accept, at least over part of them, some degree of foreign

control. That means, if the creditor country has also
political ambitions, the almost certain loss of its independence. There are also States like Turkey which
stand in need of expert advice for the reorganization
of their finances, but dread the consequences of admitting any foreigner, who may perhaps think more of the
interests of European finance and of his own mother-
land, than of those of the country which employs him.
To draw the full advantage from the international machinery at The Hague, there ought to be evolved a permanent Credit Bureau to which weak and timid States
might apply. It might conduct enquiries into their sol-
vency, lend them experts to reorganize their finances,
help them to negotiate loans in neutral markets on fair
terms, and in case of need provide the commissioners who
would control their mortgaged revenues. It would act
as a trustee or as a Court of Chancery towards its wards.
It could have no political ambitions to further, and the
country which applied to it need not tremble for its
independence. Persia or Egypt, had this Bureau existed, might have turned to The Hague for help. If, in
the end, owing to civil war, or the hopeless incapacity
of native statesmen, forcible intervention became inevitable, it would lie not with any interested Power, but
with The Hague itself, to take the initiative of summoning a European Conference to prescribe the nature and
limits of the interference. It is even possible that the
Bureau might be used as an arbitrator at the request
of a State like China, hard pressed by the rivalry of Empires competing for concessions, to decide between them
in its name, and to appoint a neutral adviser or board of
advisers, who would stand between it and the greedy
Powers in the allotment of its financial patronage.

A Europe which has organized itself for peace will
be at no loss for expedients wherewith to reconcile the

20

appetites of capital with the rights of nationality. A spectator of the moving cosmopolitan drama which is played, the world over, around this central motive of the export of capital, can readily invent attractive schemes for the regulation of the process. But such exercises tempt one to ignore the dynamics of the problem. The same primitive forces of greed which in earlier centuries inspired conquests and migrations are still strong enough to grip diplomacy and build navies. Our first task is to win at home the power to control this export of capital, to check it where it disregards the current ethical standards, to rebuff it where it would lead us into international rivalry, and at last to use it as the potent servant of a humane diplomacy. It can be forbidden to carry the devastations of slavery into distant continents. It can be checked in its usurer's practises upon simple States. It can be used, if it be firmly mastered, to starve into submission a semi-civilized Empire which meditates aggressive war, or draws from Western stores the funds to finance its own oppressions.

H. N. Brailsford, "The War of Steel and Gold," pp. 241–253.

THE PROBLEM OF DIPLOMACY

The chief
problem of
diplomacy is
the weak
State.

This whole business of jockeying for position is at first glance so incredibly silly that many liberals regard diplomacy as a cross between sinister conspiracy and a meaningless etiquette. It would be all of that if the stakes of diplomacy were not real. Those stakes have to be understood, for without such an understanding diplomacy is incomprehensible and any scheme of world peace an idle fancy.

The chief, the overwhelming problem of diplomacy seems to be the weak state—the Balkans, the African sultanates, Turkey, China, and Latin America, with the possible exception of the Argentine, Chile, and Brazil. These states are "weak" because they are industrially backward and at present politically incompetent. They are rich in resources and cheap labor, poor in capital, poor in political experience, poor in the power of defense. The government of these states is the supreme problem of diplomacy. Just as the chief task of American politics to the Civil War was the organization of the unexploited West, so the chief task of world diplomacy to-day is the organization of virgin territory and backward peoples. I use backward in the conventional sense to mean a people unaccustomed to modern commerce and modern political administration.

This solicitude about backward peoples seems to many

22

good democrats a combination of superciliousness and greed. . . .

And yet the plain fact is that the interrelation of peoples has gone so far that to advocate international laissez-faire now is to speak a counsel of despair. Commercial cunning, lust of conquest, rum, bibles, rifles, missionaries, traders, concessionaires have brought the two civilizations into contact, and the problem created must be solved, not evaded.

The great African empires, for example, were not created deliberately by theoretical imperialists. Explorers, missionaries, and traders penetrated these countries. They found rubber, oil, cocoa, tin; they could sell cotton goods, rifles, liquor. The native rulers bartered away enormous riches at trivial prices. But the trading-posts and the concessions were insecure. There were raids and massacres. No public works existed, no administrative machinery. The Europeans exploited the natives cruelly, and the natives retaliated. Concession hunters and merchants from other nations began to come in. They bribed and bullied the chiefs, and created still greater insecurity. An appeal would be made to the home government for help, which generally meant declaring a protectorate of the country. Armed forces were sent in to pacify, and civil servants to administer the country. These protectorates were generally sanctioned by the other European governments on the proviso that trade should be free to all. . . .

It is essential to remember that what turns a territory into a diplomatic "problem" is the combination of natural resources, cheap labor, markets, defenselessness, corrupt and inefficient government. The desert of Sahara is no "problem," except where there are oases and trade routes. Switzerland is no "problem," for Switzerland is a highly organized modern state. But Mexico is a

23

problem, and Haiti, and Turkey, and Persia. They have the pretension of political independence which they do not fulfil. They are seething with corruption, eaten up with "foreign" concessions, and unable to control the adventurers they attract or safeguard the rights which these adventurers claim. More foreign capital is invested in the United States than in Mexico, but the United States is not a "problem" and Mexico is. The difference was hinted at in President Wilson's speech at Mobile. Foreigners invest in the United States, and they are assured that life will be reasonably safe and that titles to property are secured by orderly legal means. But in Mexico they are given "concessions," which means that they secure extra privileges and run greater risks, and they count upon the support of European governments or of the United States to protect them and their property.

The weak states, in other words, are those which lack the political development that modern commerce requires. To take an extreme case which brings out the real nature of the "problem," suppose that the United States was organized politically as England was in the time of William the Conqueror. Would it not be impossible to do business in the United States? There would be an everlasting clash between an impossible legal system and a growing commercial development. And the internal affairs of the United States would constitute a diplomatic "problem."

This, it seems to me, is the reason behind the outburst of modern imperialism among the Great Powers. It is not enough to say that they are "expanding" or "seeking markets" or "grabbing resources." They are doing all these things, of course. But if the world into which they are expanding were not politically archaic, the growth of foreign trade would not be accompanied

24

by political imperialism. Germany has "expanded" only through order and political control. wonderfully in the British Empire, in Russia, in the United States, but no German is silly enough to insist on planting his flag wherever he sells his dyestuffs or stoves. It is only when his expansion is into weak states—into China, Morocco, Turkey, or elsewhere that foreign trade is imperialistic. This imperialism is actuated by many motives—by a feeling that political control insures special privileges, by a desire to play a large part in the world, by national vanity, by a passion for "ownership," but none of these motives would come into play if countries like China or Turkey were not politically backward.

Imperialism in our day begins generally as an attempt to police and pacify. This attempt stimulates national pride, it creates bureaucrats with a vested interest in imperialism, it sucks in and receives added strength from concessionaires and traders who are looking for economic privileges. There is no doubt that certain classes in a nation gain by imperialism, though to the people as a whole the adventure may mean nothing more than an increased burden of taxes.

Some pacifists have attempted to deny that a nation could ever gain anything by political control of weak states. They have not defined the "nation." What they overlook is that even the most advanced nations are governed, not by the "people," but by groups with special interests. These groups do gain, just as the railroad men who controlled American legislatures gained. A knot of traders closely in league with the colonial office of a great Power can make a good deal of money out of its friendships. Every government has contracts to be let, franchises to give; it establishes tariffs, fixes railroad rates, apportions taxes, creates public works, builds roads. To be favored by that power is to be

The
backward
States are
the arenas of
international
friction

favored indeed. The favoritism may cost the mother-
land and the colony dear, but the colonial merchant is
not a philanthropist. . . .

The whole situation might be summed up by saying
that the commercial development of the world will not
wait until each territory has created for itself a stable
and fairly modern political system. By some means or
other the weak states have to be brought within the
framework of commercial administration. Their independence and integrity, so-called, are dependent upon
their creating conditions under which world-wide business can be conducted. The pressure to organize the
globe is enormous. . . .

Out of this complexity of motive there is created a
union of various groups on the imperial program: the
diplomatic group is interested primarily in prestige; the
military group in an opportunity to act; the bureau-
cratic in the creation of new positions; the financial
groups in safeguarding investments; traders in securing
protection and privileges, religious groups in civilizing
the heathen, the "intellectuals," in realizing theories of
expansion and carrying out "manifest destinies," the
people generally in adventure and glory and the sense
of being great. These interested groups severally control public opinion, and under modern methods of publicity public opinion is easily "educated."

Who should intervene in backward states, what the
intervention shall mean, how the protectorate shall be
conducted—this is the bone and sinew of modern diplomacy. The weak spots of the world are the arenas of
friction. This friction is increased and made popular
by frontier disputes over Alsace-Lorraine or Italia Irredenta, but in my judgment the boundary lines of Europe are not the grand causes of diplomatic struggle.
Signor Ferrero confessed recently that the present gen-

eration of Italians had all but forgotten Italia Irredenta, War is for sake of prestige in undeveloped countries. and the Revanche has been a decadent French dream until the Entente and the Dual Alliance began to clash in Morocco, in Turkey, in China. Alsace-Lorraine has no doubt kept alive suspicion of Germany, and predisposed French opinion to inflicting diplomatic defeats in Morocco. But the arena where the European Powers really measure their strength against each other is in the Balkans, in Africa, and in Asia. . . .

This war is fought not for specific possessions, but for that diplomatic prestige and leadership which are required to solve all the different problems. It is like a great election to decide who shall have the supreme power in the Concert of Europe. Austria began the contest to secure her position as a great Power in the Balkans; Russia entered it to thwart this ambition; France was engaged because German diplomatic supremacy would reduce France to a "second-class power," which means a power that holds world power on sufferance; England could not afford to see France "crushed" or Belgium annexed because British imperialism cannot alone cope with the vigor of Germany; Germany felt herself "encircled," which meant that wherever she went—to Morocco, Asia Minor, or China— there a coalition was ready to thwart her. The ultimate question involved was this: whenever in the future diplomats meet to settle a problem in the backward countries, which European nation shall be listened to most earnestly? What shall be the relative prestige of Germans and Englishmen and Frenchmen and Russians; what sense of their power, what historical halo, what threat of force, what stimulus to admiration shall they possess? To lose this war will be like being a Republican politician in the solid South when the Democrats are in

World
problem is
due to com-
petition for
unorganized
territory.
power at Washington. It will mean political, social, and economic inferiority.

Americans have every reason to understand the dangers of unorganized territory, to realize clearly why it is a "problem." Our Civil War was preceded by thirty or forty years of diplomatic struggle for a balance of power in the West. Should the West be slave or free, that is, should it be the scene of homesteads and free labor, or of plantations and slaves? Should it be formed into States which sent senators and representatives to support the South or the North? We were virtually two nations, each trying to upset the balance of power in its own favor. And when the South saw that it was beaten, that is to say "encircled," when its place in the Western sun was denied, the South seceded and fought. Until the problem or organizing the West had been settled, peace and federal union were impossible.

The world's problem is the same problem tremendously magnified and complicated.

The point I have been making will, I fear, seem a paradox to many readers,—that the anarchy of the world is due to the backwardness of weak states; that the modern nations have lived in an armed peace and collapsed into hideous warfare because in Asia, Africa, the Balkans, Central and South America there are rich territories in which weakness invites exploitation, in which inefficiency and corruption invite imperial expansion, in which the prizes are so great that the competition for them is to the knife.

This is the world problem upon which all schemes for arbitration, leagues of peace, reduction of armaments must prove themselves. The diplomats have in general recognized this. It was commonly said for a generation that Europe would be lucky if it escaped a general war over the breakup of Turkey in Europe. The Sick Man

28

has infected the Continent. Our own "preparedness" Need of European legislatures to deal with problem. campaign is based on the fear that the defenselessness of Latin America will invite European aggression, that the defenselessness of China will bring on a struggle in the Pacific. Few informed people imagine for a moment that any nation of the world contemplates seizing or holding our own territory. That would be an adventure so ridiculous that no statesman would think of it. If we get into trouble it will be over some place like Mexico, or Haiti, or the Philippines, or the Panama Canal, or Manchuria, or Hawaii. . . .

Europe has also recognized that some kind of world government must be created. The phrase world government, of course, arouses immediate opposition; the idea of a European legislature would be pronounced utopian. Yet there have been a number of European legislatures. The Berlin Conference of 1885 was called to discuss "freedom of commerce in the basin and mouths of the Congo; application to the Congo and Niger of the principles adopted at the Congress of Vienna with a view to preserve freedom of navigation on certain international rivers . . . and a definition of formalities to be observed so that new occupations on the African coasts shall be deemed effective." The Powers represented made all sorts of reservations, but they managed to pass a "General Act of the West African Conference." The Congo Free State was recognized. As Mr. Harris says: "Bismarck saw in this a means of preventing armed conflict over the Congo Basin, of restricting the Portuguese advance, and of preserving the region to free trade." What was it that Bismarck saw? He saw that the great wealth of the Congo and its political weakness might make trouble in Europe unless the Congo was organized into the legal structure of the world.

The Conference at Algeciras was an international legislature in which even the United States was represented; the London Conference after the Balkan wars was a gathering of ambassadors trying to legislate out of existence the sources of European trouble in the Balkans. But all these legislatures have had one great fault. They met, they passed laws, they adjourned, and left the enforcement of their mandate to the conscience of the individual Powers. The legislature was international, but the executive was merely national. The legislature moreover had no way of checking up or controlling the executive. The representatives of all the nations would pass laws for the government of weak territories, but the translation of those laws into practise was left to the colonial bureaucrats of some one nation.

If the law was not carried out, to whom would an appeal be made? Not to the Conference, for it had ceased to exist. There was no way in which a European legislature could recall the officials who did not obey its will. Those officials were responsible to their home government, although they were supposed to be executing a European mandate. Those who were injured had also to appeal to their home government, and the only way to remedy an abuse or even sift out the truth of an allegation was by negotiation between the Powers. This raised the question of their sovereignty, called forth patriotic feeling, revived a thousand memories, and made any satisfactory interpretation of the European Act or any criticism of its administration a highly explosive adventure.

Suppose, for example, that Congress had power to pass laws, but that the execution of them was left to the States. Suppose New York had its own notions of tariff administration. How would the other States compel the New York customs officials to execute the spirit and let-

30

ter of the Federal law? Suppose every criticism by Pennsylvania of a New York Collector was regarded as an infringement of New York's sovereignty, as a blow at New York's pride, what kind of chaos would we suffer from? Yet that is the plight of our world society.

The beginnings of a remedy would seem to lie in not disbanding these European conferences when they have passed a law. They ought to continue in existence as a kind of senate, meeting from time to time. They ought to regard themselves as watchers over the legislation which they have passed. To them could be brought grievances, by them amendments could be passed when needed. The colonial officials should at least be made to report to this senate, and all important matters of policy should be laid open to its criticism and suggestion. In this way a problem like that of Morocco, for example, might be kept localized to a permanent European Conference on Morocco. Europe would never lose its grip on the situation, because it would have representatives on the spot watching the details of administration, in a position to learn the facts, and with a real opportunity for stating grievances.

The development of such a senate would probably be towards an increasing control of colonial officials. At first it would have no power of appointment or removal. It would be limited to criticism. But it is surely not fantastic to suppose that the colonial civil service would in time be internationalized; that is to say, opened to men of different nationalities. The senate, if it developed any traditions, would begin to supervise the budget, would fight for control of salaries, and might well take over the appointing power altogether. It would become an upper house for the government of the protected territory, not essentially different perhaps from the American Philippine Commission. The lower house

Prevention
of war by
international
commissions
for unorgan-
ized regions. would be native, and there would probably be a minority
of natives in the senate. . . .

An organization of this kind would meet all the difficulties that our Continental Congress or that any other
primitive legislature has had to deal with. There would
be conflicts of jurisdiction, puzzling questions of interpretation, and some place of final appeal would have to
be provided. It might be the Senate of European representatives; but if the Senate deadlocked, an appeal
might be taken to The Hague. The details of all this
are obviously speculative at the moment.

The important point is that there should be in existence permanent international commissions to deal with
those spots of the earth where world crises originate.
How many there should be need not be suggested here.
There should have been one for Morocco, for the Congo,
for the Balkan Peninsula, perhaps for Manchuria; there
may have to be one for Constantinople, for certain countries facing the Caribbean Sea. Such international governing bodies are needed wherever the prizes are great,
the territory unorganized, and the competition active.

The idea is not over-ambitious. It seems to me the
necessary development of schemes which European diplomacy has been playing with for some time. It represents an advance along the line that governments, driven
by necessity, have been taking of their own accord.
What makes it especially plausible is that it grasps the
real problems of diplomacy, that it provides not a pana-
cea but a method and the beginnings of a technique. It
is internationalism, not spread thin as a Parliament of
Man, but sharply limited to those areas of friction where
internationalism is most obviously needed.

*Walter Lippmann, "The Stakes of Diplomacy," pp.
87–135.*

SOCIALISTS AND IMPERIALISM

Possibly we shall learn nothing from the war; at the present moment it looks that way. For all the world, including Socialists, seem to be divided between militarists and pacifists. By pacifism I mean of course the movement Socialists have attacked for fifty years— up to the present war—under the name of "bourgeois pacifism," the idea that disarmament, the Hague Tribunal, and similar devices could put an end to militarism and war. Peace impossible without solution of economic conflicts.

In one sense of course every internationalist, whether Socialist or Democrat, is a pacifist. Every internationalist is opposed to war. But from the days of Marx and before, up to the present time, all Socialists have been prepared for certain war-producing contingencies which can be abolished neither by calling them "illusions," as Norman Angell has done, nor by any other phrases or exorcisms. Nor can the economic causes of national conflict be avoided by disarmament, Hague tribunals, international police, or abolition of secret diplomacy, as proposed by the Women's Peace Party, the British Union of Democratic Control, the Independent Labor Party, etc. In a word, no measure dealing with military affairs or with mere political forms can *in the long run* have any effect whatever—as long as the present conflict of economic interests between the nations remains. The whole effort of the bourgeois pacifist from

33

the Socialist standpoint is to attempt—in spite of the horrible and tremendous lessons of the present war—to close our eyes resolutely to the great task that lies before us, namely, to find a way either in the near future or ultimately to bring the conflict of national economic interests to an end.

There are two economic forces in the world which can not be conjured away either by words, by mere political rearrangements, or by any action whatever with regard to arms—whether making for more armament or less armament. There is no power at present which can prevent a great independent nation like Russia or Japan, Germany or Austria, where the political conditions are in whole or in part those of the eighteenth century, from declaring wars of conquest either against helpless, backward or small countries, or against the economically more advanced and more democratic countries like England, France, or the United States. It is true that industrial capitalism now preponderates in Germany, but no German publicist has ever denied the tremendous influence of the landlord nobility, both over the government and over the economic and political structure of German society. It is true also that these great agricultural estates are partially operated under capitalistic conditions, but the position of agricultural labor throughout enormous districts of Prussia is certainly semi-feudal. This is equally true of Austria, and the landlord nobility is perhaps even more predominant in Hungary than in Prussia.

The second fact which can not be conjured away by phrases or mere political rearrangements is that—under the present system of society—there is a direct conflict of interests between all nations, even the most civilized. This is why Norman Angell, in his new book ("Arms and Industry"), is at such great pains to deny that na-

34

tions are economic units and "competing business firms." His denial is futile.

Even under individualistic capitalism all elements of the capitalist class have a greater or less interest in the business of the nation to which they belong; under the State Socialist policy, which is spreading everywhere, this community of interests is still closer. Moreover, under State Socialism even the working classes gain a share (of course, a small one) of whatever profits accrue from the successful competition of one's own nation with other nations, and especially from such competition in its aggressive form, "imperialism."

Socialists have sometimes denied that the economic interests of the working people of the various nations conflict.

Otto Bauer, of Austria, the world's leading Socialist authority on Imperialism—who was to report on the subject for the International Socialist Congress to have been held in Vienna last summer—is of the contrary opinion. He believes that one of the worst features of the present system is that, under capitalism, the immediate economic interests of the working people of the various nations *do* conflict.

Only in so far as the working people attach greater importance to attaining Socialism than to anything they can gain under the present society, are their interests in all nations the same. In so far as the working people aim at an improvement of their condition *this side of Socialism* their economic interests are often in conflict.

Moreover, State Socialism, political democracy, and social reform, since they tend to give the working people a slightly greater share in the prosperity of each nation, intensify the workers' nationalism and aggravate the conflict of immediate economic interests. This is why all the labor union parties of the world are tending in

35

the same direction as that in which the German Party
has been so clearly headed since the war—a tendency
very clearly formulated by *Vorwaerts* when it recently
asked whether the German Party was not becoming a
"nationalistic social reform labor party."

The bourgeois pacifists consider war to be the "great
illusion." In favoring war, under any conditions, they
say, the capitalists, the middle classes, and the working
classes are all mistaken. The only people that gain are
the officers of armies and navies, and armament manufacturers. It is needless for Socialists—believers in the
economic interpretation of politics—to point out that
such a conclusion can only be reached by an abandonment of the economic point of view.

In the opinion of internationalists, war can be abolished neither by armament or disarmament, nor by any
measures leading in either direction. War can be
abolished only by abolishing the causes of war, which
every practical man admits are economic. By strengthening already existing and natural economic tendencies
which are slowly bringing the nations together, the
causes of war may be gradually done away with.

The outlook therefore is very hopeful—provided the
intelligent (if selfish) ruling classes of the great capitalistic nations (England, France, America) decide once
and for all to place no hopes either on militarism or
pacifism. These natural economic tendencies indeed
would already have made war impossible if they had not
been impeded by artificial obstacles, such as tariff walls,
immigration restriction, financial concessions to favored
nations, etc.

Socialists relied upon natural economic forces to
abolish competition, establish the trusts, bring about
government ownership, and prepare the way for democratic ownership. They rely upon similar economic

36

forces to bring the nations together; reciprocal lowering of tariffs, the common development of the backward countries by the leading nations, the neutralization of canals—and last but not least, the modernization of Russia, Japan, Prussia, and Austria, that is, the full establishment in these countries of industrial capitalism and the semi-democratic political institutions that accompany it—as we see them in Great Britain, France, and America.

And the modernization of undemocratic countries.

William English Walling, "The Great Illusions," The New Review, June 1, 1915.

THE HIGHER IMPERIALISM

Cause of
all wars
found in
economic
motives :—

When the Socialists in the belligerent countries voted for the war budgets and took their seats in the war cabinets, their whole attitude towards war underwent a fundamental change. It is true that in Germany and elsewhere the Socialists berated the capitalists and militarists for bringing on the conflict, but having made this protest, they acted exactly as did every one else. They excused themselves on the ground that the war was defensive. But the Kaiser and the Czar and the President of the French Republic all made the same excuse. It was not that the Socialists did not have power to put obstacles in the way of their governments. They did not have the will. They were forced into a painful position, where their love of country struggled against their adherence to the proletariat of the world. Despite themselves they were moved by idealistic considerations, which according to their theory should have had no weight.

For according to socialist doctrine the great events of the world are determined by economic factors. The idealists may speak of national honor and national duty, of the inviolability of treaties and the sacred rights of small nations, but the cause of all wars is really to be traced to the clash of economic motives. If we are to establish peace, we must found it on the customary reactions of selfish men, who want things and are willing to fight for them. Peace must be a peace between men

38

as they are. It will not come by preaching, nor by na- that is, in competition of nationalist capitalistic groups. tions surrendering their ambitions. It will not come through non-resistance, through the submission of the meek to the overbearing. It will not come through the nations joyously disarming as the light of reason breaks through the clouds. Reason is not so simple nor so un-related a thing, for the material things that each nation wants, and the means by which the nation gets them, seem to the nation preeminently just and reasonable. However pompous the superstructure of ethics and ideals, the solid foundation of war, as of other social developments, is economic. So long as nations, or at all events their ruling groups, have conflicting economic interests, war is inevitable.

According to the Socialist, therefore, war and capital-ism were inseparable. War must continue so long as the wage-system continued. The argument was simple. The great owners of capital, earning more than they could consume or profitably invest in home industries, were compelled to send their surplus to colonies and de-pendencies, where a new profit could be made. With the rapid increase of capital, however, the competition between the industrial nations for the possession of these agricultural dependencies became keener. Such com-petition meant war. As capitalism approached its cli-max wars were bound to become more frequent, destruc-tive, and violent.

If this theory had been true it would have followed that the interests of capital would make for war and the interests of labor would make for peace. The day laborer, with no money in the bank, would not be inter-ested in capital investments in Morocco, Manchuria, or Asia Minor. He would have no national interests what-ever. But, as we may read in the admirable book on "Socialists and the War," by William English Walling,

But now
competitive
imperialism
makes way
for imperial-
ism by com-
bination.
a few Socialists have for some time begun to recognize
that wage-earners do have special national interests and
that these interests may be directly opposed to the interests of wage-earners in an adjoining country. If
Serbia is completely shut off from the sea, her wage-
earners suffer as acutely as do her peasants. If Switzerland is surrounded by a wall of hostile tariffs, if Holland and England are deprived of their colonies, the
loss is felt not only by great capitalists but by the man
who works with a trowel or a lathe. The ultimate interests of German and British wage-earners are identical,
but if their immediate interests conflict, there will grow
up a spirit of nationalism in both countries, and wage-
earners will clamor for a national policy which may
lead to war.

This seems to shut a door that leads to peace. But in
shutting this door the newer Socialist thought has opened
another. It assumes that the capitalists themselves are
increasingly likely to profit by peace, to desire peace,
and to achieve peace. According to the German Socialist, Karl Kautsky, we are approaching a new stage in
the industrial development of the world. At first capitalists exploited the resources of their own country.
Then they competed nationally for the exploitation of
colonies and dependencies, and this policy led to imperialism and war. Now they are beginning to unite
for the joint exploitation of all backward lands. Competitive imperialism is making way for imperialism by
combination, just as competitive industry gave way to
the trust. English, French, German, and Belgian capitalists will unite to exploit dependencies, will have joint
spheres of influence, and the result will be peace with
profits. Imperialism in the old sense will die out, and
its place will be taken by a pacific super-imperialism,
a higher imperialism.

40

What this theory actually means is that the normal de- This higher imperialism fraught with dangers. velopment of industry and finance will automatically bring about international peace, and that socialism and even democracy are quite unessential to that end. Socialists may cry for peace, but they might as well cry for free air. But the theory concedes too much and goes too far. It is tainted with the same ultrarationalistic spirit as is the earlier socialist theory, from which it is a reaction. War is not fought for economic motives alone, although these are important. Serbia would have been less vindictive had Austria conceded her an outlet for her trade, but in any case Serbia would not willingly be ruled by Austria, nor Bulgaria by Greece. Racial pride, religious prejudice, ancient traditions of all sorts still divide nations irrespective of economic interest. You cannot reduce a nation to a single unit thinking only in economic terms.

Moreover, even on the purely economic side there are infinite chances for war in the distribution of the profits of joint enterprises among the capitalists of the various nations. We all know how "gentlemen's agreements" are broken as soon as it is profitable for the gentlemen to break them, and we cannot wholly trust irresponsible magnates, whether industrial or political, to be even intelligently selfish. Moreover, in the present state of the world the higher imperialism is a policy fraught with the very dangers and difficulties which it seeks to evade. If the capitalists of Europe were determined to exploit South America under a joint European control, the decision might directly lead to war. There are too many vested national interests in colonies, dependencies and spheres of influence to make internationalization of investment an immediate specific against war.

But in this matter of the higher imperialism we are less concerned to know how false than how true it is.

41

It is a thing to be desired if it circumscribes war, even
though it does not end war, if it tends towards peace,
even though it does not by itself alone assure peace.
We believe that this present war is not unlikely to end
in a combination of great nations with enormous capital,
willing to enter upon foreign investments jointly. The
great capitalists, who influence if they do not rule our
modern industrial nations, will often discover that it
is cheaper to divide than to fight. It will be better to
have twenty per cent. of a Chinese loan without going to
war than thirty per cent.—or nothing at all—after a
war. They will strive for the peace of "understanding"
—the peace of give and take.

If the big speculators can thus merge their interests
and deal across national boundaries, the little investors
who have less to gain and more to lose by war will be
even more pacific. Farmers and wage-earners have a
still more attenuated interest in war, and a still more
obvious interest in peace. Once great liens of peace are
established, moreover, many of the incitements to war
will of themselves disappear. . . .

In the end, however, any internationalization of investment will be only a single step in the direction of
peace. There are many other steps to be taken. Education, commerce, the development of an international
morality, the creation of machinery for dealing with
international disputes, are all essential to the evolution
of peace. Industrial and political democracy are above
all necessary. Men must be given a full life and a real
stake in the wealth that peace provides, and they who
bear the burdens of war must actually determine the
national policies which make for war or peace.

The New Republic, June 5, 1915.

42

PRINCIPLES OF THE SETTLEMENT: POLITICAL

NATIONALITY AND THE FUTURE

For the first time in our lives, we find ourselves in complete uncertainty as to the future. To uncivilized people the situation is commonplace; but in twentieth-century Europe we are accustomed to look ahead, to forecast accurately what lies before us, and then to choose our path and follow it steadily to its end; and we rightly consider that this is the characteristic of civilized men. The same ideal appears in every side of our life: in the individual's morality as a desire for "Independence" strong enough to control most human passions: in our Economics as Estimates and Insurances: in our Politics as a great sustained concentration of all our surplus energies (in which parties are becoming increasingly at one in aim and effort, while their differences are shrinking to alternatives of method), to raise the material, moral, and intellectual standard of life throughout the nation. From all this fruitful, constructive, exacting work, which demands the best from us and makes us the better for giving it, we have been violently wrenched away and plunged into a struggle for existence with people very much like ourselves, with whom we have no quarrel.

We must face the fact that this is pure evil, and that we cannot escape it. We must fight with all our

War has shattered our constructive effort.

43

It has
roused the
instinct of
revenge.

strength: every particle of our energy must be absorbed in the war: and meanwhile our social construction must stand still indefinitely, or even be in part undone, and every class and individual in the country must suffer in their degree, according to the quite arbitrary chance of war, in lives horribly destroyed and work ruined. . . .

The psychological devastation of war is even more terrible than the material. War brings the savage substratum of human character to the surface, after it has swept away the strong habits that generations of civilized effort have built up. We saw how the breath of war in Ireland demoralized all parties alike. We have met the present more ghastly reality with admirable calmness; but we must be on our guard. Time wears out nerves, and War inevitably brings with it the suggestion of certain obsolete points of view, which in our real, normal life, have long been buried and forgotten.

It rouses the instinct of revenge. "If Germany has hurt us, we will hurt her more—to teach her not to do it again." The wish is the savage's automatic reaction, the reason his perfunctory justification of it: but the civilized man knows that the impulse is hopelessly unreasonable. The "hurt" is being at war, and the evil we wish to ban is the possibility of being at war again, because war prevents us working out our own lives as we choose. If we beat Germany and then humiliate her, she will never rest till she has "redeemed her honor," by humiliating us more cruelly in turn. Instead of being free to return to our own pressing business, we shall have to be constantly on the watch against her. Two great nations will sit idle, weapon in hand, like two Afghans in their loopholed towers when the blood feud is between them; and we shall have sacrificed deliberately and to an ever-increasing extent (for the blood feud grows by geometrical progression), the very freedom for which we are now giving our lives.

Another war instinct is plunder. War is often the savage's profession: " 'With my sword, spear and shield I plow, I sow, I reap, I gather in the vintage.' If we beat Germany our own mills and factories will have been at a standstill, our horses requisitioned and our crops unharvested, our merchant steamers stranded in dock if not sunk on the high seas, and our 'blood and treasure' lavished on the war: but in the end Germany's wealth will be in our grasp, her colonies, her markets, and such floating riches as we can distrain upon by means of an indemnity. If we have had to beat our plowshares into swords, we can at least draw some profit from the new tool, and recoup ourselves partially for the inconvenience. It is no longer a question of irrational, impulsive revenge, perhaps not even of sweetening our sorrow by a little gain. To draw on the life-blood of German wealth may be the only way to replenish the veins of our exhausted Industry and Commerce." So the plunder instinct might be clothed in civilized garb: "War," we might express it, "is an investment that must bring in its return."

The first argument against this point of view is that it has clearly been the inspiring idea of Germany's policy, and history already shows that armaments are as unbusinesslike a speculation for civilized countries as war is an abnormal occupation for civilized men. We saw the effect of the Morocco tension upon German finance in 1911, and the first phase of the present war has been enough to show how much Germany's commerce will inevitably suffer, whether she wins or loses.

It is only when all the armaments are on one side and all the wealth is on the other, that war pays; when, in fact, an armed savage attacks a civilized man possessed

45

of no arms for the protection of his wealth. Our Afghans in their towers are sharp enough not to steal each other's cows (supposing they possess any of their own) for cows do not multiply by being exchanged, and both Afghans would starve in the end after wasting all their bullets in the skirmish. They save their bullets to steal cows from the plainsmen who cannot make reprisals.

If Germany were really nothing but a "nation in arms," successful war might be as lucrative for her as an Afghan's raid on the plain, but she is normally a great industrial community like ourselves. In the last generation she has achieved a national growth of which she is justly proud. Like our own, it has been entirely social and economic. Her goods have been peacefully conquering the world's markets. Now her workers have been diverted *en masse* from their prospering industry to conquer the same markets by military force, and the whole work of forty years is jeopardized by the change of method.

Fighting for trade and industry is not like fighting for cattle. Cattle are driven from one fastness to another, and if no better, are at least no worse for the transit. Civilized wealth perishes on the way. Our economic organization owes its power and range to the marvelous forethought and cooperation that has built it up; but the most delicate organisms are the most easily dislocated, and the conqueror, whether England or Germany, will have to realize that, though he may seem to have got the wealth of the conquered into his grip, the total wealth of both parties will have been vastly diminished by the process of the struggle.

The characteristic feature of modern wealth is that it is international. Economic gain and loss is shared by the whole world, and the shifting of the economic

46

balance does not correspond to the moves in the game of diplomatists and armies. Germany's economic growth has been a phenomenon quite independent of her political ambitions, and Germany's economic ruin would compromise something far greater than Germany's political future—the whole world's prosperity. British wealth, among the rest, would be dealt a deadly wound by Germany's economic death, and it would be idle to pump Germany's last life-blood into our veins, if we were automatically draining them of our own blood in the process.

But issues greater than the economic are involved. The modern "Nation" is for good or ill an organism one and indivisible, and all the diverse branches of national activity flourish or wither with the whole national well-being. You cannot destroy German wealth without paralyzing German intellect and art, and European civilization, if it is to go on growing, cannot do without them. Every doctor and musician, every scientist, engineer, political economist and historian, knows well his debt to the spiritual energy of the German nation. In the moments when one realizes the full horror of what is happening, the worst thought is the aimless hurling to destruction of the world's only true wealth, the skill and nobility and genius of human beings, and it is probably in the German casualties that the intellectual world is suffering its most irreparable human losses.

With these facts in our minds, we can look into the future more clearly, and choose our policy (supposing that we win the war, and, thereby, the power to choose) with greater confidence. We have accepted the fact that war itself is evil, and will in any event bring pure loss to both parties: that no good can come from the war itself, but only from our policy when the war is

Germany's economic ruin would compromise world-prosperity.

over: and that the one good our policy can achieve,
without which every gain is delusive, is the banishing of
this evil from the realities of the future. This is our
one supreme "British interest," and it is a German
interest just as much, and an interest of the whole world.

This war, and the cloud of war that has weighed
upon us so many years before the bursting of the
storm, has brought to bankruptcy the "National State."
Till 1870 it was the ultimate ideal of European politics,
as it is still in the Balkans, where the Turk has broken
Time's wings. It was such a fruitful ideal that it has
rapidly carried us beyond itself, and in the last generation the life of the world has been steadily finding new
and wider channels. In the crisis of change from nationalism to internationalism we were still exposed to the
plague of war. The crisis might have been passed without it, and war banished for ever between the nations of
civilized Europe. Now that the catastrophe has happened (it is childish to waste energy in incriminations
against its promoters) we must carry through the change
completely and at once: we cannot possibly afford to
be exposed to the danger again.

No tool, machine, or idea made by men has an im-
mortal career. Sooner or later they all run amuck,
and begin to do evil instead of good. At that stage
savage or unskilful men destroy them by force and replace them by their opposite: civilized men get them
under control, and build them into something new and
greater. Nationality will sink from being the pinnacle
of politics only to become their foundation, and till the
foundations are laid true, further building is impossible.
But the bases of nationality have never yet been laid
true in Europe. When we say that "nationality was
the political ideal of the nineteenth century," and that
1870 left the populations of Europe organized in na-

tional groups, we are taking far too complacent a view of historical facts. The same century that produced a united Italy and Germany, saw out the whole tragedy of Poland, from the first partition in 1772 to the last revolt in 1863. Human ideas do not spring into the world full-grown and shining like Athena: they trail the infection of evil things from the past.

In the Dark Ages Europe's most pressing need and only practicable ideal was strong government. Strong government came with its blessings, but it brought the evil of territorial ambitions. The Duke of Burgundy spent the wealth of his Netherland subjects in trying to conquer the Swiss mountaineers. Burgundy succumbed to the king of France. But the very factor that made the French kings survive in the struggle for existence between governments, the force of compact nationality which the French kingdom happened to contain, delivered the inheritance of the kings to the Nation.

The French Nation in the Revolution burst the chrysalis of irresponsible government beneath which it had grown to organic life, but like a true heir it took over the Royal Government's ideal: "Peace within and piracy without." France had already begun aggression abroad before she had accomplished self-government at home, and in delivering herself to Napoleon she sacrificed her liberty to her ambition. Napoleon's only enduring achievements outside France were the things he set himself to prevent, the realization, by a forceful reaction against force, of German and Italian nationality. Nationalism was converted to violence from the outset, and the struggle for existence between absolute governments has merely been replaced by a struggle between nationalities, equally blind, haphazard, and non-moral, but far more terrific, just because the virtue of self-government is to focus and utilize human energy so

49

Intra-
national
oppression
has been
a chief
cause
of war.

much more effectively than the irresponsible government
it has superseded.

Naturally the result of this planless strife has been no
grouping of Europe on a just and reasonable national
basis. France and England, achieving racial frontiers
and national self-government early, inherited the Earth
before Germany and Italy struggled up beside them,
to take their leavings of markets and colonial areas.
But the government that united Germany had founded
its power on the partition of Poland, and in the second
Balkan War of 1913 we saw a striking example of the
endless chain of evil forged by an act of national injustice.

The Hungarians used the liberty they won in 1867
to subject the Slavonic population between themselves
and the sea, and prevent its union with the free prin-
cipality of Serbia of the same Slavonic nationality.
This drove Serbia in 1912 to follow Hungary's example by seizing the coast of the non-Slavonic Albanians;
and when Austria-Hungary prevented this (a right act
prompted by most unrighteous motives), Serbia fought
an unjust war with Bulgaria and subjected a large Bulgarian population, in order to gain access to the only
seaboard left her, the friendly Greek port of Salonika.

Hungary and Serbia are nominally national states:
but more than half the population in Hungary, and perhaps nearly a quarter in Serbia, is alien, only held
within the state by force against its will. The energy
of both states is perverted to the futile and demoraliz-
ing work of ''Magyarizing'' and ''Serbizing'' subject
foreign populations, and they have not even been successful. The resistance of Southern Slav nationalism on
the defensive to the aggression of Hungarian nationalism has given the occasion for the present catastrophe.

The evil element in nationalism under its many names,

50

"Chauvinism," "Jingoism," "Prussianism," is the one thing in our present European civilization that can and does produce the calamity of war. If our object is to prevent war, then, the way to do so is to purge Nationality of this evil. This we cannot do by any mechanical means, but only by a change of heart, by converting public opinion throughout Europe from "National Competition" to "National Cooperation." Public opinion will never be converted so long as the present system of injustice remains in force, so long as one nation has less and another more than its due. The first step towards internationalism is not to flout the problems of nationality, but to solve them.

The most important practical business, then, of the conference that meets when war is over, will be the revision of the map of Europe. . . .

If we do not think about nationality, it is simply because we have long taken it for granted, and our mind is focussed on posterior developments; but it is increasingly hard to keep ourselves out of touch with other countries, and though our blindness has been partly distraction, it has also been in part deliberate policy. We saw well enough that the present phase of the national problem in Europe carried in it the seeds of war. We rightly thought that war itself was the evil, an evil incomparably greater than the national injustices that might become the cause of it. We knew that, if these questions were opened, war would follow. We accordingly adopted the only possible course. We built our policy on the chance that national feeling could be damped down till it had been superseded in the public opinion of Europe by other interests, not because Nationalism was unjustified, but because it endangered so much more than it was worth. Knowing that we had passed out of the nationalist phase ourselves, and that

51

The map of Europe must be justly revised.

from our present political point of view war was purely,
evil, we hoped that it was merely a question of time for
the Continental populations to reach the same standpoint. Notably in Germany, the focus of danger, we
saw social interests coming more and more to the front
at the expense of militarism. We threw ourselves into
the negative task of staving off the catastrophe in the in-
terim, by a strenuous policy of compromise and conciliation, which has been successful on at least two critical occasions. Now that the evil has been too powerful
and the catastrophe has happened, the reasons for this
policy are dead. Nationalism has been strong enough
to produce war in spite of us. It has terribly proved
itself to be no outworn creed, but a vital force to be
reckoned with. It is stronger on the Continent than
social politics. It is the raw material that litters the
whole ground. We must build it into our foundations,
or give up the task, not only of constructive social
advance beyond the limits we have already reached, but
even of any fundamental reconstruction of what the
war will have destroyed.

Perhaps we might have foretold this from the case of
Ireland immediately under our eyes. Failure to solve
her national problem has arrested Ireland's development since the seventeenth century, and imprisoned her
in a world of ideas almost unintelligible to an English-
man till he has traveled in the Balkans. This has been
England's fault, and we are now at last in a fair way to
remedy it. The moment we have succeeded in arranging that the different national groups in Ireland govern
themselves in the way they really wish, the national
question will pass from the Irish consciousness; they
will put two centuries behind them at one leap, and
come into line with ourselves. The Dublin strike, contemporary with the arming of the Volunteers, shows

how the modern problems are jostling at the heels of Nationality is subjective not material. the old. Although "Unionist" and "Nationalist" politicians could still declare that their attitude towards the strike was neutral, the parliament of the new Irish state will discuss the social problem and nothing else.

Ireland, then, has forced us to think about the problem of nationalism; and our Irish experience will be invaluable to us when peace is made, and we take in hand, in concert with our allies, the national questions of the rest of Europe. To begin with, we already have a notion of what Nationality is. Like all great forces in human life, it is nothing material or mechanical, but a subjective psychological feeling in living people. This feeling can be kindled by the presence of one or several of a series of factors: a common country, especially if it is a well defined physical region, like an island, a river basin, or a mountain mass; a common language, especially if it has given birth to a literature; a common religion; and that much more impalpable force, a common tradition or sense of memories shared from the past.

But it is impossible to argue *a priori* from the presence of one or even several of these factors to the existence of a nationality: they may have been there for ages and kindled no response. And it is impossible to argue from one case to another: precisely the same group of factors may produce nationality here, and there have no effect. Great Britain is a nation by geography and tradition, though important Keltic-speaking sections of the population in Wales and the Highlands do not understand the predominant English language. Ireland is an island smaller still and more compact, and is further unified by the almost complete predominance of the same English language, for the Keltic speech is incomparably less vigorous here than in Wales; yet the

53

absence of common tradition combines with religious differences to divide the country into two nationalities, at
present sharply distinct from one another and none the
less hostile because their national psychology is strikingly the same. Germany is divided by religion in precisely the same way as Ireland, her common tradition is
hardly stronger, and her geographical boundaries quite
vague: yet she has built up her present concentrated
national feeling in three generations. Italy has geography, language and traditions to bind her together;
and yet a more vivid tradition is able to separate the
Ticinese from his neighbors, and bind him to people of
alien speech and religion beyond a great mountain
range. The Armenian nationality does not occupy a
continuous territory, but lives by language and religion.
The Jews speak the language of the country where they
sojourn, but religion and tradition hold them together.
The agnostic Jew accepts not only the language but all
the other customs of his adopted countrymen, but tradition by itself is too strong for him: he remains a Jew
and cannot be assimilated.

These instances taken at random show that each case
must be judged on its own merits, and that no argument
holds good except the ascertained wish of the living
population actually concerned. Above all we must be
on our guard against ''historical sentiment,'' that is,
against arguments taken from conditions which once
existed or were supposed to exist, but which are no
longer real at the present moment. They are most
easily illustrated by extreme examples. Italian newspapers have described the annexation of Tripoli as ''recovering the soil of the Fatherland'' because it was
once a province of the Roman Empire; and the entire
region of Macedonia is claimed by Greek chauvinists on
the one hand, because it contains the site of Pella,

54

the cradle of Alexander the Great in the fourth century B. C., and by Bulgarians on the other, because Ohhrida, in the opposite corner, was the capital of the Bulgarian Tzardom in the tenth century A.D., though the drift of time has buried the tradition of the latter almost as deep as the achievements of the "Emathian Conqueror," on which the modern Greek nationalist insists so strongly.

The national problems of Europe are numerous, and each one is beset by arguments good, bad, and indifferent, some no more specious than the above, some so elaborately staged that it requires the greatest discernment to expose them. Vast bodies of people, with brains and money at their disposal, have been interested in obscuring the truth, and have used every instrument in their power to do so. It is therefore essential for us in England to take up these hitherto remote and uninteresting national problems in earnest, to get as near to the truth as we possibly can, both as to what the respective wishes of the different populations are, and as to how far it is possible to reconcile them with each other and with Geography; and to come to the conference which will follow the war and is so much more important than the war itself, with a clear idea of the alternative solutions and a mature judgment upon their relative merits.

To accomplish this we need a coordination of knowledge on a large scale, knowledge of history, geography, religion, national psychology and public opinion. . . .

With the growth of civilization the human and the territorial unit become less and less identical. In a primitive community the members are undifferentiated from one another: the true human unit is the total group, and not the individual, and the territory this group occupies is a unit too, self-sufficing and cut off from intercourse with the next valley. In modern Eu-

55

rope every sub-group and every individual has developed a "character" or "individuality" of its own which must have free play; while the growth of communications, elaboration of organization, and economic interdependence of the whole world have broken down the barriers between region and region. The minimum territorial block that can be organized efficiently as a separate political unit according to modern standards is constantly growing in size: the maximum human group which can hold together without serious internal divergence is as steadily diminishing.

This would look like an *impasse,* were it not corrected by the virtues of civilization itself. We started with the fact that the essence of civilization was "Forethought" and its ideal the "power of free choice": the complementary side of this ideal, on the principle "Do as you would be done by," is to allow free choice to others when they are in your power. It is a virtue with as many names as there are spheres of human life: "Forbearance," "Toleration," "Constitutionalism." . . .

*Arnold J. Toynbee, "Nationality and the War,"
chap. I.*

NATIONALITY AND SOVEREIGNTY

The old Europe is dead, the old vision vanished, and we are wrestling in agony for new inspiration. . . .

We must have new forms of guarantee.

We must beware of putting our new wine into old bottles. While guarantees hold, they conserve their charge: when they break, the destruction is worse than if they had never existed. Unless we can ensure that the sovereign States of Europe respect European guarantees hereafter in other fashion than Germany at the present crisis, we must modify the formula or else discard it altogether.

Can the mechanism of the European system be safeguarded against its individual members? . . .

We have asked our question and must accept the answer. It is useless to fortify our new European organism by guarantees of the old order, because we cannot fortify such guarantees themselves against the sovereign national State. Whenever it chooses, the sovereign unit can shatter the international mechanism by war. We are powerless to prevent it: all we can do is to abandon our direct attack, and look for the causes which impel States to a choice as terrible for themselves as for their victims.

"You ask," the Germans say, "why we broke our contract towards Belgium? It would be more pertinent to ask how we were ever committed to such a contract at all.

"The heart of modern Germany is the industrial world of the Rhineland and Westphalia. The Belgian frontier and the Belgian tariff-wall rob this region of its natural outlet at Antwerp, yet the contract expressly forbids us to right this economic and geographical wrong by uniting the sea-port to its hinterland.

"The chief need of modern Germany is a source of raw produce and a market for her finished products in the tropical zone. Belgium has staked out for herself the one important region in Africa which was not already occupied by France or Great Britain. She can do nothing with it, while we—but this contract expressly forbids us to kick the Belgian dog out of the manger.

"Because of this Belgian guarantee we must go in want of almost everything we need, yet meanwhile our great neighbors on either flank have conspired to take from us even the little we possess already. The struggle with France and Russia on which we are now engaged has been impending for years, and on our part it is a struggle for existence, but even here the same remorseless contract operates to paralyze our efforts. On the scale of modern warfare the Western battle-front must extend from Switzerland to the North Sea, yet the greater part of this immense zone is neutralized by natural and artificial obstacles on either side. From Switzerland to the Ardennes there will be stalemate: the decision will be reached in the open country between the Ardennes and the coast. Here, as soon as war broke out, France and our own fatherland had to concentrate the terrific energy of their armaments, yet we had contracted away our initiative in this vital area, for it lies within the frontiers of the Belgian State. The Government we had guaranteed might prepare the ground for France and ruin it for ourselves, yet because of the guarantee we must look on passively at the digging of our grave. We must provide for national growth.

"Why, then, had we suffered ourselves to be bound hand and foot? We had not: our grandfathers had entailed the bonds upon us. When they signed the contract in 1839, they knew not what they did. At that time Germany had no industry, Belgium had no colonies, and the Franco-German frontier between the Ardennes and the Jura was not closed to field operations by two continuous lines of opposing fortifications. Had their signature been demanded in 1914, they would have refused it as indignantly as we should have refused it ourselves. To us no choice was offered, and if we have asserted for ourselves the right to choose, who dares in his heart to condemn us? Who will impose a changeless law upon a changing world?"

This is Germany's argument about Belgium. Her facts may be true or false, the arguments she builds on them valid or fallacious. That is not the point. Behind arguments and facts there looms an idea that can inspire an individual nation to make war on Europe. We must do justice to this idea, if it is not to play the same havoc again.

Humanity has an instinctive craving for something eternal, absolute, petrified. This seems to be a fundamental factor in our psychology: it has obtruded itself equally in spheres as diverse as religion and politics, but it has been especially dominant in diplomacy.

Whenever the European organism proves its instability by breaking down, we start in quest of a perfect mechanism, a "permanent settlement." We are invariably disappointed, but invariably we return to the quest again. The Congress of statesmen at Vienna followed this will-o'-the-wisp in 1814: in 1915 the belligerent democracies are preparing to lead themselves the same

59

The
European
organism
is full of
dynamic
life.

dance. "Europe is in a mess," we are all saying: "Let
us tidy her up 'once for all,' and then we can live comfortably ever after."

We might as well expect a baby to "live comfortably
ever after" in its swaddling clothes. . . .

So it is with the European organism. It is as full of
life, as perpetually in transformation, as the individual
national molecules of which it is woven, yet we confuse
it in turn with each of its transitory garments. If we
are to find a satisfactory issue out of the present crisis,
we must begin by correcting our standpoint.

The impending settlement will not be permanent, and
the better it fits the situation, the less permanent will it
be. . . .

Our real work will be to regulate this immediate
settlement so that it varies in harmony with the subsequent growth of Europe and modifies its structure and
mechanism to meet the organism's changing needs.

We have now discovered the flaw in guarantees of
the old order. They were framed for rigidity, and
therefore were doomed to crack. Our new guarantees
must be elastic: they must be forged of steel not cast in
iron.

How can we frame guarantees of this malleable character? . . .

(i.) Firstly, we propose guarantees of political
independence and integrity in the case of the three
Scandinavian States, the Slovene Unit, the Greek islands
off Anatolia, Persia, and the Sultanate of Oman. The
autonomy guaranteed to Poland within the Russian Empire comes under the same head.

(ii.) Secondly, we propose to guarantee economic
rights-of-way to one State across the political territory
of another. Instances of this type are the Russian railway through Norway to the Atlantic and through Persia

to the Indian Ocean; Poland's title to free trade down No settlement can be permanent.
the Vistula, and to the enjoyment of a free port at
Danzig; and Germany's similar claim to an unhampered
outlet at Trieste.

Both these classes of guarantee are adapted from the
international machinery invented during the nineteenth
century. The first class is an extension of the political
guarantee given to Belgium in 1839, the second of the
economic right-of-way secured to .her through Dutch
waters, in order to furnish the commerce of Antwerp
with a free passage down the estuary of the Scheldt to
the open sea.

Our standpoint towards these two classes is inevitably
prejudiced by their associations. We envisage them as
embodied "once for all," like their nineteenth-century
precedents, in a contract, and like nineteenth-century
diplomacy we tend to regard such contracts as so many
girders in a "permanent settlement."

(iii.) There is a third class, however, which has no precedent in the past, and which will react upon our standpoint in the very opposite direction: our proposed guarantee of alien minorities within the national State. . . .

The German populations transferred with Schleswig
to Denmark and with the Eastern frontier-zone to Autonomous Poland; the Poles abandoned to Germany in
West Prussia; the Germans and Slovaks who cannot be
disentangled from Hungary; the Christian elements in
Anatolia and Arabia—these are a few out of many instances, and each one of them is a refutation of
"finality."

The fact that such minorities must inevitably be left
on our hands compels us to recognize that beyond a
certain degree the economic and the national factor are
not commensurable. Here is an essential imperfection
in the best settlement we can possibly devise.

61

But elastic
guarantees
will
further
racial
toleration.

The fact that these minorities require a guarantee reveals a deficiency still more grave than the other, inasmuch as it is not environmental but psychological. It means that hardly a single national society in Europe has yet become capable of national toleration. Just as people were persecuted for their religious beliefs in the sixteenth century and for their political opinions in the nineteenth, so they are still in the twentieth century almost universally exposed to persecution for their national individuality. In this sphere the social evolution of Europe is exceptionally backward, and the problem of nationality will never be solved till this psychological incongruity is removed.

This at once reduces to their proper proportion both the immediate geographical settlement of the problem which we have elaborated in this book and that guarantee of alien minorities which we have found to be its necessary supplement. In this light, the contracts in which such guarantees are enshrined appear as the transitory scaffolding they are. Weakened by the morbid hypertrophy of nationalism which has been preying upon her for years, exhausted by the convulsion of war in which the malady has culminated, Europe must walk on crutches now or else collapse; yet she will not be a cripple forever. Relieved by these guarantees from the immediate strain of unmitigated national friction, she will be able to concentrate all her energy upon her spiritual convalescence. As soon as she has trained herself to national toleration, she will discard the guarantees and walk unaided.

So far from constituting a "permanent settlement," our third type of guarantee is an intimation that the problem still remains unsettled. The work will not be complete until we can dispense with the instrument, but the instrument will not accomplish the work unless it is

wielded by a craftsman's hand.   Not only are guarantees of our third type merely the means to an end beyond
themselves: the contract in which it is embodied is in this
case the least important part of the guarantee.

The
changing
organism
needs a
new form of
international
executive.

When we guarantee a national minority we have of
course to define certain liberties which it is to enjoy—
liberties, for instance, of religion, education, local self-
government—and all the parties to the Conference must
contract responsibility for the observance of such stipulations; yet when we have done this, we cannot simply deposit our document in some international "Ark of the
Covenant" and go our ways.   The essence of the guarantee is its subsequent interpretation.

The relation between the different elements in a country is continually changing.   One church dwindles while
another makes converts; one race advances in culture
while another degenerates; man's indefatigable struggle to dominate his physical environment alters the natural boundaries between localities: a barrier that once
seemed insurmountable is pierced, and leaves one for-
merly insignificant in relative prominence.   Each of
these modifications demands an adjustment of the guarantee, and since they are an infinite series, the guarantee
itself requires ceaseless manipulation if it is to perform
its function aright.

This need cannot be satisfied by the original *fiat* of
the International Conference: it can only be met by the
appointment of a standing international committee with
executive powers, empowered, that is, to administer and
interpret the contracts to which the members of the
Conference have originally subscribed.   Our third type
of guarantee has thus presented us with the clue we
sought.   The letter of international law has proved ineffective hitherto because it has lacked the inspiration of
a living spirit, and this spirit can only be breathed

into it by a human organ of international authority.

Supposing that such an organ were called into existence, what kind of international relations would naturally fall within its scope? We can analyze its probable sphere of activity into several departments.

(i.) The first branch would of course be those guarantees of national minorities which have just taught us the necessity for its existence.

(ii.) The second branch would include the two subjects of guarantee we dealt with first, namely, "Political Independence" and "Rights of Way." We can see now that their administration by a representative international executive would eliminate that defect of rigidity which has always proved fatal to them heretofore.

Between them these two branches would cover all the machinery we have suggested for our regenerated European organism. Are there any further spheres of national interaction over which our international organ might properly assume control? It would be logical to assign to it, if possible, all relations between sovereign national States which are peculiarly subject to change.

Change is a harmonization of two rhythms—Growth and Decay. Some sovereign units are continually waxing in population, material wealth and spiritual energy: such are Great Britain and Germany, France and the Russian Empire. Others, like the Ottoman Empire or Spain, are as continually waning in respect of the same factors.

This ebb and flow in the current of life causes, and must cause, a perpetual readjustment of the relations between units in the two complementary phases. Units in the positive phase inevitably absorb the fibers and trespass upon the environment of those which have passed over into the negative rhythm. We cannot arrest this process any more than we can abolish change

64

itself: what we can do is to regulate it on the lines of How this international organ would function. civilization, instead of letting it run riot in a blind struggle for existence.

The current radiates in an almost infinite variety of interactions. Great Britain, Germany, and India are discharging surplus population into the empty lands of the New World; Great Britain and France are applying surplus wealth to evoke the latent resources of countries with no surplus of their own; Great Britain and Russia are putting forth spiritual energy to inspire primitive peoples with the vitality of civilization.

Our international organ can handle no more than a fraction of this world-wide interchange.

(i.) We may exclude at once from its competence every interaction that is confined within the limits of a single sovereign unit. Within the British Empire, for example, it is patently impracticable to "internationalize" the problems of Indian emigration to Vancouver or the Transvaal, of the closure of the Australian labor-market against labor from the British Isles, of commercial exploitation in Nigeria or Rhodesia, of autonomy in Ireland or the Asiatic Dependencies. The Empire may handle its own problems well or ill, but it will never consent to waive its sovereignty in respect of them. We should regard the proposition of international intervention as a menace to the Empire's existence. We should undoubtedly fight rather than submit to it, and every other sovereign State would do the same under similar circumstances. In purely internal affairs international authority will never obtain a footing at the expense of the individual unit.

(ii.) We may likewise exclude interactions between two or more sovereign States in spheres that fall entirely within their respective sovereignty. The Dominion of Canada or the U. S. A. would never submit to international regulation the question of Japanese immigration along their Pacific seaboard. If Russia wished to float a loan, she would never allow our international organ to decide where and in what proportions it should be placed: she would insist on keeping her hands free, and making the best bargain for herself both from the financial and the political point of view. Italy and the Argentine would never relinquish their respective sovereign rights over the Italian laborers who cross the Atlantic every year to reap the South American harvests. International authority would be flouted as uncompromisingly in these instances as in the former.

(iii.) There are some units, however, so raw in their growth or so deeply sunk in their decay as to lack the attribute of sovereignty altogether—units which through want of population, wealth, spiritual energy, or all three together are unable to keep the spark of vitality aglow. Such dead units are the worst danger that threatens the peace of the world: each one of them is an arena enticing the living units around to clash in conflict, a vacuum. into which the current of life swirls like a maelstrom. In these ''no-man's-lands'' where no sovereignty exists, our international organ can and must assert its own sovereignty against the sovereign States outside.

(*a*) In every such area the standing international executive should regulate immigration from over-populated sovereign units—German colonization, for instance, in Anatolia, or Indian settlement on the alluvium of Irak.

(*b*) It should likewise regulate the inflow of capital. . . .

(*c*) In areas where the pressure of spiritual energy is so low that the population cannot save itself by its own efforts from political anarchy, the international executive should be prepared to step in and organize ''strong government.'' . . .

66

Morocco, the Balkans, the Ottoman Empire—the present war is not really being waged to settle these problems: it is being waged because they have been settled already, and settled on such unjust and injudicious lines that all parties concerned have found it worth while to stake their existence for the reversal of the settlement. No one need have been involved by such problems in a struggle for life. They were all problems of expansion, and their solution ought at worst to have disappointed the expectation of immoderate gains: it ought never, as it has done, to have threatened the parties with the loss of what they possessed already before the problems were probed.

Such an executive could have prevented the war of diplomacy and of arms.

Why has the contrary occurred? Because, just for lack of that international executive with the sovereign authority we postulate, these issues that were not vital have been fought out, like issues of life and death, by war—not by the war of arms which has descended upon us now like some recurrent plague, into which we relapse at rarer and rarer intervals as we advance in civilization, but by the unobtrusive, unremittent war of diplomacy which is being waged year in and year out between the sovereign States of Europe, and which has increased appallingly in violence during the last generation.

In this disastrous diplomatic warfare our opponents in the present war of arms have been uniformly the aggressors. If Austria-Hungary is now struggling for existence, it is because she deliberately embarked nearly forty years ago upon a diplomatic campaign of aggrandizement against South-Slavonic nationality. If Germany is fighting back to back with her in the same ghastly struggle, it is because Germany has wielded diplomatic weapons still more ruthlessly against her other European neighbors.

67

For the terrible embitterment of the diplomatic contest Germany herself is entirely responsible, but she has inevitably exposed herself to reprisals as severe as her own provocative blows. She opened the battle over Morocco by forcibly intruding upon a sphere where she had no shadow of claim to expansion: thereby she drew France and Great Britain into diplomatic alliance against her, and laid herself open to the humiliation of 1911, when Franco-British diplomacy mobilized its financial forces and drove her to retreat by cutting off her supplies. In Turkey she might easily have satisfied her needs without any battle at all. The untenanted area was vast, the claims staked out on it were singularly narrow: when German enterprise circumvented the enterprise of Great Britain and France, and secured all the railway-concessions in the virgin hinterland of Anatolia, French and British diplomacy grumbled but did not attempt to open hostilities. Yet instead of reaping her harvest in peace, Germany again precipitated a diplomatic conflict by extending her ambitions to Bagdad and the Persian Gulf. The moment she aspired to absorb the whole Ottoman Empire, Great Britain and Russia entered into diplomatic cooperation, and opposed her purpose with all their might. Germany's Arabian venture has jeopardized her Anatolian gains, and if she is defeated in the present struggle, she will probably be excluded from the Ottoman area altogether.

The diplomatic warfare over three secondary issues, which ought never to have been settled by fighting at all, has thus left none of the combatants unscathed. On the contrary, the wounds inflicted then have festered till their poison has threatened each combatant with the pains of dissolution, and made that quack-physician the diplomatist call out in panic for the knife of that quack-surgeon the war lord.

68

This diplomatic warfare is the objective of our new international organization. Upon diplomacy we can and must make a direct attack. If we can draw this monster's teeth, we shall no longer be troubled by its still more monstrous offspring—War.

Arnold J. Toynbee, "Nationality and the War," chap. XII.

THE GOVERNMENTAL THEORY

International politics dominated by a theory.   The position I intend to put forward and defend is
this: War is made—this war has been made—not by
any necessity of nature, any law beyond human control, any fate to which men must passively bow; it is
made because certain men who have immediate power
over other men are possessed by a certain theory. Sometimes they are fully conscious of this theory. More
often, perhaps, it works in them unconsciously. But it
is there, the dominating influence in international politics. I shall call it the governmental theory, because it
is among governing persons—Emperors, Kings, Ministers, and their diplomatic and military advisers—that
its influence is most conspicuous and most disastrous.
But it is supported also by historians, journalists, and
publicists, and it is only too readily adopted by the ordinary man, when he turns from the real things he knows
and habitually handles to consider the unknown field of
foreign affairs.

Very briefly, and, therefore, crudely expressed, the
theory is this: "The world is divided, politically, into
States. These States are a kind of abstract beings, distinct from the men, women, and children who inhabit
them. They are in perpetual and inevitable antagonism
to one another; and though they may group themselves
in alliances, that can be only for temporary purposes to
meet some other alliance or single power. For States
are bound by a moral or physical obligation to expand

indefinitely, each at the cost of the others. They are nat- ural enemies, they always have been so, and they always will be; and force is the only arbiter between them.

Artificiality of the governmental theory. That being so, war is an eternal necessity. As a necessity, it should be accepted, if not welcomed, by all sound-thinking and right-feeling men. Pacifists are men at once weak and dangerous. They deny a fact as fundamental as any of the facts of the natural world. And their influence, if they have any, can only be disastrous to their State in its ceaseless and inevitable contest with other States.''

Stated thus briefly, and in its most uncompromising terms, this is what I have called the governmental theory. I propose to criticize it in detail. But before doing so I will ask the reader to compare with it the ordinary attitude of the plain men and women who inhabit these States, and who have to bear the burden of the wars in which the theory involves them. These ordinary people, in the course of their daily lives, do not think at all in terms of the State. They think about the people they come in contact with, about their business, their friends, and their families. When they come across foreigners, as many of them do, in business or in travel, they may like or dislike them, but they do not regard them as pre-destined enemies. On the contrary, if they are intelligent, they know themselves to be cooperating with them in innumerable complicated ways, implying mutual advantage. Differences of language and of social habit make it easier for most people to associate with their fellow-countrymen than with foreigners. But that is all. There are, of course, among these men and women real enmities and spontaneous quarrels. But these do not occur because men belong to different States. They occur because they really have injured one another, or hate one another; and they occur, naturally, for the most part, be-

71

tween men of the same State, because it is these who most
often come into direct contact with one another. It is
not, therefore, these enmities of ordinary men that give
rise to wars.

Wars are made by governments, acting under the influence of the governmental theory. And of this fact—
for a fact it is among civilized Western peoples in
modern times—no better example could be given than
the present war. Before it broke out nobody outside
governmental and journalistic circles was expecting it.
Nobody desired it. And though, now that it is being
waged, all the nations concerned are passionately interested in it, and all believe themselves to be fighting in
a righteous cause, yet no ordinary citizen, in the days
preceding its outbreak, would have maintained that there
was any good reason for war, and few even knew what
the reasons alleged were or might be. Even now the different nations have quite opposite views as to which Government was responsible. We believe it was the German
Government; and with equal conviction Germans believe it was the British. But nobody believes that it was
the mass of the people in any nation. The millions who
are carrying on the war, at the cost of incalculable suffering, would never have made it if the decision had
rested with them. That is the one indisputable fact.
How can such a fact occur? How is it possible for Governments to drag into war people who did not desire war
and who have no quarrel with one another?

The immediate answer is simple enough. In no country is there any effective control by the people over foreign policy. That is clear in the case of the great military empires. But it is true also of France and of England, where, in other respects, government is more or
less under popular control. The country has no real
choice, for it gets its information only after the decisive

action has been taken. That is an important truth which But peoples are also obsessed by the theory. ought to lead to important changes in our methods of conducting foreign affairs. But it is only part of the truth. For we have now to notice this further fact: that in all countries, in Germany no less than in England and France, no sooner is the war declared than it is supported by the whole nation. The voice of criticism is silenced, and every one, whatever his opinion about the origin of the war, gives his help to see it through. Why is that? The reason is obvious. As soon as war is made, the people of one country, conscious just before of no cause of enmity, do really become enemies of the people of another country; for armed populations are marching on armed populations to massacre them. Everybody, therefore, is bound to fight in self-defense. It is too late to ask whether there was any real cause of quarrel; for, quarrel or no, there is real and imminent danger. To meet that danger becomes, therefore, the immediate necessity which overbears every other consideration. And that is the deepest reason why wars made by governments without, and even against, the will of peoples, will always be supported by peoples.

But though that is the most powerful reason, it is not the only one. There is a further fact. The ordinary man, though he does not live under the obsession of the governmental theory, is not protected against it by any knowledge or reflection. As far as he is concerned, he knows no reason for war, and, left to himself, would never make it. But he has a blank mind open to suggestion; and he has passions and instincts which it is easy to enlist on the side of the governmental theory. He has been busy all his life; and he has no education, or one that is worse than none, about those issues which, in a crisis like that which has come upon us, suddenly reveal themselves as the issues of life and death. His-

tory, no doubt, should have informed him. But history,
for the most part, is written without intelligence or conviction. It is mere narrative, devoid of instruction, and
seasoned, if at all, by some trivial, habitual, and second-
hand prejudice of the author. History has never been
understood, though it has often been misunderstood. To
understand it is perhaps beyond the power of the human
intellect. But the attempt even has hardly begun to be
made.

Deprived, then, of this source of enlightenment, the
ordinary man falls back upon the press. But the press
is either an agent of the very governments it should exist
to criticize (it is so notoriously and admittedly on the
Continent, and, to an extent which we cannot measure,
also in England), or else it is (with a few honorable ex-
ceptions) an instrument to make money for certain individuals or syndicates. But the easiest way for the
press to make money is to appeal to the most facile emotions and the most superficial ideas of the reader; and
these can easily be made to respond to the suggestion that
this or that foreign State is our natural and inevitable
enemy. The strong instincts of pugnacity and self-ap-
probation, the nobler sentiment of patriotism, a vague
and unanalyzed impression of the course of history,
these and other factors combine to produce this result.
And the irony is that they may be directed indifferently
against any State. In England, for instance, a hundred
years ago, it was France against whom they were mar-
shaled; sixty years ago it was Russia; thirty years ago
it was France again; now it is Germany; presently, if
governments have their way, it will be Russia again.

The foreign offices and the press do with nations what
they like. And they will continue to do so until ordinary people acquire right ideas and a machinery to
make them effective. . . .

74

The governmental theory holds that States are the great realities, and that they are natural enemies. My reply is that States are unreal abstractions; that the reality is the men and women and children who are the members of the States; and that as soon as you substitute real people for the abstract idea that symbolizes them you find that they have no cause of quarrel, no interests or desires of a kind to justify or necessitate aggressive war. And, if there were no aggressive war, there could, of course, be no cause for defensive war. . . .

G. Lowes Dickinson, "The War and the Way Out,"
Atlantic Monthly, January, 1915.

THE WAY OUT OF WAR

No aggran-
dizement!

We will to perpetuate European peace. How are we to accomplish it? By keeping in view and putting into effect certain clear principles.

First, the whole idea of aggrandizing one nation and humiliating another must be set aside. What we are aiming at is, not that this or that group of States should dominate the others, but that none should in future have any desire or motive to dominate. With that view, we must leave behind the fewest possible sores, the least possible sense of grievance, the least possible humiliation. The defeated States, therefore, must not be dismembered in the hope of making or keeping them weak; and that means, in detail, that, if the Allies win, the English and the French must not take the German colonies, or the Russians the Baltic Coast, the Balkans, or Constantinople; and that, if Germany wins, she must not dismember or subordinate to her system France or England or the neutral powers. That is the first clear condition of the future peace of Europe.

Secondly, in rearranging the boundaries of States—and clearly they must be rearranged—one point, and one only, must be kept in mind: to give to all peoples suffering and protesting under alien rule the right to decide whether they will become an autonomous unit, or will join the political system of some other nation. Thus, for example, the people of Alsace-Lorraine should be allowed to choose whether they will remain under

76

Germany, or become an autonomous community, or be
included in France. The same principles shall be applied to the Poles. The same to Schleswig-Holstein. The same to the Balkan States. The same to the Slav communities included in Austria-Hungary. There would arise, of course, difficulties in carrying this principle through. For, in the Balkan States, in Bohemia, and elsewhere, there is an almost inextricable tangle of nationalities. But with good-will these difficulties could be at least partially met.

Even the wholesale transference of peoples of one nationality from one location to another is a possibility; and, indeed, it is now going on. In any case the principle itself is clear. Political rule must cease to be imposed on peoples against their will in the supposed interest of that great idol, the abstract state. Let the Germans, who belong together, live together under the same government, pursuing in independence their national ideal and their national culture. But let them not impose that ideal and that culture on reluctant Poles and Slavs and Danes. So, too, let Russia develop her own life over the huge territory where Russians live. But let her not impose that life on unwilling Poles and Finns. The English, in history, have been as guilty as other nations of sacrificing nationality to the supposed exigencies of the State. But of late they have been learning their lesson. Let them learn it to the end. Let no community be coerced under British rule that wants to be self-governing. The British have had the courage, though late, to apply this principle to South Africa and Ireland. There remains their greatest act of courage and wisdom —to apply it to India.

A Europe thus rearranged, as it might be at the peace, on a basis of real nationality instead of on a basis of States, would be a Europe ripe for a permanent league.

And by such a league only, in my judgment, can its future peace, prosperity, happiness, goodness, and greatness be assured. There must be an end to the waste upon armaments of resources too scanty, at the best, to give to all men and women in all countries the material basis for a good life. But if States are left with the power to arm against one another they will do so, each asserting, and perhaps with truth, that it is arming in defense against the imagined aggression of the others. If all are arming, all will spend progressively more and more on their armaments, for each will be afraid of being outstripped by the others. This circle is fatal, as we have seen in the last quarter of a century.

To secure the peace of Europe the peoples of Europe must hand over their armaments, and the use of them for any purpose except internal police, to an international authority. This authority must determine what force is required for Europe as a whole, acting as a whole in the still possible case of war against powers not belonging to the league. It must apportion the quota of armaments between the different nations according to their wealth, population, resources, and geographical position. And it, and it alone, must carry on, and carry on in public, negotiations with powers outside the league. All disputes that may arise between members of the league must be settled by judicial process. And none of the forces of the league must be available for purposes of aggression by any member against any other.

With such a league of Europe constituted, the problem of reduction of armaments would be automatically solved. Whatever force a united Europe might suppose itself to require for possible defense would clearly be far less than the sum of the existing armaments of the separate States. Immense resources would be set free for the general purposes of civilization, and especially for those

78

costly social reforms on the accomplishment of which And we must prepare public opinion for the idea. depends the right of any nation to call itself civilized at all. And if any one insists on looking at the settlement from the point of view of material advantage—and that point of view will and must be taken—it may be urged, without a shadow of doubt, that any and every nation, the conquerors no less than the conquered, would gain from a reduction of armaments far more than they could possibly gain by pecuniary indemnities or cessions of territory which would leave every nation still arming against the others with a view to future squandering of resources in another great war. This is sheer common sense of the most matter-of-fact kind.

A League of Europe is not Utopian. It is sound business.

Such a league, it is true, could hardly come into being immediately at the peace. There must be preparation of opinion first; and, not less important, there must be such changes in the government of the monarchic States as will insure the control of their policy by popular opinion; otherwise we might get a league in which the preponderating influence would be with autocratic emperors. But in making peace the future league must be kept in view. Everything must be done that will further it, and nothing that will hinder it. And what would hinder it most would be a peace by which either there should be a return to the conditions before the war—but of that there is little fear—or by which any one power, or group of powers, should be given a hegemony over the others. For that would mean a future war for the rehabilitation of the vanquished.

The mood, therefore, which seems to be growing in England, that the British must "punish" Germany by annihilating her as a political force; the mood which seems to be growing in Germany, that she must annihilate

the British as the great disturbers of the peace—all
such moods must be resolutely discouraged. For on
those lines no permanent peace can be made. Militarism
must be destroyed, not only in Germany but everywhere.
Limitation of armaments must be general, not imposed
only on the vanquished by victors who propose themselves to remain fully armed. The view of peoples must
be substituted once for all for the view of governments,
and the view of peoples is no domination, and, therefore, no war, but a union of nations developing freely
on their own lines, and settling all disputes by arbitration.

*G. Lowes Dickinson, "The War and the Way Out,"
Atlantic Monthly, Jan. 1915.*

LOWES DICKINSON'S PLAN

Writing in the *Atlantic Monthly*, Mr. Lowes Dickinson attempts to point the moral of the war and to offer a way out. His theory is that wars are made by governments without the consent and against the interest of their subjects; they are made because the governmental mind is obsessed with the illusion that States are "natural enemies," that they have always been so and always will be, that force is the only arbiter between them. This fantasy of the governing caste, says Mr. Dickinson, is what rules the State, and through control of foreign policy and the press drags the population to slaughter. The remedy is to shatter the illusion, to assert against the criminal nonsense of the governing mind the humanity and commonsense of ordinary people. . . .

Mr. Dickinson's plan lacks hardheadedness.

Now peace will have to be built on a very hard-headed basis or it will be fragile and illusory. But it is just this hard-headedness which Mr. Dickinson's argument seems to lack. In our opinion he himself is building on an illusion, and if his doctrine prevails among the workers for peace their passion will be misdirected, and their disappointment will be as deep as their hopes are high.

To prove these assertions, we need not go beyond the example which Mr. Dickinson uses, the case of Russia and her desire to hold Constantinople. Mr. Dickinson dismisses this ambition with the statement that "for all purposes of trade, for all peace purposes, the Darda-

nelles are open. And it is the interest of all nations
alike that they should remain so.'' What he is assuming
here is that it makes no economic difference whether Constantinople is under one political government or another.
This is the center of Mr. Dickinson's argument, and it
rests on the doctrine of Norman Angell that ''political
power is a consideration irrelevant to economic power.''

Is it irrelevant in a case like that of the Dardanelles?
The Black Sea region is already a great agricultural
exporting region; it is destined most probably to become the industrial center of Russia. But to carry out
goods, Russian ships must pass through a narrow Turkish
strait. Mr. Dickinson says that for all ''peace purposes'' the passage is free. Is it? Let us suppose that
Mexico held New York harbor, or that Ecuador held
Liverpool. Would these harbors be free to American
and English commerce? They would be free if Mexico
and Ecuador were highly efficient governments imbued
with the doctrine of absolute free trade. Then commerce
might pass through easily. But if Mexicans or Ecua-
dorians took it into their heads to exercise sovereignty
by setting up a tariff zone around New York or Liverpool, who would regard political power as irrelevant to
economic power? Certainly not the Manchester ex-
porter as he paid his customs tax to the pleasant official
from Ecuador.

Although England is in no danger from Ecuador,
there are nations in the world which suffer just as fan-
tastically. There is the case of Servia, shut off from a
''window on the sea.'' Servia exports pigs, when she
isn't fighting for the privilege of exporting them. But
to export anything she has to run the gauntlet of an
Austrian tariff to the north, Albanian and Greek discrimination to the west and south. Shut off from the
sea, she is like a man trying to get out of a restaurant

who has still to tip the waiter, the headwaiter, the girl who took care of his hat, and the boy who brushed it.

Political power is not in the least irrelevant to economic power. Mr. Dickinson has no doubt heard of a thing which we Americans call vulgarly "dollar diplomacy." European powers do not call it that, but they practise it. They call it staking out "spheres of influence," and there is nothing sentimental or illusory about it. The nation that can secure political control of an undeveloped country can decide who shall receive the mining rights and the railroad franchises, can fix railroad rates to favor its own manufacturers, can use all the methods which Americans describe as restraint of trade. It may have been dishonest, it certainly wasn't a delusion, when capitalists in those dreadful early days of this republic bought political power to further economic ends. A legislature or a governor was generally worth the price in this country, and we presume that they would be worth the price in Asia Minor. If German bureaucrats governed Morocco, they would, we suppose, be good to their friends, almost all of whom have at least a nominal residence east of Belgium, and French capitalists might then be prospecting fresh mines and pastures new.

Mr. Dickinson ignores these considerations when he speaks of national antagonisms arising "because a few men of the military and diplomatic caste have a theory about States, their interests and destinies." He ignores the monopolies, the use of tariffs, the special privileges of which political power is the instrument. He does not face the fact that in every country there are exporters of goods and capital, concession-hunters and traders, who stand to gain by the use of governmental power in half developed territory. To them at least it is not a matter of indifference whether Germany is politically supreme in say India or China. Since Germany has brought the

83

doctrine of protection to its highest point, it would make
a very great difference to the commerce of other nations
if Germany developed a world-empire.

How little reality there is in Mr. Dickinson's contention may be seen by analyzing his concrete proposals. Apart from the shattering of the great illusion of
the governmental mind by a propaganda, he suggests
a settlement of Europe on the basis of nationality, capped
by a League of Europe to maintain the peace.

Now there are all sorts of reasons for trying to found
States on nationality, and the only reason against the
proposal is the reason on which Mr. Dickinson's article
is built. He tells us on one page that "ordinary people, in the course of their daily lives, do not think at all
in terms of the state." Then what difference does it
make to people of the same nationality that they should
be under different governments, and how is the world's
peace to be assured by gathering into one State people
who do not care about the State? Either the people have
an interest in the State or they have not, but surely it is
futile for Mr. Dickinson to argue in one place against
the German contention that their emigrants are "lost,"
and in another that the Danes of Schleswig-Holstein
should go back to Denmark. And what does he mean
by telling us that in the event of an Austro-German
victory "Italy and the Balkans will be pillaged to
the benefit of Austria, and Russia rolled back—though
that would be all to the good—from her ambition to expand in the West." Is Mr. Dickinson also afflicted with
the "governmental mind," that he should talk of "benefit" to Austria and pronounce it good that "Russia" be
rolled back? What does he mean by telling us that
"the English and the French must not take the German
colonies, or the Russians the Baltic coast, the Balkans,
or Constantinople," for what difference does it make,

84

except to the "governmental mind," who exercises political power?

As for the League of Europe, surely no one here would
wish to obstruct the plan. But if the League is to be
based on nothing more realistic than an absence of governmental thinking, it will be a very precarious league.
Every argument advanced by Mr. Dickinson is based on
the assumption of absolute free trade in the world, yet
in his plan of peace he says not one syllable about how
tariffs and discriminations and monopolies are to be
wiped out. The conflict between Germany and England
is world-wide, yet Mr. Dickinson is thinking only
of rectified frontiers in Europe.

When he proposes so readily a League of Europe with
a police force to carry out its jurisdiction, has he considered the possibility of civil war within the League?
If Germany and Austria rebelled against the League,
they would presumably be attacked on all sides. But
they are now attacked on all sides. We had on this continent a league of States with a central government, a
Supreme Court, and an army. In 1861 some of the
States seceded, and the struggle which followed, called a
Civil War, was a terrible conflict. Has Mr. Dickinson
faced the fact that a League of Europe would be based
on the *status quo,* would be a sort of legalization of every
existing injustice? And how does he propose to amend
peacefully the constitution of Europe if some nation objects too seriously?

The New Republic, Jan. 2, 1915.

THE MORROW OF THE WAR

In time
of war,
prepare
for peace.

This country (Great Britain) is at war, and has for the moment one overwhelming preoccupation: to render safe our national inheritance.

The Union of Democratic Control has been founded for the purpose of trying to secure for ourselves and the generations that succeed us a new course of policy which will prevent a similar peril ever again befalling our Empire. Many men and women have already joined us holding varying shades of opinion as to the origins of the war. Some think it was inevitable, some that it could and should have been avoided. *But we believe that all are in general agreement about two things: First, it is imperative that the war, once begun, should be prosecuted to a victory for our country. Secondly, it is equally imperative, while we carry on the war, to prepare for peace. Hard thinking, free discussion, the open exchange of opinion and information are the duty of all citizens to-day, if we are to have any hope that this war will not be what most wars of the past have been—merely the prelude to other wars.*

Our contribution to this necessary discussion are the principles put forward for consideration by the Union of Democratic Control.

The Union of Democratic Control has been created to insist that the following policy shall inspire the actual

86

conditions of peace, and shall dominate the situation
after peace has been declared:

1. No Province shall be transferred from one Government to another without consent by plébiscite or otherwise of the population of such Province.

2. No Treaty, Arrangement, or Undertaking shall be entered upon in the name of Great Britain without the sanction of Parliament. Adequate machinery for ensuring democratic control of foreign policy shall be created.

3. The Foreign Policy of Great Britain shall not be aimed at creating Alliances for the purpose of maintaining the "Balance of Power"; but shall be directed to the establishment of a Concert of the Powers and the setting up of an International Council whose deliberations and decisions shall be public, part of the labor of such Council to be the creation of definite Treaties of Arbitration and the establishment of Courts for their interpretation and enforcement.

4. Great Britain shall propose as part of the Peace settlement a plan for the drastic reduction by consent of the armaments of all the belligerent Powers, and to facilitate that policy shall attempt to secure the general nationalization of the manufacture of armaments, and the control of the export of armaments by one country to another.

It is the purpose of this pamphlet to elaborate and explain the considerations which underlie the policy outlined above.

I

No Province shall be transferred from one Government to another without the consent of plébiscite of the population of such Province.

87

There
must be
general
recognition
of principle
of plébiscite.

This condition has been placed first because if adhered to practically and in spirit, and if recognized by the European Powers as a principle that must guide all frontier rearrangements, it would help to put an end to European war.

If no province were retained under a Government's power against the will of its inhabitants, the policy of conquest and the imposition of political power would lose its *raison d'être*.

The subject as a whole is wrapped up, of course, with the principle of democratic government and is not merely a problem of international but of internal politics, and could not be treated briefly in a mere outline like the present. But any one who reflects carefully on the subject will see that the peace in Europe ultimately depends upon the acceptance of this idea.

It is obvious that there are many difficulties of detail in its application; that a plébiscite may be a mere form and not reflect the real wishes of the population concerned, and under military control it can be used as an instrument for obtaining an apparent sanction for oppression, and that in populations of mixed race it is very difficult of application. But it should not be impossible to guard against the defeat of the principle through defects in the working machinery. Plébiscites, where used at the end of the war, might be carried out under international supervision. The essential is that the principle involved should be clearly enunciated.

Fortunately the Government has already given the country a valuable lead in this matter. For Mr. Churchill, speaking on September 11, said:

"Now the war has come, and when it is over let us be careful not to make the same mistake or the same sort of mistake as Germany made when she had France prostrate at her feet in 1870. [Cheers.] Let us, what-

88

ever we do, fight for and work towards great and sound principles for the European system, and the first of those principles which we should keep before us is the principle of nationality—that is to say, not the conquest or subjugation of any great community, or of any strong race of men, but the setting free of those races which have been subjugated and conquered; and if doubt arises about disputed areas of country we should try to settle their ultimate destination in the reconstruction of Europe which must follow from this war with a fair regard to the wishes and feelings of the people who live in them.''

One nation must not be allowed to dominate another.

We agree with Mr. Churchill that the terms of peace should secure that there shall in the future be no more Alsace-Lorraines to create during half a century resentment, unrest, and intrigues for a *revanche*. The power of the victorious parties must not be used for vindictive oppression and dismemberment of beaten nationalities, but for the creation, by cooperation with all the belligerents, victors and vanquished alike, of a true society of nations, banded together for mutual security. The future relationship of the States of Europe must be not that of victor and vanquished, domination or subserviency, but of partnership. The struggle of one nation for domination over another must be replaced by the association of the people for their common good.

II

No Treaty, Arrangement, or Undertaking shall be entered upon in the name of Great Britain without the sanction of Parliament. Adequate machinery for ensuring democratic control of foreign policy shall be created.

89

The peoples of all constitutionally-governed countries
are justified in demanding that diplomatic relations
with their neighbors shall be conducted with the main
object of maintaining friendly international intercourse.
The increasing social and economic interdependence, the
ramifications of the credit system, the facility and ra-
pidity of intercommunication, the developing community
of intellectual interest, the growth of a collective social
consciousness, are combining to minimize the significance
of the purely political frontiers which divide civilized
States. For these reasons the world is moving towards
conferences when political difficulties arise as a substitute for war. The determination to preserve national
ideals and traditions offers no real obstacle. But the
common interest of civilized democracies cannot be advanced by a secret diplomacy out of touch with democratic sentiment.

The anomaly of such practises in a democratic State
has only to be understood to be condemned. All the domestic activities of a constitutional Government are
tested in the crucible of public analysis and criticism.
But the Government department charged with the supervision of the nation's intercourse with its neighbors,
which if wrongly handled may react with ruinous effect
upon the whole field of its domestic activities and upon
the future of its entire social economy, *not only escapes
efficient public control, but considers itself empowered
to commit the nation to specific courses and to involve
it in obligations to third parties entailing the risk of war,
without the nation's knowledge of consent.*

During the past eight years particularly, the management of the Foreign department has become avowedly
and frankly autocratic. Parliamentary discussion of
foreign policy has become so restricted as to be perfunctory. It is confined to a few hours' roving debate

90

on one day in each session. The eliciting of information by means of questions, never satisfactory, is rendered extremely difficult by the ingenuity employed in evading the issues it is attempted to raise. Advantage has been taken, of the wholesome desire that discussion of foreign policy should not partake of mere party recriminations, to burke discussion altogether, and this process has received the endorsement of both Front Benches. A claim to ''continuity'' has been further evolved to stifle debate on foreign affairs, whereas in point of fact, if one feature more than another has characterized British foreign policy of recent years, it has been its bewildering fluctuations. Parliamentary paralysis has had its counterpart in the country. The present Government's tenure of office has been marked by an almost complete abstention from public reference to foreign affairs. The public has been treated as though foreign affairs were outside—and properly outside—its ken. And the public has acquiesced. Every attempt to shake its apathy has been violently assailed by spokesmen of the Foreign Office in the press. The country has been told that its affairs were in the wisest hands, and that mystery and silence are the indispensable attributes to a successful direction of foreign policy. The caste system which prevails in the diplomatic service, and which has survived unimpaired the democratizing of the majority of the public services, facilitates these outworn political dogmatisms. Appointment is made by nomination and selection. Candidates are required to possess an income per annum of £400. The natural result is that the vast bulk of the national intelligence is debarred from the diplomatic field of employment. A study of the Foreign Office list will disclose the fact that over 95 per cent. of the British diplomatic staff is composed of members of the aristocracy and landed gentry.

Connection
between
politics
and busi-
ness is
ignored.

Inevitable exile from their country results in our
diplomatic representatives abroad losing touch with the
center of affairs and living in a mental atmosphere remote from the popular and progressive movements of the
time. Another pronounced characteristic of the system
is the indifference displayed by the Foreign Office to the
business interests of the nation. Our vast commercial
interests, so intimately affected by our relations with
foreign Powers, are regarded as lying outside the orbit
of diplomatic considerations. The connection between
politics and business—and by business we mean the
entire framework of peaceful commerce upon which the
prosperity of this country depends—appears to be ignored, or, at least, treated with indifference and something like contempt. The services of our Consuls abroad
are not sufficiently utilized, and the Consular machinery
requires complete overhauling. Such questions as, for
instance, the effect upon British commercial interest of
British diplomacy supporting the acquisition of undeveloped areas of the world's surface by a Power like
France, which imposes differential tariffs upon British
goods, and opposing the acquisition of such areas by a
Power like Germany, which admits British goods on
terms of equality, does not appear to enter into Foreign
Office calculations.

In the last few years also has been added another institution which modifies national policy without coming
under Parliamentary control, the Committee of Imperial
Defense. Its influence upon the Cabinet is nominally
indirect, and its activities confined to the discussion of
hypothetical events. But no one can doubt that its
recommendations exercise a powerful effect on the executive decisions of the Government. No criticism of the
advice given by the Committee is possible in Parliament.
Momentous military and naval schemes are prepared

there on which hang the issues of peace and war, as in the case of our recent relations to France. It is an intimate and powerful means of framing Government policy according to the ideas of military experts, without the knowledge and control of Parliament.

In the various ways indicated, opportunities of evincing an intelligent concern in its foreign policy has been increasingly withdrawn from the nation. The work of the Department escapes all outside control, loses all sense of contact with national life, and tends more and more to become an autocratic institution, contemptuous of the efforts of a small group of members in the House to acquire information, and utilizing a powerful section of the press to mold public opinion in the direction it considers public opinion should travel.

The nation awoke with a shock to the evils of this state of affairs in the summer of 1911, when it suddenly found itself on the very brink of war with Germany over a Franco-German quarrel about Morocco, and became cognizant of the existence of diplomatic entanglements of which it had no previous intimation.

It is obviously impossible to attempt here a full presentment of the Moroccan crisis of 1911. But the story is inseparably intertwined with the avowals to the House of Commons on August 3rd, 1914, of the secret understanding with France which has played so capital a part in bringing about British intervention in the present war.

So long as this situation prevails it must be perfectly clear to any man of ordinary intelligence that the system of government under which we live is not a democratic system, but its antithesis. It cannot be too often insisted upon that the domestic concerns of the nation, its constitutional liberties, its social reforms, all its internal activities in short, depend upon the preservation of peaceful relations with its neighbors. War in which this country is involved is certain to prove a serious check to social progress. Hence it is a matter of absolutely vital concern to the nation that the machinery of its Foreign Office should be thoroughly capable of performing its functions, and that the policy pursued by that department should be pursued with the knowledge and the consent of the nation. It is imperative not only that a treaty with a foreign Power should require endorsement by Parliament, but that no agreement or understanding possessing binding force and postulating the use of the national military and naval forces should be valid without the assent of Parliament. The nation should insist upon this essential reform, and should seriously apply itself to considering what other steps are needed to ensure some mechanical means whereby a greater national control of foreign policy can be secured; whether by the establishment of a permanent Committee of the House of Commons, by the adaptation to suit our needs of the American system under which a two-thirds majority of one branch of the Legislature is required for the validity of international agreements, or other procedure. *But real and permanent reforms will not be obtained unless the nation is determined to assert its fundamental right to participate in the formation of its own foreign policy.*

III

The Foreign Policy of Great Britain shall not be aimed at creating Alliances for the purpose of maintaining the "Balance of Power"; but shall be directed to the establishment of a Concert of Europe and the setting up of an International Council whose deliberations and decisions shall be public.

94

What does the "Balance of Power" mean?

It is popularly supposed to mean that no single Power or group of Powers should, in the interests of international peace, be allowed to acquire a preponderating position in Europe, and that the policy of Great Britain should be directed against such a consummation. British policy during the past few years has been based upon the assumption that Germany had attained, or was seeking to attain, that position of eminence.

It is that idea which, in the minds of masses of our people, justifies the present war.

But if this policy has been right in the past, what prospect does the future hold? The victory of the Allies —which is a vital necessity—must enormously upset the "balance" by making Russia the dominant military power of Europe, possibly the dictator both in this Continent and in Asia.

Russia can draw upon vast sources of human military material, only partly civilized. At present she is governed by a military autocracy which is largely hostile to Western ideas of political and religious freedom. There is hope in the minds of Western Liberals that the war may bring political liberation to Russia. At present that is only a hope. For wars have as often been a prelude to tyranny as to liberty. It is only too likely that after a victorious war our national feeling may revert to its old anti-Russian channel, and we shall again have the "Balance of Power" invoked to protect Europe and India against a new Russian preeminence.

Speaking generally, the "Balance of Power" is little more than a diplomatic formula made use of by the mouthpieces of the interests from whose operations war comes. It signifies nothing more than that, at a given moment, in a given country, there is an effort to hold up to the public gaze the Government and the people of an-

95

other country as being intent upon the destruction of its
neighbors. At one moment it is Russia, at another
France, and at another Germany. The "Balance of
Power" was invoked for several years and down to
within a few weeks of the Crimean War to inflame British public opinion against France. It was invoked
against Russia to justify the Crimean War, and France
was chosen as the ally with which to fight Russia! No
sooner had peace been signed than France became once
more the potential threat to the "Balance of Power";
and again during the period of rivalry in West and Central Africa, and in the Far East, in the late nineties.

Once the ball has been set rolling in the required direction, influences of all kinds are brought to bear for the
purpose of permanently fixing this idea in the public
mind. A flood of innuendo, denunciation, and distorted
information is let loose. Every dishonorable motive and
the most sinister of projects are attributed to the Government and the people selected for attack. The public
becomes the sport of private ambitions and interests, of
personal prejudices and obscure passions, which it can
neither detect nor control, and, for the most part, does
not even suspect. The power for mischief wielded by
these forces is to-day immense, owing to a cheap press
and to the concentration of a large number of newspapers, possessing in the aggregate an enormous circula-
tion, under one directing will. At the present moment
the editorial and news columns of some fifty British
newspapers echo the views of one man, who is thus able
to superimpose in permanent fashion upon public thought
the dead weight of his own prejudices or personal aims
and intentions, and to exercise a potent influence upon
the Government of the day.

For the last few years these newspapers have striven
with unceasing pertinacity to create an atmosphere of

ill-will and suspicion between Great Britain and Germany. The effort has been continuous, systematic, and magnificently organized, and inferential evidence is not lacking that it has been pursued with the approval and even with the assistance of certain official influences, and to the satisfaction of certain foreign Governments. This propaganda has had, needless to say, its counterpart in Germany. *The net result of the latest recrudescence of the "Balance of Power" policy with its Alliances and Ententes as the dominating factor in international relationships is now visible to all men. A quarrel (whose culminating episode was the murder in a Bosnian town of the heir to the Austrian throne last June) between Austria and Serbia, to which the Russian Government determined to become a party, has already involved the peoples of France, Belgium, Britain, and Germany, the first three of whom were not even remotely concerned, in a terrible and desolating war.* How the "Balance of Power" works.

Japan and Montenegro have also become involved, and the same fate may overtake Holland, Italy, the other Balkan States, and the Scandinavian Powers. But for the policy of the "Balance of Power" the results of the quarrel would almost certainly have been confined to the parties immediately affected, and an early mediation by the neutral Powers would have been possible.

Bright's scathing denunciation of the fetish of the "Balance of Power" appeals with even greater force to us to-day:

"You cannot comprehend at a thought what is meant by this balance of power. If the record could be brought before you—but it is not possible to the eye of humanity to scan the scroll upon which are recorded the sufferings which the theory of the balance of power has entailed upon this country. It rises up before me when I think of it as a ghastly phantom . . . which has

It must be
superseded
by a council
of nations.
loaded the nation with debt and with taxes, has sacrificed the lives of hundreds of thousands of Englishmen,
has desolated the homes of millions of families, and has
left us, as the great result of the profligate expenditure
which it has caused, a doubled peerage at one end of the
social scale, and far more than a doubled pauperism
at the other.''

For a system therefore which carries with it the implication that the interests of nations are necessarily in
constant conflict and which involves the permanent division of Europe into two hostile competing groups, we
must substitute machinery which will facilitate cooperation and a reasonable solution of differences between all
the peoples of the world.

The objective should be a real council of the nations
with at first very limited powers, rather an expansion
of an alliance of three Powers against three, into a
league of six Powers, designed to act against any one
recalcitrant member which might threaten the peace of
the whole. To this ideal, indeed, the pronouncement of
Mr. Asquith in his Dublin speech has already pointed,
while it is noteworthy that Sir Edward Grey himself
seems in a significant passage of one of his despatches
to admit the failure of the balance principle and to indicate that the nations must ''start afresh'' on the basis of
a general council. This passage is as follows:

''If the peace of Europe can be preserved, and the
present crisis safely passed, my own endeavor will be to
promote some arrangement to which Germany could be
a party, by which she could be assured that no aggressive or hostile policy would be pursued against her or
her allies by France, Russia, and ourselves, jointly or
separately. I have desired this and worked for it as
far as I could through the last Balkan crisis; and Germany having a corresponding object, our relations sen-

98

sibly improved. The idea has hitherto been too Utopian
to form the subject of definite proposals, but if this
present crisis, so much more acute than any Europe has
gone through for generations, be safely passed, I am
hopeful that the relief and reaction which will follow
may make possible some more definite *rapprochement*
between the Powers than has been possible hitherto.''

Armaments,
the instru-
ment of
diplomacy,
must be
reduced.

It is from some such simple beginning, pursued with
good will and perseverance by all parties, that the nations may hope to arrive at a system of cooperation to
replace the system of hostile alliances, the fruits of
which are the present war.

It is essential, of course, if the negotiations of such a
council are to be lifted out of the atmosphere of diplomatic intrigue which the secrecy of negotiations always
involves, that its deliberations be public. Publicity will
at one and the same time be a guarantee of openness, of
good faith, and of democratic control.

IV

*Great Britain shall propose as part of the Peace settle-
ment a plan for the drastic reduction by consent of the
armaments of all the belligerent Powers, and to facilitate that policy shall attempt to secure the general nationalization of the manufacture of armaments, and the
control of the export of armaments by one country to
another.*

The theory of the ''Balance of Power'' and secret
diplomacy are two factors which, in combination, make
for war.

Two other factors intimately connected with these
ensure its certainty. They are: a constant progression
in expenditure upon armaments, and the toleration of a
private armament interest.

99

Competitive
armaments
mean the
bankruptcy
of states-
manship.

It would be labor wasted to endeavor to apportion responsibility between the various European Governments for the insane competition in armaments which of recent years has attained incredible proportions. No government can escape liability. Each government has defended its policy on the ground that its neighbor's action compelled it to do so. Many of the governing statesmen of the world have alternately confessed their helplessness, attacked their rivals, appealed to public opinion, and blamed the warlike tendencies inherent in the people whose destinies they control. Every government, without exception, has proceeded on the assumption that in order to ensure peace it had to be stronger than its neighbor, a philosophy which could have but one possible outcome—war. In pursuance of this phantom, a considerable proportion of the wealth of the European States has been wasted, and activities have been withdrawn from the constructive work of the world, to prepare for the world's destruction. And with every fresh outburst of expenditure, responding to some diplomatic check or alarmist propaganda, fresh fagots have been piled around Europe's powder magazine. The disaster which has fallen upon Europe is the fitting sequel to the bankruptcy of statesmanship which this policy embodies.

The more extensive the armaments, the greater the temptation to seize an opportunity for testing their efficiency; the greater the nervousness and irritation of Governments when negotiating; the greater the pressure upon those Governments of the powerful professional and other interests concerned in armament construction.

The policy of gigantic armaments cannot in the very nature of things ensure any final settlement of disputes between States. It leads, and can only lead, to an in-

100

tolerable situation from which war comes to be regarded Armament industry rests in government demand, by diplomacy as the only escape.

An all-round limitation of armaments must follow the present war if the world is to be permanently relieved of the nightmare which has weighed upon it for so long. We can no longer afford to listen to arguments as to the impracticability of such a course from those whose claims to the possession of human wisdom and experienced guidance have so utterly broken down.

The difficulty of compelling a change in the policy of European Governments has been intensified by the conditions under which armament construction is carried on in this and other countries. Every one is familiar with the fact that the object of a commercial firm is to push its wares in every legitimate manner, to advertise them, and systematically to tout for orders both at home and abroad. Every one is aware that there exists a powerfully-equipped industry for the manufacture of military and naval engines and instruments of offense. Disguise it as we may, that industry waxes and wanes, the profits its management derives rise and fall, the dividends earned by its shareholders increase and dwindle in the measure of the demand for the articles it produces. That demand does not emanate from members of the public. It emanates from the military and naval departments of the public services. The industry relies, therefore, for its existence and for its profits not upon a private demand, but upon a Government demand, and the extent of that Government demand will depend upon the view which the Government may take of the number and nature of these articles required to ensure the national safety. Such a condition of affairs is a permanent and terrible danger both to democratic government and to international peace. What are its implications?

There is created in every country an economic force
101

in private hands directly interested in war and in the preparation for war; directly interested in assisting to bring about a general atmosphere advantageous to an industry which, were wars to cease or the expenditure on armaments to be substantially reduced, would suffer accordingly. What the successful prosecution of an ordinary commercial undertaking requires this industry also requires. The demand for the article must be created. That basic situation engenders effects which can only be appreciated in their cumulative significance. It is not at all necessary to attribute sinister machinations to individuals. These effects are automatic. An industry disposing, as does this one, of an enormous aggregate of capital possesses almost unlimited power of influence and suggestion. For such purposes the press is a potent instrument ready at hand. Many of those most closely associated with this great industry are men of considerable influence. Some have been in the public service and have acquaintances in the Government Departments. Others may be on friendly and perfectly honorable terms with the proprietors or editors of newspapers or associations of newspapers. The proprietor of a newspaper may be honestly convinced, or may by arguments be persuaded, that an agitation for increased armaments is advisable. If he is acquainted with one of the directors of the armament industry that acquaintance will hardly act as a deterrent to his entertaining those views. He may be furnished with special information, accurate or otherwise, as to the projects, real or alleged, of other Governments, which will be familiar to the director through his connection with Continental branches of the same industry. The press may be utilized in a similar manner by certain permanent officials in the nation's Foreign Department, who feel that their views of the international situation can be best

102

served by a press campaign of a certain kind. The in- fluence of the industry which stands to gain from the existence of these views, and the willingness of newspaper editors and proprietors to push them on to the public, cannot be expected to intervene against their propagation. Again, an ambitious Minister, in charge of one of the fighting branches of the public service, desirous of placing his personality in the limelight and focusing public attention upon the affairs of his Department, will be from that circumstance a readier listener to representations from the industry in question. Those representations may quite legitimately take the form of pointing out that heavy expenses have been incurred in providing a certain type of machinery or special accommodation for the construction of a particular kind of offensive instrument, that the orders have not kept pace with the expenditure, and that if further orders be not forthcoming losses will ensue and future facilities for production be necessarily restricted. There would be nothing indefensible in representations of this character. And again, it is not unlikely that a member of Parliament, convinced of certain public dangers associated with the existing system, but representing a constituency where this great industry is established and employs, perhaps, not an inconsiderable section of the local labor, may find his freedom of speech considerably curtailed lest he should be accused of taking the bread from the mouths of some of his constituents.

Endless, indeed, are the ramifications of a *private* industrial interest so wealthy and so well organized, and dependent for its profits upon *national* expenditure in instruments of warfare, and, consequently, in the ultimate resort, upon war itself. *The general influence exerted upon public life as a whole by the very fact that this industry is a private one, and possesses a large body*

103

*of shareholders usually belonging to the upper strata
of society, cannot be regarded otherwise than as an un-
healthy and dangerous element in the nation.* Emphasis is lent to this aspect of the case when it is borne in
mind that the armaments industry has of late years become internationalized to a remarkable degree. Recent
disclosures, the accuracy of which has not been disputed,
in Germany, France, England, and Japan, have clearly
shown an inter-connection of the armament interest pro-
ductive of repellent accompaniments. This inter-connection of interest has, for example, made it possible for
a body of British shareholders, including prominent ec-
clesiastics, members of Parliament, and even Cabinet
Ministers, to be financially interested in enterprises engaged in the manufacture of engines of destruction
impartially used in the slaughter of Englishmen, Frenchmen, Germans, and Russians.

But however revolting this may be, it is insignificant
compared with the graver peril to which precedent allusion has been made. *Reflection must bring with it the
conviction that the armament industry is not one which
the nation can safely permit to be retained in private
hands and to be the subject of private profit.*

What, then, is to be our policy in connection with the
war? First and foremost we must be victorious. That
is a prime necessity upon which the nation is unanimous.
We must win not only because many British institutions
of the highest value would be destroyed by our defeat,
not only because Prussia, our principal enemy, is the
leading exponent of that doctrine of military domination and intolerance which is incompatible with a permanently peaceful Europe; but also because we must
see justice done, as far as may be, to the least powerful
of our Allies. *Ample compensation must be secured for*

104

Belgium to repair her material loss and in recognition *of the wrong done to her.*

What of the future? What lessons do the incompetence and secretiveness, the jealousies and vanities of that vaunted European statecraft which has plunged the world in war convey to the peoples who are its victims?

What can the people do to amend a system under which they are used as pawns in a game of chess?

They can begin to understand what that system is and that its existence is their undoing. They can begin to understand the monstrous errors and fallacies which underlie the whole teaching imposed upon their intelligence. They can begin to understand that this immunity from public control enjoyed by the small group of professional men who manipulate international relations has led to the establishment amongst the latter of a standard of conduct which would not be tolerated in the ordinary affairs of a well-ordered community. They can begin to understand that "high politics" in the diplomatic world has become a synonym for intrigue; that a code of morals is therein practised which, in other branches of the public service, would entail dismissal, and in the business world would involve disgrace.

They can force themselves to a mental effort which shall lead them to the realization of the complete artificiality of the conditions under which they suffer, the remoteness from their real and vital needs of the issues for which they are asked to sacrifice all that they hold dear. *They can rid themselves of the paralyzing belief that their relations with their neighbors are so complicated and mysterious as to be beyond their comprehension. They can bring themselves to grasp a plain and demonstrable truth, and to appreciate its full significance, which is that those to whom they have looked for guidance, those who have told them that in the pre-*

*servation of the "Balance of Power," and in the multi-
plication of colossal armaments lay the one chance of
international peace, have been utterly, hopelessly, calam-
itously wrong. They can put to themselves these simple
issues.*

"By the terrible logic of events which now confront
us we see that the methods advocated by those to whose
training and wisdom we trusted to ensure peace among
the nations have entirely failed. The system which we
were induced reluctantly to support, far from preserving
peace, has precipitated us into the greatest conflict in
history, a conflict we passionately desired to avoid, and
for the avoidance of which we made heavy sacrifices
because, we were told, that therein lay our hope of
averting it. The system was wrong. We must evolve
another."

The idea of a federalized Europe, regulated by an
Areopagus, involving the disappearance, or substantial
reduction, of standing armies and navies, and the submission of all disputes to a Central Council, is not to
be dismissed. It is the ultimate goal to aim at. But it
cannot be attained until the constitutionally governed
democracies of the West are brought to realize how impossible it is that their moral and spiritual development
and their happiness and well-being can be secured under
a system of government which leaves them at the mercy
of the intrigues and imbecilities of professional diplomatists and of the ambitions of military castes; helpless,
too, in the face of an enormously powerful and internationalized private interest dependent for its profits
upon the maintenance of that "armed peace" which is
the inevitable prelude to the carnage and futility of
war.

To awaken these sentiments among the democracies of
this and other countries, to instil into them these con-

victions, to ensure the cooperation of all forces in all Democracies in the different countries must cooperate. countries working to that end—is the task to which we must all turn our attention.

Potentates, diplomatists, and militarists made this war. They should not be allowed to arrange unchecked and uncontrolled the terms of peace and to decide alone the conditions which will follow it. The mass of the people who suffer from their blunders and their quarrels must claim the ineradicable right of participating in the future settlement.

And, when peace has come, the democratic parties of Europe must set before themselves a new province of political effort. That peace will be permanently preserved only if our artisans and industrialists keep up with the artisans and industrialists of other countries a constant and deliberate communication through their political parties and other organizations which will prevent misunderstandings and subdue the hatreds out of which war ultimately comes.

"The Morrow of the War," Union of Democratic Control, London, Bulletin No. 1.

NO PEACE WITHOUT FEDERATION

The great war has now been going on long enough to enable mankind to form approximately correct views about its vast extent and scale of operations, its sudden interference with commerce and all other helpful international intercourse, its unprecedented wrecking of family happiness and continuity, its wiping out, as it proceeds, of the accumulated savings of many former generations in structures, objects of art, and industrial capital, and the huge burdens it is likely to impose on twentieth-century Europe. From all these points of view, it is evidently the most horrible calamity that has ever befallen the human race, and the most crucial trial to which civilization has been exposed. It is, and is to be, the gigantic struggle of these times between the forces which make for liberty and righteousness and those which make for the subjection of the individual man, the exaltation of the State, and the enthronement of physical force directed by a ruthless collective will. It threatens a sweeping betrayal of the best hopes of mankind.

Each of the nations involved, horrified at the immensity of the disaster, maintains that it is not responsible for the war; and each Government has issued a statement to prove that some other Government is responsible for the outbreak. This discussion, however, relates almost entirely to actions by monarchs and Cabinets between July 23 and August 4—a short period of

108

hurried messages between the chancelleries of Europe —actions which only prove that the monarchs and ministers for foreign affairs could not, or at least did not, prevent the long-prepared general war from breaking out. The assassination of the Archduke and Duchess of Hohenberg, on the 28th of June, was in no proper sense a cause of the war, except as it was one of the consequences of the persistent aggressions of Austria-Hungary against her southeastern neighbors. Neither was Russian mobilization in four military districts on July 29 a cause of the war; for that was only an external manifestation of the Russian state of mind toward the Balkan peoples, a state of mind well known to all publicists ever since the Treaty of Berlin in 1878. No more was the invasion of Belgium by the German army on August 4 a true cause of the war, or even the cause, as distinguished from the occasion, of Great Britain's becoming involved in it. By that action, Germany was only taking the first step in carrying out a long-cherished purpose, and in executing a judicious plan of campaign prepared many years in advance. The artificial panic in Germany about its exposed position between two powerful enemies, France and Russia, was not a genuine cause of the war; for the General Staff knew they had crushed France once, and were confident they could do it again in a month. As to Russia, it was, in their view, a huge nation, but very clumsy and dull in war.

The real causes of the war are all of many years' standing; and all the nations now involved in the fearful catastrophe have contributed to the development of one or more of these effective causes. The fundamental causes are: (1) The maintenance of monarchical Governments, each sanctioned and supported by the national religion, and each furnished with a Cabinet selected by the monarch,—Governments which can make war with-

109

The most
potent
cause is
the lust
for world-
empire.
out any previous consultation of the peoples through their elected representatives; (2) the constant maintenance of conscript armies, through which the entire able-bodied male population is trained in youth for service in the army or navy, and remains subject to the instant call of the Government till late in life, the officering of these permanent armies involving the creation of a large military class likely to become powerful in political, industrial, and social administration; (3) the creation of a strong, permanent bureaucracy within each nation for the management of both foreign and domestic affairs, much of whose work is kept secret from the public at large; and finally (4) the habitual use of military and naval forces to acquire new territories, contiguous or detached, without regard to the wishes of the people annexed or controlled. This last cause of the war is the most potent of the four, since it is strong in itself, and is apt to include one or more of the other three. It is the gratification of the lust for world-empire.

Of all the nations taking part in the present war, Great Britain is the only one which does not maintain a conscript army; but, on the other hand, Great Britain is the earliest modern claimant of world-empire by force, with the single exception of Spain, which long since abandoned that quest. Every one of these nations except little Servia has yielded to the lust for empire. Every one has permitted its monarch or its Cabinet to carry on secret negotiations liable at any time to commit the nation to war, or to fail in maintaining the peace of Europe or of the Near East. In the crowded diplomatic events of last July, no phenomenon is more striking than the exhibition of the power which the British people confide to the hands of their Foreign Secretary. In the interests of public liberty and public welfare no official should possess such powers as Sir Edward Grey

110

used admirably—though in vain—last July. In all Germany has been the leader in imperialism. three of the empires engaged in the war there has long existed a large military caste which exerts a strong influence on the Government and its policies, and on the daily life of the people.

These being the real causes of the terrific convulsion now going on in Europe, it cannot be questioned that the nation in which these complex causes have taken strongest and most complete effect during the last fifty years is Germany. Her form of government has been imperialistic and autocratic in the highest degree. She has developed with great intelligence and assiduity the most formidable conscript army in the world, and the most influential and insolent military caste. Three times since 1864 she has waged war in Europe, and each time she has added to her territory without regard to the wishes of the annexed population. For twenty-five years she has exhibited a keen desire to obtain colonial possessions; and since 1896 she has been aggressive in this field. In her schools and universities the children and youth have been taught for generations that Germany is surrounded by hostile peoples, that her expansion in Europe and in other continents is resisted by jealous Powers which started earlier in the race for foreign possessions, and that the salvation of Germany has depended from the first, and will depend till the last, on the efficiency of her army and navy and the warlike spirit of her people. This instruction, given year after year by teachers, publicists, and rulers, was first generally accepted in Prussia, but now seems to be accepted by the entire empire as unified in 1871.

The attention of the civilized world was first called to this state of the German mind and will by the triumphant policies of Bismarck; but during the reign of the present Emperor the external aggressiveness of Ger-

The
German
ethics is
the ethics of
valor and
the State.

many and her passion for world-empire have grown to much more formidable proportions. Although the German Emperor has sometimes played the part of the peacemaker, he has habitually acted the war-lord in both speech and bearing, and has supported the military caste whenever it has been assailed. He is by inheritance, conviction, and practise a divine-right sovereign whose throne rests on an "invincible" army, an army conterminous with the nation. In the present tremendous struggle he carries his subjects with him in a rushing torrent of self-sacrificing patriotism. Mass-fanaticism and infectious enthusiasm seem to have deprived the leading class in Germany, for the moment, of all power to see, reason, and judge correctly—no new phenomenon in the world, but instructive in this case because it points to the grave defect in German education—the lack of liberty and, therefore, of practise in self-control.

The twentieth-century educated German is, however, by no means given over completely to material and physical aggrandizement and the worship of might. He cherishes a partly new conception of the State as a collective entity whose function is to develop and multiply, not the free, healthy, and happy individual man and woman, but higher and more effective types of humanity, made superior by a strenuous discipline which takes much account of the strong and ambitious, and little of the weak or meek. He rejects the ethics of the Beatitudes as unsound, but accepts the religion of Valor, which exalts strength, courage, endurance, and the ready sacrifice by the individual of liberty, happiness, and life itself for Germany's honor and greatness. A nation of sixty millions holding these philosophical and religious views, and proposing to act on them in winning by force the empire of the world, threatens civilization with more formidable irruptions of a destroying host than any that

112

history has recorded. The rush of the German army into Belgium, France, and Russia and its consequences to those lands have taught the rest of Europe to dread German domination, and—it is to be hoped—to make it impossible.

The real cause of the present convulsion is, then, the state of mind or temper of Germany, including her conception of national greatness, her theory of the State, and her intelligent and skilful use of all the forces of nineteenth-century applied science for the destructive purposes of war. It is, therefore, apparent that Europe can escape from the domination of Germany only by defeating her in her present undertakings; and that this defeat can be brought about only by using against her the same effective agencies of destruction and the same martial spirit on which Germany itself relies. Horrible as are the murderous and devastating effects of this war, there can be no lasting peace until Europe as a whole is ready to make some serious and far-reaching decisions in regard to governmental structures and powers. In all probability the sufferings and losses of this widespread war must go farther and cut deeper before Europe can be brought to the decisions which alone can give securities for lasting peace against Germany on the one hand and Russia on the other, or to either of these nations, or can give security for the future to any of the smaller nations of Continental Europe. There can, indeed, be no security for future peace in Europe until every European nation recognizes the fact that there is to be no such thing in the world as one dominating nation—no such thing as world-empire for any single nation—Great Britain, Germany, Russia, Japan, or China. There can be no sense of security against sudden invasion in Europe so long as all the able-bodied men are trained to be soldiers, and the best possible

armies are kept constantly ready for instant use. There
can be no secure peace in Europe until a federation of
the European States is established, capable of making
public contracts intended to be kept, and backed by an
overwhelming international force subject to the orders
of an international tribunal. The present convulsion
demonstrates the impotence toward permanent peace of
secret negotiations, of unpublished agreements, of treaties and covenants that can be broken on grounds of military necessity, of international law if without sanctions,
of pious wishes, of economic and biological predictions,
and of public opinion unless expressed through a firm
international agreement, behind which stands an international force. When that international force has been
firmly established it will be time to consider what proportionate reductions in national armaments can be pru-
dently recommended. Until that glorious day dawns,
no patriot and no lover of his kind can expect lasting
peace in Europe or wisely advocate any reduction of
armaments.

The hate-breeding and worse than brutal cruelties and
devastations of the war with their inevitable moral and
physical degradations ought to shock mankind into attempting a great step forward. Europe and America
should undertake to exterminate the real causes of the
catastrophe. In studying that problem the coming European conference can profit by the experience of the
three prosperous and valid countries in which public
liberty and the principle of federation have been most
successfully developed—Switzerland, Great Britain, and
the United States. Switzerland is a democratic federation which unites in a firm federal bond three different
racial stocks speaking three unlike languages, and divided locally and irregularly between the Catholic
Church and the Protestant. The so-called British Em-

114

pire tends strongly to become a federation; and the A federalized Europe is possible, even if the road is long. methods of government both in Great Britain itself and in its affiliated commonwealths are becoming more and more democratic in substance. The war has brought this fact out in high relief. As to the United States, it is a strong federation of forty-eight heterogeneous States which has been proving for a hundred years that freedom and democracy are safer and happier for mankind than subjection to any sort of autocracy, and afford far the best training for national character and national efficiency. Republican France has not yet had time to give this demonstration, being encumbered with many survivals of the Bourbon and Napoleonic régimes, and being forced to maintain a conscript army.

It is an encouraging fact that every one of the political or governmental changes needed is already illustrated in the practise of one or more of the civilized nations. To exaggerate the necessary changes is to postpone or prevent a satisfactory outcome from the present calculated destructions and wrongs and the accompanying moral and religious chaos. Ardent proposals to remake the map of Europe, reconstruct European society, substitute republics for empires, and abolish armaments are in fact obstructing the road toward peace and goodwill among men. That road is hard at best.

The immediate duty of the United States is presumably to prepare, on the basis of its present army and navy, to furnish an effective quota of the international force, servant of an international tribunal, which will make the ultimate issue of this most abominable of wars, not a truce, but a durable peace.

Charles W. Eliot, "The Road Toward Peace," chap. XI.

115

PART II
A LEAGUE OF PEACE

PART II. A LEAGUE OF PEACE

BASES FOR CONFEDERATION

After this war is over, will the nations fall back again The substitution of partnership for force. into the armed peace, the rival alliances, the Balance of Power with competing armaments, the preparations for another war thus made "inevitable," or will they go forward to the realization of the idea of "public right," as expounded by Mr. Asquith, "the substitution for force, for the clash of competing ambitions, for groupings and alliances and a precarious equipoise, of a real European partnership, based on the recognition of equal rights and established and enforced by the common will?" The preservation and progress of civilization demand that the peoples go forward. But how shall "public right" be realized?

The issue is, perhaps, best approached by putting a narrower, more concrete question: How can nations be got to reduce their armaments? For this action will be the best test and pledge of the establishment of "public right" and the reliance on a pacific future. Could a conference of Powers bring about a reduction of armaments by agreement? Surely not unless the motives which have led them in the past to arm are reversed. These motives are either a desire to be stronger than some other Power, in order to take something from him by force—the aggressive motive; or a desire to be strong enough to prevent some other Power from acting in this way to us—the defensive motive. Now how can these

119

The League
of Peace must
become an In-
ternational
government. motives be reversed? Nations may enter into a solemn
undertaking to refer all differences or disputes that may
arise to arbitration or to other peaceful settlement. If
they can be got to adhere to such a general agreement,
international law and public right will take the place of
private force, and wars of aggression and defense will
no longer happen. But what will ensure the fulfilment
of their undertaking by all the signatory Powers? Public opinion and a common sense of justice are found in-
adequate safeguards. There must be an executive power
enabled to apply an economic boycott, or in the last resort an international force. If this power is adequate,
it will secure the desired reversal of the offensive and the
defensive motives to armaments, and will by a natural
process lead to a reduction of national forces.

But it is not safe for the League of Nations to wait
until difficulties ripen into quarrels. There must be
some wider power of inquiry and settlement vested in a
representative Council of the Nations. This will in substance mean a legislative power. For peace cannot be
secured by adopting a purely statical view of the needs
and rights of nations in relation to one another. New
applications of the principles of political "autonomy"
and of "the open door" will become necessary, and some
international method of dealing with them is essential.
So there emerges the necessity of extending the idea of a
League of Peace into that of an International Government.

The new era of internationalism requires the replace-
ment of the secret diplomacy of Powers by the public
intercourse of Peoples through their chosen representatives. If the Peace which ends this war is to be durable,
it must be of a kind to facilitate the setting-up of these
new international arrangements. No timid, tentative
quarter measures will suffice. Courage and faith are

120

needed for a great new extension of the art of government. . . .

Almost everybody hopes that, when this war is over, it will be possible to secure the conditions of a lasting peace by reducing the power of militarism and by setting the relations between nations on a better footing. To watchers of the present conflict it seems an intolerable thought that, after the fighting is done, we should once more return to a condition of "armed peace," with jealous, distrustful, and revengeful Powers piling up armaments and plotting singly or in groups against their neighbors until Europe is plunged into another war more terrible, more bloody, and more costly than this. Yet nothing is more certain than that this will happen unless the Peoples which are so vitally concerned are able to mobilize their powers of clear thought, sane feeling, and goodwill in carefully considered plans for a cooperative policy of nations.

The first great obstacle to the performance of this task is the state of mind of those who seem to think that all that is required is "to crush German militarism," and that, this incubus once removed, the naturally pacific disposition of all other nations will dispose them to live together in amity. It is not easy to induce such persons to consider closely what they mean by "crushing German militarism," or how its destruction, whatever it does mean, would secure the peace of Europe, we will not say in perpetuity, but for a single generation. But let us suppose the most complete success for the arms of the Allies, the slaughter or the capture of great German forces, the invasion of Germany, and the dictation of terms of peace by the Allies at Berlin. Such terms as were imposed might cripple her military power of aggression or revenge for some years. But would it kill what we know as German militarism? If our accepted

121

political analysis be right, the German militarism that must be crushed is not an army and a navy, but a spirit of national aggression, proud, brutal, and unscrupulous, the outcome of certain intellectual and moral tendencies embodied in the "real" politics and the "real" culture of the nation. Can we seriously suppose that this evil spirit will be exorcised by a crushing defeat on land and sea, followed by a humiliating peace? If Germany could be permanently disabled from entertaining any hopes of recovering her military strength, or from exercising any considerable influence in the high policy of Europe, her feelings of resentment and humiliation might perhaps be left to rankle in impotence, or to die out by lapse of time. But nothing which the Allies can do to Germany will leave her in such long-lasting impotence. Even if stripped of her non-Teutonic lands and populations, she will remain a great Power—great in area, population, industry, and organizing power— and no temporary restrictions or guarantees can long prevent her from once more developing a military strength that will give dangerous meaning to her thirst for vengeance. Whether the hegemony of Prussia over a confederation of German States (possibly including Austria) be retained or not, Europe can have no security that the same passions which stirred France to the most strenuous efforts to recover her military strength after 1870 will not be similarly operative throughout Germany. We cannot feel sure that the experience of the most disastrous war will effectively destroy the hold of Prussianism, and that the efficiency of intellect and will which constitute that power will not be able to reassert their sway over a broken Germany.

The fear of such a revival of German strength will remain ever-present in her neighbors, and will compel them to maintain great military preparations. A beaten

122

Germany, with a ring of military Powers round her, watching every phase of her recovery with suspicion, and always liable to quarrel among themselves, will not give peace to Europe. Even, therefore, if we assign to Germany a monopoly of the spirit of aggressive militarism, European peace is not secured by crushing Germany. A saner review of the situation, however, will recognize that Germany has no such monopoly of the spirit of aggression, though that spirit has in her recent policy found its most formidable and most conscious expression. If the craving for a colonial Empire with "places in the sun" was, as seems likely, the principal factor in the aggressive designs of Germany, can we confidently assert that no other State has in the past harbored such designs, or may not harbor them again? The expansive Imperialism of Great Britain, France, Russia, and even more recently of Japan, gives the lie to any such assertion. Pan-Slavism is in spirit identical with the Pan-Teutonism which has contributed to this *débâcle,* and Great Britain and France are already sated with the overseas Empire which Germany was craving. History shows that, in every militarist State, aggressive and defensive motives and purposes are present together in different degrees at all times. While, therefore, we may reasonably think that the aggressive militarism of Germany held increasing sway in the political direction of that Empire during recent years, and was the direct efficient cause of the present conflict, we cannot hold that, with the defeat or even the destruction of the military and naval power of Germany, militarism would tend to disappear from the European system, and that the relations between nations would henceforth undergo so radical a change as to secure the world against all likelihood of forcible outbreaks in the future.

Clearly, it is not German militarism alone, but mili-

123

tarism in general that must be broken. The real question is how to change the inner attitude of nations, their beliefs and feelings towards one another, so as to make each nation and its rulers recognize that it is no longer either desirable or feasible to seek peculiar advantages for itself by bringing force to bear upon another nation.

But it may be urged, granted that disarmament may not be set afoot spontaneously and separately by the different nations, mutual disarmament can occur by arrangement between the Powers, which, after the menace of German aggression is removed, will be disposed to take this step in concert. Such disarmament, it is usually conceived, will not stand alone, but will form an important feature of a larger international policy, by which the Powers will agree among themselves to settle any differences that may arise by reference to courts of conciliation or of arbitration, and perhaps also to concert measures of common action in dealing with States and territories not within their jurisdiction. Such a concert of European Powers has hitherto appeared to many to yield an adequate basis for the peace of Europe, if it could be brought about. It has also seemed to most men the utmost limit of the actually attainable. The idea of the possibility of any closer relation between sovereign independent States has been dismissed as chimerical.

Now in any discussion of the feasibility of such a concert of European or world Powers as will by mutual agreement secure disarmament and a settlement of differences by judicial methods, it must be recognized at the outset that this war may make the successful pursuance of such a policy more difficult than it would have been before. A Balance of Power, whatever may have been its other disadvantages, seemed in itself favorable to the possibilities of an agreement in which each nation, or group of nations, might be an equal gainer. But a decisive victory in war, which leaves the Allied nations with a strong preponderance of power, is less likely to yield a satisfactory basis of agreement for a mutual disarmament. Is it likely that they will readily consent to a reduction in their several military and naval forces equivalent to the reduction they will demand in the forces of the nations that have been their enemies? To put the difficulty in concrete terms: Would France consent to an early reduction of her army upon terms which would leave her fighting-strength as compared with that of Germany relatively the same as before the war? Would Great Britain consent to reduce her navy in the same proportion as the reduction she required of Germany? Even if the Allies believed that the proportionate reduction would be duly carried out by Germany, would they regard such an arrangement as affording the desired security? Obviously not. It may, of course, be urged that an agreed basis of reduction might be reached, according to which the relative strength of army and navy assigned to Germany would be smaller than before. But the more closely the proposition is examined the less feasible does it appear. What basis for the size of armies could reasonably, or even plausibly, be suggested which would not assign to Germany a larger preponderance over France in number of soldiers than she possesses at present? Size of population, or of frontiers, the two most reasonable considerations for apportioning defensive needs, would tell in favor of Germany against France. True it would tell even more strongly in favor of Russia, assigning her, in fact, a relatively larger military predominance in Europe than she has ever claimed. But would either France or Germany regard the new military situation as safe or desirable? Nor would there be any permanence in an arrangement based on such a mutable factor as population, according to which the

125

German preponderance over France and of Russia over
Germany would be continually increasing. If area of
territory, as well as population and frontiers, were taken
into consideration in fixing a basis, France would come
off a little better in relation to Germany, but the size of
Russia, even if her European lands were alone included,
would give her an overwhelming advantage. If, as
might not unreasonably be claimed, the extra-European
possessions of Russia, Great Britain, and France must be
reckoned in, either on a basis of territory or of population, Great Britain and Russia would possess a superi-
ority of military strength which would give them, acting
together, a complete control over the politics of Europe
and Asia. Or, were the United States to come into the
arrangement, the military strength of Anglo-Saxondom
might too obviously surpass that of any likely combination of other Powers.

Again, what basis of naval strength would be satisfactory? Great Britain would not think of accepting
the area, population, or frontier factors unless the Empire as well as the British Isles were counted in. On the
other hand, her proposal, that volume of shipping and of
foreign trade should count heavily in the basis, might
give her for the time being an even greater preponderance over other navies than she has hitherto possessed.

If the comparison of the military and naval strength
of nations were conducted, as in the past, by direct consideration of the numerical strength and the fighting
value of the several items of an army and a navy, agreement upon a basis of reduction would be manifestly impossible. The discovery and acceptance of any standard
unit of naval or military value applicable to changing
conditions of modern warfare are found to be impracticable. For though every military budget implies the acceptance of some scale of values by which the worth of a

126

battery of artillery is compared with that of a battalion of infantry, while every naval budget involves a calculation of the worth of a submarine or a seaplane as compared with an armored cruiser and a super-Dreadnought, no two budgets would be found to support the same scale of values. It is quite manifest that no agreement for reducing armaments could be attained by stipulations as to the number, size, or quality of the several forces and arms employed. This difficulty in itself, however, is not fatal to the proposal. For a far simpler and more satisfactory method of agreement might be found by disregarding the concrete armaments and accepting a financial basis of expenditure which would leave each nation complete liberty to apply the money prescribed to it as a maximum expenditure on armaments in whatever way it chose. Though each nation, considering its defense, would doubtless have to take into account the sort of preparations for possible attack its neighbors might be making, it would be entitled to spend as large a proportion of its authorized expenditure upon guns, torpedo-boats, aircraft, Dreadnoughts, as it chose.

The real difficulty, therefore, turns upon the agreement upon a basis of comparative expenditure. Now this difficulty appears insuperable, if reduction of armaments be regarded as the sole, or the chief, mainstay of a durable peace. For so long as the motives which have hitherto impelled nations to increase their armaments still retain the appearance of validity in any nation or group of nations, no agreed basis for reduction will be reached, or, were it reached, no reliable adherence to its terms could be expected. For the reduction of armaments involves the acceptance of and the adherence to a principle of reduction by all the Great Powers. If any single Great Power refused to come into the agreement, or, coming in, was suspected of evading the fulfilment of

127

its pledge by concealing some of its expenditure on armaments, this method would have failed *pro tanto*, both as
an economy and a security. For each of the would-be
pacific nations would have to make adequate provision
against the warlike outsider or suspect. Now, that a
mere agreement for mutual disarmament would thus be
baffled is almost certain. So long as a Power, by simply
refusing to come in, could retain full liberty to pile up
arms with a view to a future policy of menace or aggression, would there not be Governments which would
find some more or less plausible excuses for declining
the invitation to come in? Or could we feel complete
assurance that a Power with an aggressive past, after entering into such an agreement, would faithfully fulfil it
when so many facilities of evasion present themselves?
Nay, there would be a positive incentive to an aggressive or revengeful Power either to stay outside, or, entering in, to violate secretly its obligations. For, by
either course, it would be enabled to steal a march in
military strength over its intended enemy, if the latter
were a faithful adherent to such a treaty. The slight-
est reflection suffices to show that a mere agreement for
disarmament or reduction of armament must be futile.

But, it will be contended, these difficulties may be
overcome by extending the agreement so as to bind the
signatory Powers to bring their united force to bear
upon any member convicted of a wilful evasion or in-
fraction of the agreement. That is to say, they must
engage to secure the agreement by an ultimate sanction of physical force. The administration of such an
agreement would, of course, involve the setting up of
some standing Court or Committee of Inquiry, vested
with full rights of inspection and judgment, and en-
dowed with a power of armed executive.

But if a treaty of reduction of armaments could be

128

secured by such a guarantee of collective force, it would still find itself confronted by the problem of the lawless outsider. So long as an aggressive outsider were at liberty to threaten or coerce a member of the League without involving the hostility of the other members, this danger would compel members of the League to maintain large armaments, though they were secure against internal hostility. A single Power, such as Germany, Russia, or Japan, standing out for its absolute right to determine its own expenditure and policy, would cancel nearly all the economy of the agreement. It would become self-evident that the Powers entering such an agreement must bind themselves to a common defense against such an outsider. They would be impelled to this course by a double motive. In no other way could each member gain that security which would win his consent to a basis of reduction that would lower his separate defensive power. Again, by pledging themselves to united action against an aggressive outside Power, they would diminish, perhaps destroy, the aggressive design or policy of such a Power. For such aggressive policy and the armed force which supports it are only plausible upon the assumption that they can be successfully applied to gain a selfish national end. If the united strength of the Treaty Powers remained so great as to render the pursuance of its aggressive designs impossible or too dangerous, the lawless Powers might learn the lesson of the law, and, abandoning its hopes of aggression, come into the League.

In a word, the proposal for reduction of armaments only becomes really feasible when it is linked with a provision for reversing the *motives* which lead nations to increase their armed forces. Once bring to bear upon the Governments of States a clear recognition of the two related facts: first, that by no increase of their armed

Must make it
too dangerous
for one Power
to attack
another.

force will they be reasonably likely to succeed in any aggressive design upon a neighbor; second, that by the pledged cooperation of their cosignatories they are not dependent for defense upon their own force alone, then obvious motives of economy and self-interest will lead them to reduce their armaments. Though the military caste may still plead the instability of pacific agreements and the disciplinary advantages of National Service, while contractors for armaments do their best to sow dissension among the leagued Powers and to arouse the military ambitions of new nations, these war interests would no longer be able to play as heretofore upon the fears and passions of the peoples. For whatever the secret political and business policy behind the race for armaments, its engineers could only make that policy effective by periodic appeals to the menace of invasion. Once make it manifest that no evil-minded foreigner can threaten aggression against one country without meeting an overwhelming strength of leagued forces, to which one particular contribution is not of determinant importance, and the balance of national motives leans heavily and constantly towards smaller and less expensive forces.

The absolute strength of the rational and moral case against war and militarism has in some degree obscured the fact that, so long as pushful statesmen and diplomatists, ambitious soldiers, covetous financiers, and war-traders were able to stimulate and carry out aggressive policies of conquest and aggrandizement on the part of stronger against weaker States, the apprehensions upon which these same interests played in urging the necessity of large expenditure upon defense were not unreasonable. It is only by making it too obviously difficult and dangerous for any one Power to attack any other Power that the balance of reasonable motives is

130

firmly weighted against armaments. This can only be achieved by substituting for a world of isolated independent States, or of Balances of Power, a world in which the united strength of a sufficient number of States is brought to bear immediately and certainly against any disturber of the public peace. A confederation for security against aggression.

"Splendid isolation" is no longer practicable in the modern world of international relations. Group alliances in pursuit of the Balance of Power are seen to be nothing else than an idle feint. For the sole and constant aim of each such group and Power is not to achieve or to maintain the balance, but to weight it on one side. Such an alternating and oscillating balance gives the maximum of insecurity, and thus plays most effectively the game of war and armaments. The only possible alternative is the creation of such a concert or confederation of Powers as shall afford to each the best available security against the aggression of another within the concert and the best defense of all against aggression from outside.

The general form in which a cooperation of nations for these objects presents itself is that of a League or Confederation. The primary object of such a League is to bind all its members to submit all their serious differences to arbitration or some other mode of peaceful settlement, and to accept the judgment or award thus obtained. Some advocates of a League of Peace think that the sense of moral obligation in each State, fortified by the public opinion of the civilized world, would form a valid sanction for the fulfilment of such undertakings, and would afford a satisfactory measure of security. But most hold that it is advisable or essential that the members of such a League should bind themselves to take joint action against any member who breaks the peace.

Assuming that a considerable body of nations entered

131

Success
depends on
the size of
the nucleus
of leagued
States.

such a League with good and reliable intentions, how far
would it be likely to secure the peace of the world and a
reduction of armed preparations? The answer to this
question would depend mainly upon the number and
status of the Powers constituting the League, and their
relations to outside nations. If, as is not unlikely, at
first only a small number of nations were willing to enter
such a League, the extent of the pacific achievement
would be proportionately circumscribed. If, say, Britain, France, and the United States entered the League,
undertaking to settle all their differences by peaceful
methods, such a step, however desirable in itself, would
not go far towards securing world-peace or enabling
these leagued Powers to reduce their national armaments. This is so obvious that most advocates of the
League of Peace urge that the leagued Powers should not
confine their undertakings to the peaceful settlement of
differences among themselves, but should afford a united
defense to any of their members attacked by any outside
Power which was unwilling to arbitrate its quarrel. A
defensive alliance of three such Great Powers (for that
is what the League of Peace would amount to at this
stage of development) would no doubt form a force which
it would be dangerous for any nation, or combination of
nations, to attack. But it would secure neither peace
nor disarmament. Nor would it, as an earnest advocate
of this procedure argues, necessarily, or even probably,
form a nucleus of a larger League drawing in other nations. A few nations forming such a League would not
differ substantially from the other nominally defensive
alliances with which the pages of history are filled.
Their purely defensive character would be suspected by
outside Powers, who would tend to draw together into
an opposing alliance, thus reconstituting once more the
Balance of Power with all its perils and its competing

armaments. Nay, if such a League of Peace were constituted in the spirit of the Holy Alliance of a century ago, or of the resurrection of that spirit which Mr. Roosevelt represents in order "to back righteousness by force" in all quarters of the earth, such an opposition of organized outside Powers would be inevitable. The League of Peace idea, in order to have any *prima facie* prospect of success, must at the outset be so planned as to win the adherence of the majority of the Great Powers, including some of those recently engaged in war with one another. For until there was an absolute preponderance of military and naval strength inside the League, the relief from internal strife would do very little, if anything, to abate the total danger of war, or to enable any country to reduce its armed preparations. Further, it would seem essential that such a League should in its relations to outside Powers assume a rigorously defensive attitude, abstaining from all interference in external politics until they encroached directly upon the vital interests of one or more of its members. Such an encroachment it would presumably treat as an attack upon the League, and would afford the injured member such power of redress as was deemed desirable by the representatives of the Powers forming the League.

League of Peace must have absolute preponderance of force.

Before entering upon the fuller consideration of the practicability of a League of Nations formed upon these lines, it may be well to set forth in a brief, formal manner the nature of the chief implications which appear to be contained in the proposal. We shall then be in a position to examine *seriatim* the various steps which the advocates of this method of securing world-peace and disarmament desire to take, and the many difficulties which are involved.

The signatory Powers to the Treaty or Agreement establishing such a League of Peace would undertake:

What the joint Powers would undertake.

(1) To submit to arbitration or conciliation all disputes or differences between them not capable of settlement by ordinary processes of diplomacy, and to accept and carry out any award or terms of settlement thus attained.

(2) To bring joint pressure, diplomatic, economic, or forcible, to bear upon any member refusing to submit a disputed matter to such modes of peaceable settlement, or to accept and carry out the award, or otherwise threatening or opening hostilities against any other member.

(3) To take joint action in repelling any attack made by an outside Power, or group of Powers, upon any of the members of the League.

(4) To take joint action in securing the redress of any injury which, by the general assent of the signatory Powers, had been wrongfully inflicted upon any member of the League.

J. A. Hobson, "Towards International Government," pp. 5–27.

134

EXISTING ALLIANCES AND A LEAGUE
OF PEACE

The war has converted the belligerent world to that kind of pacifism which consists in a grim determination that the present Armageddon shall never be repeated, however long it may be necessary to fight in order to ensure this outcome. To perpetuate the peace, however, a strong League of Nations is indispensable, and various plans for such a league are forming. Some of these rely on an extension of treaties of arbitration and conciliation, some would fortify these treaties by giving to the league a power to coerce recalcitrant members, and still others would create a world State with a central government, an army and a navy. The first question to be answered is, What kind of international union *can* be secured? since, in the case of any new league of this kind, the more ambitious the plan, the less probable it is that nations will adopt it. In many minds grave doubt exists whether even a modest plan will be carried into execution. In the face of this doubt I wish to express the audacious opinion that something having the characteristics of a league of peace is rapidly evolving and in all probability will, at the close of the war, require only a small modification to enable it to prevent, so long as it lasts, the recurrence of a great war on the Continent of Europe.

It is not necessary to create a league of peace *de novo* and without reference to combinations which now

135

exist. Two great leagues have been formed, each embracing powerful States and each so firmly held together that it acts toward the outer world much as a single great empire would do. Since they are now waging against each other the greatest war in history, the conclusion is much too lightly reached that such unions are, *by their nature,* war-breeders. Defensive unions, however, are in line with the whole trend of political evolution. Great nations, created by combining smaller ones, are in the order of the day, and so are federations of a looser kind, such as those which preceded the German Empire and our own Federal State.

Every such consolidation involves a risk that, if a war occurs, it will be larger than it might otherwise be; but it reduces the frequency with which wars occur. Peace between great States continues through longer periods than it does between warring districts which later unite in such States. The prospect that peace shall ever be universal depends on its tendency to establish itself within larger and larger areas till it shall end by embracing the world. European wars have occurred in spite of alliances rather than because of them and the general effect even of imperfect unions has been to lengthen the intervals of peace. It is an even century since a war akin to this one was waging in Europe, and it is forty-four years since a war between any two great nations has taken place on that continent. The consolidating tendency in itself makes for peace.

The present leagues have several times acted as peace preservers. During the Moroccan trouble and the two Balkan wars they averted a general struggle and they might have averted the present one *if, as unions, they had been more complete than they were.* It is a safe guess that if it had been definitely known that Russia, France and England would act as a unit in opposing the invasion of Serbia, the knowledge would have delayed But countries outside of alliance or league are not safe. the invasion and possibly prevented it with all its fateful consequences. The first thing to be remembered is that these two great leagues, both formed for defense, will be in existence and probably vigorous when the war shall end.

Let us assume that peace has been made, that both the Entente and the Alliance continue to be strong and that in everything political they are the Powers which must first be reckoned with. Let us assume that, in each of them, the constituent countries are held firmly together because no single country can think of surrendering the protection which union affords. Outside of the Entente, France would be helpless against an attack by Germany and outside of the Alliance Austria would be helpless against one by Italy and Russia. Any country standing alone would have a precarious hold on its territory and its freedom.

The chief dangers that threaten a great league spring from within, while those that threaten a small league are from without. A union of all Europe would be entirely immune against foreign attack and, *for that very reason,* would be far more easily disrupted and plunged into something like civil war. Such unions as the Alliance and the Entente, each of which has a great power now arrayed against it, are held together much more firmly. The bond that unites its members is the imperative need of mutual protection.

If, as we have assumed, the war has ended neither in a draw nor in a sweeping victory for one side—if the unsuccessful league has kept most of its territories and its fighting strength—the situation will throw an enormous power into the hands of the neutral States. By joining either union they might cause it to preponderate over the other; and by joining the victorious one they

137

could make it safe against any attack and able, if it were disposed to do so, to guarantee the peace of Europe. In the smaller States of Europe the opinion is growing that for them liberty and union are one and inseparable. It may be vital for them to join a defensive league and, by their union with it, cause it to become, if it were not already, a true commonwealth of nations, great and small, and fully committed to a just and peaceful policy.

In order to be a nucleus of such a commonwealth a league should, if possible, already contain enough great States to prevent any one from dominating the others. If possible it should contain a number of the smaller States and, as a group, it should be so free from aggressive designs as to merit the confidence of States not as yet in any combination. Since the Entente now virtually includes five great States and four small ones and may soon be joined by more it already has important qualifications for becoming such a league of peace as we are suggesting—a commonwealth of nations powerful enough to preserve peace and vitally interested in doing it.

The original purpose of each of the two leagues now existing was protective. It aimed primarily to secure each of its members against attacks by other Powers, and this security, which all the members continue to need, is what the small neutral countries are also compelled to look for. What they must demand of any combination which they are asked to join is, above all else, protection. Now the more promising plans for new leagues of peace which have been suggested contain no provision for protecting their members from attacks by nations outside of their circle. They content themselves with preventing warfare between the members. On the other hand, the present combinations have no formal and constitutional machinery for settling internal disputes.

138

A true commonwealth of nations needs to be assured against both dangers and its constitution, therefore, will need to contain the best provisions that it is humanly possible to devise for settling peacefully all internal disputes and also for preventing or repelling attacks by other States. This is saying that an enlarged Entente, besides protecting its members, as it is now using all its force in doing, will need to guard itself against the perils that necessarily beset large leagues, those, namely, that originate from within. The institutions of The Hague will be for it well nigh a *sine qua non* of success, and there must be measures for compelling a resort to them in disputes between members of the league and in those arising between any of them and States outside of it. Such provisions as have been contained in the best constitutions that have been suggested for new leagues will be needed in one that may evolve out of one of the existing combinations.

If a new league should be formed without affording protection against external attacks it would be necessary that the Entente and the Alliance should continue. It would be vain to ask their members to dissolve them and trust to a new league that would leave each of them to fight its own battles. The Entente or the Alliance, as the case might be, would then constitute a union within a union—a compact defensive body within a loosely organized combination for promoting the friendly settlement of disputes. This is entirely possible. A new league of many States might conceivably be formed and either the Entente or the Alliance might join it bodily and give its own members the protection which the larger league would not give; but a simpler and more natural plan would be to enlarge one of the present leagues and adopt the needed provisions for peacefully settling all disputes of which a member is a party.

139

Power of
neutrals to
help in form-
ing such a
League.
Of a league so formed the objection that it is theoretical and utopian certainly cannot be urged. Nine
countries are already in effect in the Entente and that
combination is now fulfiling the one function that, in
making constitutions for new leagues, few persons are
bold enough to require of the members—that of lavish-
ing life and treasure in defending each other. In this
respect, the present reality outstrips our dreams. As the
leagues will almost certainly continue it should be possible to give to one of them the relatively easy function
of settling peacefully the disputes occurring within its
membership.

Herein lies the golden opportunity for the neutral
States. They have a sense of danger and the protective feature of a league will attract them, though the
chance of being involved in a general war will, in itself,
repel them. It will probably repel them less than the
danger of being conquered by some great State, and
both dangers will be at a minimum if the international
body that they join is too strong to be attacked and if
its spirit as well as its formal constitution and the
interest of its members hold it in ways of peace and
justice. It will be in the power of the neutral countries to help effectively in making it so. They can consent to join only a union of this character.

It will be hard indeed for the two leagues now in
deadly war with each other at once to unite in any single
union. Will the fact that one of them for a time holds
aloof be a source of danger? In one essential way it
will be a cause of security. It is sadly to be admitted
that, in the present moral status of the world, treaties
are not bands of steel and there is danger that they may
be broken when they are not buttressed by national interests. Against the danger of disruption a defensive
league which does not include all States of Europe may

140

be stronger than one which does so. The treaty that All Europe might eventually be consolidated. binds such a league together will be powerfully reenforced if all the members have a sense of common danger —a sense of the presence of a foe strong enough to overcome any country singly. Pressure from without means solidarity within and, while enmities are strong, a hostile nation might impart to a league more strength by remaining outside of it than by joining it.

In the long run, all Europe should be consolidated. The chance that it will become so by a single step is small, and the best beginning of a general union will be furnished by one of the existing leagues, enlarged by the adherence of neutral States and fortified against the danger of disruption from within by the exposure of any seceding State to the peril of attacks from without. The league may thrive on external hostility until the good time shall come when the desired system of settling international disputes shall be thoroughly established and peace shall prevail by the supremacy of reason. Guarding always the territory and protecting the sovereignty of its members the league will develop mutual interests so important that a new and powerful tie will bind the countries together in addition to the bond furnished by the necessity for defense. That necessity itself will grow less, armaments may be curtailed and the forces now engaged in mutual destruction may become available for raising in many ways the level of human life. Under such influences the league should become too powerful to be attacked from without and too indispensable to humanity to be weakened or disrupted from within.

For these reasons I conclude that in the leagues now at war may be afforded the most practical means of creating the league of peace. There is inspiration in this possibility and there is a terrible spur to action in what

141

Present
leagues
may be
means to
peace.

will ensue if it is not realized—desolated lands under
enormous debts with no assurance against a further
struggle; neutral lands as well as belligerent ones involved in the competition for larger armies, navies, ar-
senals, guns and fortifications; the people demanding
costly reforms by governments unable to afford them
and in peril of revolution if they refuse to do so. Only
in the relief from war and its burdens lies the possibility
of meeting such needs and giving to social progress an
upward trend. Such is the plain teaching of the pending struggle. It is as though the war demon himself
had led humanity to the parting of the roads where the
guide boards indicate, on the one side, the long way to
the Delectable Mountains and on the other, a short route
to the pit. Far reaching beyond all precedent is the
choice that humanity must soon make and lands at war
and lands at peace must participate in the decision.

*John Bates Clark, Address at Lake Mohonk Confer-
ence, 1915.*

142

PROTECTION OF SMALL NATIONS

A small nation—a nation of not more than fifteen millions, for example—can have no independent existence in Europe except as a member of a federation of States having similar habits, tendencies, and hopes, and united in an offensive and defensive alliance, or under guarantees given by a group of strong and trustworthy nations. The firm establishment of several such federations, or the giving of such guarantees by a group of powerful and faith-keeping nations ought to be one of the outcomes of the war of 1914–15. Unless some such arrangement is reached, no small State will be safe from conquest and absorption by any strong, aggressive military power which covets it—not even if its people live chiefly by mining and manufacturing as the Belgians did.

Only a firm League can protect small nations.

The small States, being very determined to exist and to obtain their natural or historical racial boundaries, the problem of permanent or any durable peace in Europe resolves itself into this: How can the small or smaller nations be protected from attack by some larger nation which believes that might makes right and is mighty in industries, commerce, finance, and the military and naval arts? The experience gained during the past year proves that there is but one effective protection against such a Power, namely, a firm league of other Powers—not necessarily numerous—which together are stronger in industries, commerce, finance, and the military and

143

naval arts than the aggressive and ambitious nation
which heartily believes in its own invincibility and cherishes the ambition to conquer and possess.

Such a league is the present combination of Great
Britain, France, Russia, Italy, and Japan against the
aggressive Central Monarchies and Turkey; but this
combination was not formed deliberately and with conscious purpose to protect small States, to satisfy natural
aspirations, and to make durable peace possible by removing both fear of invasion and fear of the cutting off
of overseas food and raw materials. In spite of the lack
of an explicit and comprehensive purpose to attain these
wise and precious ends, the solidity of the alliance during a year of stupendous efforts to resist military aggression on the part of Germany and Austria-Hungary certainly affords good promise of success for a somewhat
larger league in which all the European nations—some,
like the Scandinavian and the Balkan, by representation
in groups—and the United States should be included.
Such a league would have to act through a distinct and
permanent council or commission which would not serve
arbitrary power, or any peculiar national interest, and
would not in the least resemble the ''Concert of Europe,'' or any of the disastrous special conferences of
diplomatists and Ministers for Foreign Affairs, called
after wars since that of 1870–71 to ''settle'' the questions
the wars raised.

The experience of the past twelve months proves that
such a league could prevent any nation which disobeyed
its orders from making use of the oceans and from occu-
pying the territory of any other nation. Reduction of
armaments, diminution of taxation, and durable peace
would ensue as soon as general confidence was established that the league would fairly administer international justice, and that its military and naval forces

144

were ready and effective. Its function would be limited to the prevention and punishment of violations of international agreements, or, in other words, to the enforcement of treaty obligations, until new treaties were made.

The present alliance is of good promise in three important respects—its members refuse to make any separate peace, they cooperate cordially and efficiently in military measures, and the richer members help the poorer financially. These policies have been hastily devised and adopted in the midst of strenuous fighting on an immense scale. If deliberately planned and perfected in times of peace, they could be made in the highest degree effective toward durable peace.

The war has demonstrated that the international agreements for the mitigation of the horrors of war, made by treaties, conferences, and conventions in times of peace, may go for nothing in time of war; because they have no sanction, or, in other words, lack penalties capable of systematic enforcement. To provide the lacking sanction and the physical force capable of compelling the payment of penalties for violating international agreements would be one of the best functions of the international council which the present alliance foreshadows. Some years would probably be required to satisfy the nations concerned that the sanction was real and the force trustworthy and sufficient. The absolute necessity of inventing and applying a sanction for international law, if Europe is to have international peace and any national liberty, will be obvious to any one who has once perceived that the present war became inevitable when Austria-Hungary, in violation of an international agreement to which she was herself a party, seized and absorbed Bosnia and Herzegovina, and became general and fierce when Germany, under Prussian lead, in violation of an international agreement to which she was

145

herself a party, entered and plundered neutralized Belgium.

A strong, trustworthy international alliance to preserve the freedom of the seas under all circumstances would secure for Great Britain and her federated commonwealths everything secured by the burdensome two-navies policy which now secures the freedom of the seas for British purposes. The same international alliance would secure for Germany the same complete freedom of the seas which in times of peace between Germany and Great Britain she has long enjoyed by favor of Great Britain, but has lost in time of war with the Triple Entente. This security, with the general acceptance of the policy of the ''open door,'' would fully meet Germany's need of indefinite expansion for her manufacturing industries and her commerce, and of room ''in the sun'' for her surplus population.

It is a safe inference from the events of the past six months that the longer the war lasts the more significant will be the political and social changes which result from it. It is not to be expected, and perhaps not to be desired, that the ruling class in the countries autocratically governed should themselves draw this inference at present, but all lovers of freedom and justice will find consolation for the prolongation of the war in this hopeful reflection.

To devise the wise constitution of an international council or commission with properly limited powers, and to determine the most promising composition of an international army and an international navy are serious tasks, but not beyond the available international wisdom and goodwill, provided that the tasks be intrusted to international publicists, business men of large experience, and successful administrators, rather than to professional diplomatists and soldiers. To dismiss such a

146

noble enterprise with the remark that it is "academic," or beyond the reach of "practical" politics, is unworthy of courageous and humane men; for it seems now to be the only way out of the horrible abyss into which civilization has fallen. At any rate, some such machinery must be put into successful operation before any limitation of national armaments can be effected. The war has shown to what a catastrophe competitive national arming has led, and would probably again lead the most civilized nations of Europe. Shall the white race despair of escaping from this hell? The only way of escape in sight is the establishment of a rational international community. Should the enterprise fail after fair trial, the world will be no worse off than it was in July, 1914, or is to-day.

Such a League is our only hope.

Whoever studies the events of the past year with some knowledge of political philosophy and history, and with the love of his neighbor in his heart, will discover, amid the horrors of the time and its moral chaos, three hopeful leadings for humanitarian effort, each involving a great constructive invention. He will see that humanity needs supremely a sanction for international law, rescue from alcoholism, and a sound basis for just and unselfish human relations in the great industries, and particularly in the machinery industries. The war has brought out all three of these needs with terrible force and vividness. Somehow they must be met, if the white race is to succeed in "the pursuit of happiness," or even to hold the gains already made.

Charles W. Eliot, N. Y. Times, July 16, 1915.

A LEAGUE TO ENFORCE PEACE

The pro-
posals of
the League. Without attempting to cover details of operation
(which are, indeed, of vital importance and will require
careful study by experts in international law and diplomacy), the proposal contains four points stated as general objects. The first is that before resorting to arms
the members of the league shall submit disputes with
one another, if justiciable, to an international tribunal;
second, that in like manner they shall submit non-
justiciable questions—that is, such as cannot be decided
on the basis of strict international law—to an international council of conciliation, which shall recommend
a fair and amicable solution; third, that if any member
of the league wages war against another before submitting the question in dispute to the tribunal or council, all the other members shall jointly use forthwith
both their economic and military forces against the State
that so breaks the peace; and fourth, that the signatory
Powers shall endeavor to codify and improve the rules
of international law.

The kernel of the proposal, the feature in which it dif-
fers from other plans, lies in the third point, obliging
all the members of the league to declare war on any
member violating the pact of peace. This is the provision that provokes both adherence and opposition; and
at first it certainly gives one a shock that a people should
be asked to pledge itself to go to war over a quarrel
which is not of its making, in which it has no interest,

148

and in which it may believe that substantial justice lies The use of force to compel arbitration before war. on the other side. If, indeed, the nations of the earth could maintain complete isolation, could pursue each its own destiny without regard to the rest; if they were not affected by a war between two others or liable to be drawn into it; if, in short, there were no overwhelming common interest in securing universal peace, the provision would be intolerable. It would be as bad as the liability of an individual to take part in the *posse comitatus* of a community with which he had nothing in common. But in every civilized country the public force is employed to prevent any man, however just his claim, from vindicating his own right with his own hand instead of going to law, and every citizen is bound when needed to assist in preventing him, because that is the only way to restrain private war, and the maintenance of order is of paramount importance for every one. Surely the family of nations has a like interest in restraining war between States.

It will be observed that the members of the league are not to bind themselves to enforce the decision of the tribunal or the award of the council of conciliation. That may come in the remote future, but it is no part of this proposal. It would be imposing obligations far greater than the nations can reasonably be expected to assume at the present day; for the conceptions of international morality and fair play are still so vague and divergent that a nation can hardly bind itself to wage war on another, with which it has no quarrel, to enforce a decision or a recommendation of whose justice or wisdom it may not be itself heartily convinced. The proposal goes no further than obliging all the members to prevent, by a threat of immediate war, any breach of the public peace before the matter in dispute has been submitted to arbitration; and this is neither unreasonable

nor impracticable. There are many questions, especially
of a non-justiciable nature, on which we should not be
willing to bind ourselves to accept the decision of an
arbitration, and where we should regard compulsion by
armed intervention of the rest of the world as outrage-
ous. Take, for example, the question of Asiatic immigration, or a claim that the Panama Canal ought to be
an unfortified neutral highway, or the desire by a European Power to take possession of Colombia. But we
ought not, in the interest of universal peace, to object
to making a public statement of our position in these
matters at a court or council before resorting to arms;
and in fact the treaty between the United States and
England, ratified on November 14, 1914, provides that
all disputes between the high contracting parties, of
every nature whatsoever, shall, failing other methods of
adjustment, be referred for investigation and report to
a permanent international commission, with a stipulation
that neither country shall declare war or begin hostilities during such investigation and before the report is
submitted.

What is true of this country is true of others. To
agree to abide by the result of an arbitration, on every
non-justiciable question of every nature whatsoever, on
pain of compulsion in any form by the whole world,
would involve a greater cession of sovereignty than nations would now be willing to concede. This appears,
indeed, perfectly clear from the discussions at The
Hague Conference of 1907. But to exclude differences
that do not turn on questions of international law from
the cases in which a State must present the matter to a
tribunal or council of conciliation before beginning hostilities, would leave very little check upon the outbreak
of war. Almost every conflict between European nations for more than half a century has been based upon

150

some dissension which could not be decided by strict rules of law, and in which a violation of international law or of treaty rights has usually not even been used as an excuse. This was true of the war between France and Austria in 1859, and, in substance, of the war between Prussia and Austria in 1866. It was true of the Franco-Prussian War in 1870, of the Russo-Turkish War in 1876, of the Balkan War against Turkey in 1912, and of the present war.

No one will claim that a league to enforce peace, such as is proposed, would wholly prevent war, but it would greatly reduce the probability of hostilities. It would take away the advantage of surprise, of catching the enemy unprepared for a sudden attack. It would give a chance for public opinion on the nature of the controversy to be formed throughout the world and in the militant country. The latter is of great importance, for the moment war is declared argument about its merits is at once stifled. Passion runs too high for calm debate, and patriotism forces people to support their government. But a trial before an international tribunal would give time for discussion while emotion is not yet highly inflamed. Men opposed to war would be able to urge its injustice, to ask whether, after all, the object is worth the sacrifice, and they would get a hearing from their fellow citizens which they cannot get after war begins. The mere delay, the interval for consideration, would be an immense gain for the prospect of a peaceful settlement.

Most people who have been thinking seriously about the maintenance of peace are tending to the opinion that a sanction of some kind is needed to enforce the observance of treaties and of agreements for arbitration. Among the measures proposed has been that of an international police force, under the control of a central coun-

cil which could use it to preserve order throughout the
world. At present such a plan seems visionary. The
force would have to be at least large enough to cope with
the army that any single nation could put into the field
—under existing conditions let us say five millions of
men fully equipped and supplied with artillery and ammunition for a campaign of several months. These
troops need not be under arms, or quartered near The
Hague, but they must be thoroughly trained and ready
to be called out at short notice. Practically that would
entail yearly votes of the legislative bodies of each of the
nations supplying a quota; and if any of them failed to
make the necessary appropriation there would be great
difficulty in preventing others from following its example. The whole organization would, therefore, be in
constant danger of going to pieces.

But quite apart from the practical difficulties in the
permanent execution of such a plan, let us see how it
would affect the United States. The amount of the contingents of the various countries would be apportioned
with some regard to population, wealth, and economic
resources; and if the total were five million men, our
quota on a moderate estimate might be five hundred
thousand men. Is it conceivable that the United States
would agree to keep anything like that number drilled,
equipped, and ready to take the field on the order of an
international council composed mainly of foreign nations? Of course it will be answered that these figures
are exaggerated, because any such plan will be accompanied by a reduction in armaments. But that is an
easier thing to talk about than to effect, and especially
to maintain. One must not forget that the existing system of universal compulsory military service on the continent of Europe arose from Napoleon's attempt to limit
the size of the Prussian army. He would be a bold
152

or sanguine man who should assert that any treaty to limit armaments could not in like manner be evaded; and however much they were limited, the quantity of troops to be held at the disposal of a foreign council would of necessity be large, while no nation would be willing to pledge for the purpose the whole of its military force. Such a plan may be practicable in some remote future when the whole world is a vast federation under a central government, but that would seem to be a matter for coming generations, not for the men of our day.

Moreover, the nations whose troops were engaged in fighting any country would inevitably find themselves at war with that country.

One cannot imagine saying to some foreign State, "Our troops are killing yours, they are invading your land, we are supplying them with recruits and munitions of war, but otherwise we are at peace with you. You must treat us as a neutral, and accord to our citizens, to their commerce and property, all the rights of neutrality." In short the plan of an international police force involves all the consequences of the proposal of a league to enforce peace, with other complex provisions extremely hard to execute.

A suggestion more commonly made is that the members of the league of nations, instead of pledging themselves explicitly to declare war forthwith against any of their number that commits a breach of the peace, should agree to hold at once a conference, and take such measures—diplomatic, economic, or military—as may be necessary to prevent war. The objection to this is that it weakens very seriously the sanction. Conferences are apt to shrink from decisive action. Some of the members are timid, others want delay, and much time is consumed in calling the body together and in discussions after it meets. Meanwhile the war may have

broken out, and be beyond control. It is much easier
to prevent a fire than to put it out. The country that
is planning war is likely to think it has friends in the
conference, or neighbors that it can intimidate, who will
prevent any positive decision until the fire is burning.
Even if the majority decides on immediate action, the
minority is not bound thereby. One great Power re-
fuses to take part; a second will not do so without her;
the rest hesitate, and nothing is done to prevent the war.

A conference is an excellent thing. The proposal of a
league to enforce peace by no means excludes it; but the
important matter, the effective principle, is that every
member of the league should know that whether a conference meets or not, or whatever action it may take
or fail to take, all the members of the league have
pledged themselves to declare war forthwith on any
member that commits a breach of the peace before submitting its case to the international tribunal or council
of conciliation. Such a pledge, and such a pledge alone,
can have the strong deterrent influence, and thus furnish
the sanction, that is needed. Of course the pledge may
not be kept. Like other treaties it may be broken by the
parties to it. Nations are composed of human beings
with human weaknesses, and one of these is a disin-
clination to perform an agreement when it involves a
sacrifice. Nevertheless, nations, like men, often do have
enough sense of honor, of duty, or of ultimate self-interest, to carry out their contracts at no little immediate
sacrifice. They are certainly more likely to do a thing
if they have pledged themselves to it than if they have
not; and any nation would be running a terrible risk
that went to war in the hope that the other members of
the league would break their pledges.

The same objection applies to another alternative proposed in place of an immediate resort to military force:

154

that is the use of economic pressure, by a universal agree- ment, for example, to have no commercial intercourse with the nation breaking the peace. A threat of universal boycott is, no doubt, formidable, but by no means so formidable as a threat of universal war. A large country with great natural resources which has determined to make war, might be willing to face commercial non-intercourse with the other members of the league during hostilities, when it would not for a moment contemplate the risk of fighting them. A threat, for example, by England, France, and Germany to stop all trade with the United States might or might not have prevented our going to war with Spain; but a declaration that they would take part with all their armies and navies against us would certainly have done so.

It has often been pointed out that the threat of general non-intercourse would bear much more hardly on some countries than on others. That may not in itself be a fatal objection, but a very serious consideration arises from the fact that there would be a premium on preparation for war. A nation which had accumulated vast quantities of munitions, food, and supplies of all kinds, might afford to disregard it; while another less fully prepared could not.

Moreover, economic pressure, although urged as a milder measure, is in fact more difficult to apply and maintain. A declaration of war is a single act, and when made sustains itself by the passion it inflames; while commercial non-intercourse is a continuous matter, subject to constant opposition exerted in an atmosphere relatively cool. Our manufacturers would complain bitterly at being deprived of dye-stuffs and other chemical products on account of a quarrel in which we had no interest; the South would suffer severely by the loss of a market for cotton; the shipping firms and the exporters

155

Drastic
threats by
a League
could prob-
ably pre-
vent war.

and importers of all kinds would be gravely injured; and all these interests would bring to bear upon Congress a pressure well-nigh irresistible. The same would be true of every other neutral country, a fact that would be perfectly well known to the intending belligerent and reduce its fear of a boycott.

But, it is said, why not try economic pressure first, and, if that fails, resort to military force, instead of inflicting at once on unoffending members of the league the terrible calamity of war? What do we mean by "if that fails"? Do we mean, if, in spite of the economic pressure, the war breaks out? But then the harm is done, the fire is ablaze and can be put out only by blood. The object of the league is not to chastise a country guilty of breaking the peace, but to prevent the outbreak of war, and to prevent it by the immediate prospect of such appalling consequences to the offender that he will not venture to run the risk. If a number of great Powers were to pledge themselves with serious intent, to wage war jointly and severally on any one of their members that attacked another before submitting the case to arbitration, it is in the highest degree improbable that the *casus fœderis* would ever occur, while any less drastic provision would be far less effective.

An objection has been raised to the proposal for a league to enforce peace on the ground that it has in the past often proved difficult, if not impossible, to determine which of two belligerents began a war. The criticism is serious, and presents a practical difficulty, grave but probably not insurmountable. The proposal merely lays down a general principle, and if adopted the details would have to be worked out very fully and carefully in a treaty, which would specify the acts that would constitute the waging of war by one member upon another. These would naturally be, not the mere creat-

156

ing of apprehension, but specific acts, such as a declara- Object is to lessen chances of war. tion of war, invasion of territory, the use of force at sea not disowned within forty-eight hours, or an advance into a region in dispute. This last is an especially difficult point, but those portions of the earth's surface in which different nations have conflicting claims are growing less decade by decade.

It must be remembered that the cases which would arise are not like those which have arisen in the past, where one nation is determined to go to war and merely seeks to throw the moral responsibility on the other while getting the advantage of actually beginning hostilities. It is a case where each will strive to avoid the specific acts of war that may involve the penalty. The reader may have seen, in a country where personal violence is severely punished, two men shaking their fists in each other's faces, each trying to provoke the other to strike the first blow; and no fight after all.

There are many agreements in private business which are not easy to embody in formal contracts; agreements where, as in this case, the execution of the terms calls for immediate action, and where redress after an elaborate trial of the facts affords no real reparation. But if the object sought is good, men do not condemn it on account of the difficulty in devising provisions that will accomplish the result desired; certainly not until they have tried to devise them. It may, indeed, prove impossible to draft a code of specific acts that will cover the ground; it may be impracticable to draft it so as to avoid issues of fact that can be determined only after a long sifting of evidence, which would come too late; but surely that is no reason for failure to make the attempt. We are not making a treaty among nations. We are merely putting forward a suggestion for reducing war, which seems to merit consideration.

though the
League
could not
meet all
possible con-
tingencies.

A second difficulty that will sometimes arise is the
rule of conduct to be followed pending the presentation
of the question to the international tribunal. The continuance or cessation of the acts complained of may appear to be, and may even be in fact, more important
than the final decision. This has been brought to our
attention forcibly by the sinking of the *Lusitania*. We
should have done very wisely to submit to arbitration
the question of the right of submarines to torpedo merchant ships without warning, provided Germany abandoned the practise pending the arbitration; and Germany would probably not have refused to submit the
question to a tribunal on the understanding that the
practise was to continue until the decision was rendered,
because by that time the war would be over. This difficulty is inherent in every plan for the arbitration of international disputes, although more serious in a league
whose members bind themselves to prevent by force the
outbreak of war. It would be necessary to give the
tribunal summary authority to decree a *modus vivendi*,
to empower it, like a court of equity, to issue a temporary injunction.

In short, the proposal for a league to enforce peace
cannot meet all possible contingencies. It cannot prevent all future wars, nor does any sensible person believe
that any plan can do so in the present state of civilization. But it can prevent some wars that would otherwise take place, and if it does that it will have done much
good.

People have asked how such a league would differ
from the Triple Alliance or Triple Entente—whether
it would not be nominally a combination for peace which
might in practise have quite a different effect. But in
fact its object is quite contrary to those alliances. They
are designed to protect their members against outside

158

Powers. This is intended to insure peace among the Enough if League meant peace for its members. members themselves. If it grew strong enough, by including all the great Powers, it might well insist on universal peace by compelling the outsiders to come in. But that is not its primary object, which is simply to prevent its members from going to war with one another. No doubt if several great nations, and some of the smaller ones, joined it, and if it succeeded in preserving constant friendly relations among its members, there would grow up among them a sense of solidarity which would make any outside Power chary of attacking one of them; and, what is more valuable, would make outsiders want to join it. But there is little use in speculating about probabilities. It is enough if such a league were a source of enduring peace among its own members.

How about our own position in the United States? The proposal is a radical and subversive departure from the traditional policy of our country. Would it be wise for us to be parties to such an agreement? At the threshold of such a discussion one thing is clear. If we are not willing to urge our own government to join a movement for peace, we have no business to discuss any plan for the purpose. It is worse than futile, it is an impertinence, for Americans to advise the people of Europe how they ought to conduct their affairs if we have nothing in common with them; to suggest to them conventions with burdens which are well enough for them, but which we are not willing to share. If our peace organizations are not prepared to have us take part in the plans they devise, they had better disband, or confine their discussions to Pan-American questions. . . .

A. Lawrence Lowell, "A League to Enforce Peace," Atlantic Monthly, Sept., 1915.

159

THE CONSTITUTION OF A LEAGUE

Force for defense vs. force for aggression.

The problem of the League of Peace is actually the problem of the use of force. Force internationally expressed is measured in armaments. The chief discussion which has been waged for the past decade between the pacifists and militarists has been over the question of armaments. The militarists claim that armaments insure national safety. The pacifists declare they inevitably lead to war. Both disputants insist that the present war furnishes irrefutable proof of their contentions.

As is usual in cases of this kind the shield has two sides. The confusion has arisen from a failure to recognize the threefold function of force:

1. Force used for the maintenance of order—police force.

2. Force used for attack—aggression.

3. Force used to neutralize aggression—defense.

Police force is almost wholly good.

Offense is almost wholly bad.

Defense is a necessary evil, and exists simply to neutralize force employed for aggression.

The problem of the peace movement is how to abolish the use of force for aggression, and yet to maintain it for police purposes. Force for defense will of course automatically cease when force for aggression is abolished.

The chief problem then of a League of Peace is this:

160

Shall the members of the League "not only keep the peace themselves, but prevent by force if necessary its being broken by others," as ex-President Roosevelt suggested in his Nobel Peace Address delivered at Christiania, May 5, 1910? Or shall its force be exercised only within its membership and thus be on the side of law and order and never on the side of arbitrary will or tyranny? Or shall it never be used at all? Whichever one of these conceptions finally prevails the Great War has conclusively demonstrated that as long as War Lords exist defensive force must be maintained. Hence the League must be prepared to use force against any nations which will not forswear force. Nevertheless a formula must be devised for disarmament. For unless it is a law of nature that war is to consume all the fruits of progress disarmament somehow and some way must take place. How then can the maintenance of a force for defense and police power be reconciled with the theory of disarmament?

In this way: Let the League of Peace be formed on the following five principles:

First. The nations of the League shall mutually agree to respect the territory and sovereignty of each other.

Second. All questions that cannot be settled by diplomacy shall be arbitrated.

Third. The nations of the League shall provide a periodical assembly to make all rules to become law unless vetoed by a nation within a stated period.

Fourth. The nations shall disarm to the point where the combined forces of the League shall be a certain per cent. higher than those of the most heavily armed nation or alliance outside of the League. Detailed rules for this pro rata disarmament shall be formulated by the Assembly.

Fifth. Any member of the League shall have the

right to withdraw on due notice, or may be expelled by
the unanimous vote of the others.

The advantages that a nation would gain in becoming a member of such a league are manifest. The risk
of war would be eliminated within the League. Obviously the only things that are vital to a nation are its
land and its independence. Since each nation in the
League will have pledged itself to respect the territory
and the sovereignty of every other, a refusal to do so
will logically lead to expulsion from the League. Thus
every vital question will be automatically reserved from
both war and arbitration. All other questions are of
secondary importance and can readily be arbitrated.

By the establishment of a periodical assembly a
method would be devised whereby the members of the
League could develop their common intercourse and
interests as far and as fast as they could unanimously
agree upon ways and means. As any law could be vetoed by a single nation, no nation could have any fear
that it would be coerced against its will by a majority
vote of the other nations. By such an assembly the
League might in time agree to reduce tariffs and postal
rates and in a thousand other ways promote commerce
and comity among its members.

As a final safeguard against coercion by the other
members of the League, each member will have the right
of secession on due notice. This would prevent civil
war within the League. The right of expulsion by the
majority will prevent one nation by its veto power indefinitely blocking all progress of the League.

But it will be said that all these agreements will have
no binding effect in a crisis. A covenant is a mere
"scrap of paper" whose provisions will be violated by
the first nation which fancies it is its interest to do so.
In order to show that their faith is backed up by deeds,

however, the nations on entering the League agree to disarm to a little above the danger point, and put all their defensive power under a federal authority. This is the real proof of their conversion to the peace idea.

Thus the nations which join the League will enjoy all the economic and political advantages which come from mutual cooperation and the extension of international friendship and at the same time will be protected by an adequate force against the aggressive force of the greatest nation or alliance outside the League. The League therefore reconciles the demand of the pacifists for the limitation of armaments and eventual disarmament and the demand of the militarists for the protection that armament affords. Above all the establishment of such a league will give the liberal parties in the nations outside the League an issue on which they can attack their governments so as sooner or later to force them to apply to the League for membership. As each one enters there will be another pro rata reduction of the military forces of the League down to the armament of the next most powerful nation or alliance outside it; until finally the whole world is federated in a brotherhood of universal peace and armies and navies are reduced to an international police force.

Hamilton Holt, "The Way to Disarm," Independent, Sept. 28, 1914.

163

PACIFISM AND THE LEAGUE OF PEACE

Peace is not
mere non-
resistance.

In short, we have little faith in a pacifism which is mere *laissez-faire*, in the doctrine that peace is the vacuum created by the absence of war. Peace is something more original than that. It is a great construction, of infinite complexity, which will be aided but not consummated by good intentions. It involves dangers, failures, disappointments. The interests of the world are interwoven, and no nation can work for peace by adopting counsels of perfection in a policy of isolation. Yet that is what mere non-resistance implies. It implies an unwillingness to take the risk of participation in world politics, it trusts vaguely that by staying at home and minding our business, we can make our own little cultivated garden bloom in peace and prosperity. There is no internationalism in such a view of things. The real internationalist is one who works first of all to keep his own nation from aggressive action, who infuses his own national policy with a desire for international peace. He works to control his own government so as to make it adopt a humanely constructive foreign policy. He does not refuse to have part in the world's affairs because the world may soil his hands. He realizes that peace can be created only out of the strength of intelligent people, that even God when he fought the devil had to compromise his own perfection.

It is more than a century since Thomas Paine proposed to secure the world's peace forever by a league

164

between Britain, France and the United States. He made the suggestion on the eve of the Napoleonic wars, and it is hardly an accident that the idea was revived with a different trinity a few months before the present struggle. It was Britain, France and Germany that Jean Jaurès would have united in a League of Peace. At the parting of the ways the clear-sighted idealist has always understood that the choice is not between war and that sort of peace which is only a negation of war. The choice in both these crises lay between shattering war and constructive peace, between an open and destructive enmity and a peace based on a common will and an active partnership. Mirabeau had the same vivid perception, and what these three saw is still a vision that haunts us among the mists of war. Of the several proposals that arise inevitably in men's minds when we think of preventing the renewal of this Continental struggle, there is none which sober thinkers propound so readily and none which has been worked out with greater detail in England than this expedient of the League of Peace. There are, indeed, a few who dare to speak of the United States of Europe, and some who discuss the creation of an international police force to secure the law of nations and repress aggression. But even they do not deny the inordinate difficulties. This war has lasted long enough to teach all but the unteachable that neither side will be able to crush and dominate the other. But short of the compulsion of irresistible might, will any influence suffice to bring the enemies of to-day by their spontaneous choice into a European federation? Is any people, even the most pacific, prepared as yet to accept the surrender of sovereignty which entry into even a loosely-knit federation would involve?

The League of Peace presents itself to practical men

165

as a dream capable of an early translation into fact. The allies need only agree to join their forces against any power which persisted, after offers of arbitration or mediation (a reservation which no old-fashioned alliance ever made) in attacking any one of them. It would differ from other alliances partly by its insistence on the duty of arbitration, partly by its frank and public constitution, but mainly by the ready welcome which it would offer even to the enemy of yesterday, should he elect to enter it. The United States would rally to it, seeing in it their best hope of safety, and ultimately it might become a genuine Pan-European League. It is sometimes suggested that Paine's Anglo-Franco-American combination might form its nucleus. More often its advocates base their hopes on the Anglo-Franco-Russian entente, expanded by adhesion of some of the present neutrals. No one suggests, and this is the weakest point of the whole scheme, that Germany and Austria would be likely to join such a League at the start, though no one of this way of thinking would desire to exclude them.

Much would depend on the nucleus of the federation. Crude military considerations render an Anglo-French-American trinity impossible. Without discussing whether the United States would care to enter "the vortex of European militarism," it is enough to point out that such a combination could not hope to hold the rest of Europe in check, could not even safeguard France against Germany alone, unless one or both of the English-speaking nations adopted compulsory military service. France must ally herself to some first-rate military power; no navy can protect her land frontiers. The Anglo-Franco-Russian combination is open to other objections. It does not represent a homogeneous civilization. Every outbreak of anti-Jewish fanaticism in

166

Russia, every assault on Finland or Persia, every re- minder that official Russia still belongs to the Dark Ages, would tend to weaken the moral authority of such a League. It has, moreover, too long a history. It would seem even to charitable Germans a mere perpetuation under a new name of the combination which M. Del-cassé and King Edward were accused of forming to "pen Germany in." It would seem to be nothing better than an alliance to assure the victors in the perpetual pos-session of the fruits of victory, and the new pacifist fa-çade to the old armed fortress would only aggravate by hypocrisy the sin of success. Germany would never join this League; she would scheme with all the arts of barter and intrigue to detach Russia from it, and the old game of the Balance of Power would go on.

The fatal objection to any alliance of this kind is that it does not really meet the difficulty that no State will abandon its sovereignty. This alliance would not be a League of Peace unless it were prepared to exer-cise a very sharp supervision over the foreign policy of its members. If the old Anglo-Franco-Russian entente had been a genuine League of Peace, it would have had to say, for example, to Serbia, "You may join us, but if you do join us, you must abandon forever your Ir-redentist ambitions at the expense of Austria. We will protect you against any unprovoked attack by Austria. But you on your side must refrain from any encour-agement to those who would dismember her." It would have had to say with equal decision to France, "Join us by all means, but at the cost of refraining from any expansion in Morocco. You cannot march on Fez with-out provoking some German reply." Such a League, in short, would be a mutual insurance society, but the risks would be too high unless the society could prohibit its members from any deliberate playing with fire. It

is not enough to say, "We will murder an Archduke
once in a way, but when he is dead and buried we will
go to The Hague about him"; or, "We will, to be sure,
take places in the sun which other people covet, but
when we have taken them we shall not wantonly attack
any unsuccessful rivals." The League of Peace would
either be the old imperialistic alliance under a dishonest name, or else it would be a highly conservative
federation which would keep its members in a very
strait pacifist jacket. If great powers would really
endure such a control they might as well face at once the
limitation of sovereignty implied in a United States of
Europe.

The vice of all such schemes is that they are based
too one-sidedly on the idea of preventing wars. They
take a static view of the world. They come quite naturally from citizens of satisfied powers, weary of the burden of defending what they have got. They ignore the
fact that life is change. They make no provision for
any organic alterations in the world's structure. We
can no more prevent war by organizing a defensive
league than revolution by creating a police. We must
deal with causes, must provide some means alternative
to war by which large grievances can be redressed and
legitimate ambitions satisfied. To recur to our concrete
cases: if it is desired to insure that Serbia shall not
again embroil a continent in war, some machinery must
be provided by which Austria can be required to treat
her subject Serbs reasonably well. When a "place in
the sun" like Morocco, one of the few unappropriated
parts of the earth fit for settlement by a white race, can
no longer maintain its independence, there must be some
impartial Power which can say, "This rich potential colony ought not to go to a State like France, with two
similar colonies already under its flag and a dwindling

population at home, but rather to a State like Germany, All interests must be reconciled. with no such colony of her own, despite her teeming population, her great birth-rate, her vigorous and expansive commerce."

For such problems as this there is no solution in the quasi-legal processes of arbitration. The fundamental fact in the European history of the last twenty years has been the restless search of Germany for colonies and fields of exploitation. She felt her way in South Africa; the British Empire expanded to exclude her. She turned a timid glance to Brazil; the Monroe Doctrine was the flaming sword at the gate of that Paradise. She coveted Morocco; the British navy cleared its decks. She penetrated Turkey down the spine of the Bagdad Railway; she was met at the Gulf with opposing sea-power. A League of the Satisfied might appeal to London and Paris and Petrograd. But Berlin will ask, "What hope does it offer to me that when my population is still denser, my industry still more expansive, my need for markets and fields of exploitation for my capital even more clamant than it is to-day, your League of Peace will provide me with an outlet? You bar the future, and you call it peace."

The recent Philadelphia conference on The League to Enforce Peace was extraordinarily sensible because it recognized so clearly its own limitations. It did not propose to stop the war. It did not urge anybody to act before he was ready to act. It did not try to stampede our government or any European government into some theoretical program. It tried merely to focus the ideas which have been most common in England and America during the last ten months. Under impressive circumstances, in a hall filled with noble memories, it crystallized a number of vague ideas into an hypothesis. The conference was visibly trying to reach some mini-

169

mum agreement for the purpose of clarifying the thinking of individuals and groups all over the world.

Nobody is expected to act upon the resolutions, but
everybody is expected to give what thought and knowledge and imagination he may have towards maturing
the intentions which they expressed. The conference
did what every person must do constantly for himself
whenever he is trying to think out a long and complex
problem. It stopped for breath and for a renewal of
faith; it made a tentative proposal as a guide for the
thought which is to follow. With great sanity it took
no doctrinaire position, laid down no rule, such as peace-
at-any-price, honor-cannot-be-arbitrated, sovereignty-is-
one-and-indivisible, or any of the other assumptions
which obscure pacifist and militarist argument. The
delegates in Philadelphia were scientific in their spirit;
they did not even attempt that over-precise definition
of the final end which always results in the misleading
use of theory. They were not doctors who begin their
study of disease by trying to define the ideal healthy
man, they were not political doctrinaires who begin by
defining the ideally peaceful world. They were agreed,
as doctors are agreed, that a sounder organic constitution is required, and that pain and suffering should be
lessened as much as possible, but they did not attempt to
say that they would not inflict pain to cure pain, or
wage war to preserve the peace.

The idea which the delegates had uppermost in their
thoughts was a league of nations that should give power
to international law. It is an extension of The Hague
plan by which the nations attempt not only to set up a
court, but to compel those who have a dispute to go to
the court. As we understand the resolutions, they do
not take the added step of agreeing to enforce the decision of the court.

170

The idea is based on a tremendous compromise, as our own history shows. We were once a league of foreign States, suspicious of common action and jealous of each sovereign prerogative. On the greatest issue of our history we fought our greatest war, and the States which represented union and federalism put an end once for all to the unlimited sovereignty of any individual State. Our Civil War established the supremacy of the federal power over the States.

The United States of the World would face the same problem, though on a much more difficult scale. It will find that a court to adjust mistakes is not enough, for the really important conflicts that provoke war are not "justiciable." They are matters upon which a policy has to be declared—upon which, in brief, legislation is needed. Some kind of legislature a League of Peace would have to establish, and with a legislature and court would have to go an executive. This would open up the problem of representation, of the large and populous State as against the small ones, of the "satisfied Powers" against the "unsatisfied." For it is clear that the British Empire will not consent to give to Montenegro equal representation, or the United States to Venezuela. Here will be the question of conflicts between international and national legislation, similar to the conflicts which our Supreme Court is called upon to settle. All the problems of home rule, such as that of Ireland within the Empire, and of Ulster within Ireland, would have to be met in territory like that of the Balkans, by the League of Peace. It would have to determine whether, for example, the sovereignty of a national India was an internal question for the British Empire, or a legitimate subject for international settlement.

The League would have to work out the problem of unexploited territories, of weaker peoples, and of dis-

orderly States. Just as our original Union had the
whole West to organize, so the League would have
Africa, large parts of Asia, and the middle Americas
as a kind of international domain. It would have to
meet those who want merely to exploit, and to support
those who are liberal enough to throw about weaker peoples that protection under which they can really grow
to freedom. Nor would that be all. The League would
have to legislate about concessions, trading rights, tariffs,
about spheres of influence, about the use of great ocean
and land highways. As soon as it grappled with the
economic aspects of diplomacy, it would find, just as our
government found, that interstate commerce cannot be
regulated satisfactorily by conflicting state interests.

In other words, there is no stopping short at a league
to prevent war. Such a league would either grow to a
world federalism, or it would break up in civil war.
But that, far from being an argument against the
League, is the strongest possible argument for it. It is
the first step towards a closer world organization, and
once that step is taken, the world will have to choose
between taking some of the next steps and returning to
the anarchy of sovereign nationalities. The vast implications of the League of Peace are what make it important. And its real service to mankind may well be
that it will establish the first rallying point of a world
citizenship.

The development of such a citizenship is one of the
great moral and educational problems of this century.
It cannot mean a vague cosmopolitanism. It must mean
the training of people who have learned to modify their
national policies so that these do not make impossible
an international allegiance. This war has offered us an
example of such citizenship. The Canadians, Australians, and New Zealanders who are fighting in Flan-

ders and at the Dardanelles are living and dying for the largest political organization the world has so far known. Their allegiance in the British Empire is to a State which embraces one-quarter of the human race. Never before in history have men been loyal to so great and so diversified a unit. They have literally come from all the ends of the earth to preserve a union of democracies. They have shown by example what any World League most needs to know, that federalism on a grand scale is not an idle dream.

It would mean a new world-federalism.

The New Republic, March 20 and June 26, 1915.

THE ECONOMIC BOYCOTT

The nations
have a power-
ful non-mili-
tary weapon.
In the discussion of an International Executive entrusted with powers to compel the fulfilment of treaty
obligations, it must not be assumed that coercion can
only be exercised by the employment of armed force.
The boycott is a weapon which could be employed with
paralyzing power by a circle of nations upon an offender against the public law of the world. No nation
to-day, least of all the great industrial and military
Powers, is or can become socially and economically self-
sufficient. It depends in countless ways upon intercourse with other nations. If all or most of these ave-
nues of intercourse were stopped, it would soon be reduced to worse straits than those which Germany is now
experiencing. If all diplomatic intercourse were withdrawn; if the international postal and telegraphic systems were closed to a public law-breaker; if all inter-
state railway trains stopped at his frontiers; if no
foreign ships entered his ports, and ships carrying his
flag were excluded from every foreign port; if all coal-
ing stations were closed to him; if no acts of sale or
purchase were permitted to him in the outside world—
if such a political and commercial boycott were seriously
threatened, what country could long stand out against
it? Nay, the far less rigorous measure of a financial
boycott, the closure of all foreign exchanges to members
of the outlaw State, the prohibition of all quotations on

174

foreign stock exchanges, and of all dealings in stocks But effective use requires co-operation. and shares, all discounting and acceptances of trade bills, all loans for public or private purposes, and all payments of moneys due—such a withdrawal of financial intercourse, if thoroughly applied and persisted in, would be likely to bring to its senses the least scrupulous of States.

Assuming that the members of the League included all or most of the important commercial and financial nations, and that they could be relied upon to press energetically all or even a few of these forms of boycott, could any country long resist such pressure? Would not the threat of it and the knowledge that it could be used form a potent restraint upon the lawbreaker? Even the single weapon of a complete postal and telegraphic boycott would have enormous efficiency were it rigorously applied. Every section of the industrial and commercial community would bring organized pressure upon its Government to withdraw from so intolerable a position and to return to its international allegiance. It may be said, Why is it that such a powerful weapon of such obvious efficacy has never been applied? The answer is that the conditions for its rapid and concerted application have never hitherto existed. For in order that it may be effective, a considerable number of nations must have previously undertaken to apply it simultaneously and by common action. And, what is more, each nation must have confidence in the *bona fides* of the intention of other nations to apply it. For the detailed application of the boycott, in most points, must of necessity remain in the hands of the several national Governments. Here comes the practical difficulty. Every boycott has a certain injurious rebound. It hits back the nation that applies it. The injury of suspended intercourse is, of course, not equal, otherwise the process would be futile. If the whole circle of A's neighbors boycott him, each suffers half the loss of his separate intercourse with A, but A suffers this loss multiplied by the number of his neighbors. Now if A's intercourse with all his neighbors is of equal magnitude, each of them can probably afford easily to bear the sacrifice involved in the boycott, trusting to the early effect of their action in bringing A to terms. But if one or two of A's neighbors are in much closer relations with A than the others, and if, as may be the case, they are getting more advantage from this intercourse than A, the risk or sacrifice they are called upon to undergo will be proportionately greater. They must bear the chief brunt of a policy in the adoption of which they have not the determinant voice.

Take, for example, the case of Germany. An all-round boycott applied to her would evidently cause more damaging reactions to Holland, Belgium, and Denmark than to any of the greater nations whose united voice might have determined its application. The injury to Holland, in particular, might in the first instance be almost as grave as that sustained by Germany, the supposed object of the boycott. It would evidently be necessary to make provision against this unequal incidence by devising a system of compensations or indemnity to meet the case of such a special injury or sacrifice.

A brief allusion to the other side of the objection will suffice, viz., the fact that any such boycott would be far less potent or immediate in its pressure against some nations than against others. While Great Britain would have to yield at once to the threat of such pressure, Russia, or even the United States, could stand out for a considerable time, and China might even regard the boycott as a blessing. But it is pretty evident that in the long run no civilized nation could endure such isolation,

176

and that this weapon is one which the League might in certain cases advantageously employ.

Other aspects of the social-economic boycott raise other difficulties. While certain modes and paths of intercourse lie directly under the control of the Governments of the cooperating States, others belong to private enterprise. Though postal, railway, and telegraphic intercourse could be cut off easily by agreements between Governments, private trading could not so easily be stopped. It is not found a simple matter to stop all trading between members of nations actually at war when national sentiment sides strongly with the legal prohibition. It might be much more difficult to prevent all commercial intercourse for private gain when there was no special hostility between the two nations in question. But this is, after all, only a minor difficulty. Provided that the respective Governments were prepared to use their normal powers of control over the principal modes of communication and of transport, the potency of the boycott so established would appear exceedingly effective.

It involves, however, a risk which needs recognition. The extreme pressure of the boycott might lead to forcible reprisals on the part of the boycotted State which would, in fact, precipitate a war. Declaring what would be in effect a blockade by sea and land, it might be necessary for the League to patrol the seas in order to stop "illegal traffic," and to keep some force along the land frontiers for general purposes. A boycotted nation might, in the stress and anger of the case, begin hostilities against those of its neighbors who were most active in the operations of the boycott. In that event the economic boycott would have to be supported by armed pressure. This would also be the case where the breach of international law against which action was

177

taken consisted, not in refusing to arbitrate or concili-
ate an issue but in an actual opening of hostilities.
Such an act of war, directed necessarily against some one
or more States, could not be met merely by a boycott.
It would involve armed cooperation as well, the economic
boycott forming an accompaniment.

There is another method of bringing financial pressure
upon a law-breaking State which deserves consideration.
It is put forward in the following terms by Mr. F. N.
Keen in his able little book, ''The World in Alliance'':
''The States comprised in the international scheme
might be required to keep deposited with, or under the
control of, the International Council sums of money,
proportioned in some way to their relative populations
or financial resources, which might be made available to
answer international obligations, and an international
bank might be organized, which would facilitate the giving of security by States to the International Council
for the performance of their obligations and the enforcement of payments between one State and another (as
well as probably assisting in the creation of an international currency and discharging other useful international functions).''

The organized concentration of international finance
by the formation of an international bank is a line of
action which might immensely strengthen that body of
pacific forces the rising importance of which Mr. Norman Angell has so effectively expounded. It might con-
solidate to an almost incalculable degree the effective
unity of the International League by placing under it
the solid foundation of world-peace, while the power
which such an institution would wield, either for purposes of fiscal or financial boycott, would be enormous.

But however highly we estimate the potentialities of
178

the boycott as a valuable adjunct to the pressure of pub- lic opinion in compelling obedience to treaty obligations, it is idle to pretend that the confidence required to induce the chief nations to rely upon the due performance of these obligations by all their co-signatories will be possible without placing at their disposal, for use in the last resort, an adequate armed force to break the resistance of an armed law-breaking State. Somewhere behind international law there must be placed a power of international compulsion by arms. If that force were really adequate, it is probable that it would never be necessary to employ it for any purpose save that of repelling invasions or dangerous disorders on the part of outsiders. Its existence and the knowledge of its presence might suffice to restrain the aggressive or lawless tendencies which will survive in members of the League. But in the beginnings of the organization of international society it is at least possible, perhaps likely, that some dangerous outbreak of the old spirit of state-absolutism should occur, and that some arrogant or greedy Power, within the circle of the League, might endeavor to defy the public law.

For the States entering such a League will be of various grades of political development: some may enter with reluctance and rather because they fear to be left out than because they believe in or desire the success of the League. It is idle to imagine that a society starting with so little inner unity of status and of purpose can dispense entirely with the backing of physical force with which the most highly evolved of national societies has been unable to dispense.

What form, then, should the required international force take, and who should exercise it?

The proposal to endow some executive international body with the power of levying and maintaining a new

179

land and sea force, superior to that of any Power or combination it may be called upon to meet, scarcely merits consideration. Apart from the hopelessness of getting the Powers to consent to set up a Super-State upon this basis, the mere suggestion of curing militarism by creating a large additional army and navy would be intolerable. Nor is it any more reasonable to expect the Powers to abandon their separate national forces, simply contributing their quota towards an international force under the permanent control of an International Executive. No such abandonment of sovereign power, no such complete confidence in the new internationalism, could for a long time to come be even contemplated. Each nation would insist upon retaining within its own territory and at its own disposal the forces necessary to preserve internal order and to meet at the outset any sudden attack made from outside. It is evident, in other words, that the forces required by the International League in the last resort, for the maintenance of public law and the repression of breaches of the treaty, must be composed of contingents drawn upon some agreed plan from the national forces and placed for the work in hand at the disposal of an international command. Such armed cooperation is, of course, not unknown. Several times within recent years concerted action has been taken by several European Powers, and though the Pekin expedition in 1900 cannot be regarded as a very favorable example, it illustrates the willingness of Powers to act together for some common end which seems to them of sufficient importance. Is it too much to expect that the nations entering the Confederation will realize with sufficient clearness the importance of preserving the integrity of their international agreement to be willing to entrust a permanent executive with the duty of commandeering the forces necessary to achieve this purpose when they may be required?

It will doubtless be objected that there is a world of difference between the occasional willingness of a group of Powers to take concerted action upon a particular occasion, for which each reserves full liberty of determination as to whether and to what extent it will cooperate, and the proposal before us. It is absurd, we shall be told, to expect that States bred in the sense of sovereignty and military pride will seriously entertain a proposal which may bring them into war in a quarrel not specifically theirs and compel them to furnish troops to serve under an international staff. But many events that have seemed as absurd are brought to pass. A few decades ago nothing would have seemed more absurd than to suppose that our nation would be willing to equip an Expeditionary Force of several million men to operate upon the Continent under the supreme control of a French general. Whether, in fact, such cooperation as we here desiderate is feasible at any early period will depend upon two factors: first, the realization on the part of Governments and peoples of the civilized world of the supreme importance of the issue at stake in this endeavor to lay a strong foundation for the society of nations; secondly, the diminution in the influence of militarism and navalism as factors in national life that is likely to occur if sufficient belief in the permanence and efficacy of the new arrangement is once secured. If nations can be brought to believe that national armies and navies are too dangerous toys to be entrusted to the indiscretion of the national statesmen and generals, and are only safe if they are held in trust for the wider world community, this conviction will modify the surviving sentiments of national pride and national pugnacity and make it easier to accept the new

181

international status. Moreover, if, as the first-fruits of
the new order, a sensible reduction of national armaments can be achieved, this lessening of the part which
armed force plays within each national economy will be
attended by a corresponding increase in the willingness
to place the reduced forces at the international disposal.
For the root motive of the international policy is the
desire of each nation to get a larger amount of security
at a smaller cost than under the old order. Those,
therefore, who confidently assert that States will not
consent on any terms to entrust their national forces to
an international command for the maintenance of the
treaty obligations under the proposed scheme in effect
simply assert the permanency of the reign of unreason in
the relations between States.

For though the general agreement of States to submit their disagreements to processes of arbitration and
conciliation with pledges to abide by the results would
be a considerable advance towards better international
relations, even if no sanction beyond the force of public opinion existed to enforce the fulfilment of the obligations, it would not suffice to establish such confidence
in future peace as to secure any sensible and simultane-
ous reduction of armed preparations. No Government
would consent to any weakening of its national forces
so long as there was danger that some Power might re-
pudiate its treaty obligations. This being the case, the
burdens and the perilous influences of militarism and
navalism would remain entrenched as strongly as before
in the European system, advertising, by their very presence, the lack of faith in the efficacy of the new pacific arrangements. So long as these national armaments
remained unchecked the old conception of State absolut-
ism would still survive. There would still be danger of
militarist Governments intriguing for aggression or de-

182

fense in new groupings, and new efforts to tip the balance of armed power in their favor.

It is ultimately to the dread and despair of this alternative that I look for the motive-power to induce nations to make the abatements of national separatism necessary to establish an international society. Whether the end of this war will leave these motives sufficiently powerful to achieve this object will probably depend upon the degree of enlightenment among mankind at large upon the old ideas of States and statecraft.

J. A. Hobson, "Toward International Government," pp. 90–100.

ECONOMIC COERCION

There must
be effective
penalties for
aggression.

I want to suggest here that the forces of Europe will not be readily deterrent of aggression until the following conditions at least are fulfilled: (a) The forces placed behind a policy the first object of which shall be to deter aggression; (b) aggression so defined as to have no reference to the merits of a dispute between two nations or groups, but to consist simply in taking any belligerent action to enforce a State's claim against another without first having submitted that claim to international enquiry; (c) the economic pressure which is an essential part of military operations rendered effective by the co-operation of States which do not necessarily give military aid at all; (d) economic pressure so organized as to be capable of prolongation beyond the period of military operations; and (e) the penalties attaching to aggression made so plain as to be realized beforehand by any people whose government tends to drift towards aggression.

If the new Congress of Vienna is effective, these conditions will be fulfilled.

Any arrangement which includes them would partake of the nature of a league of mutual guarantee of integrity, and would be one in which there would be fair hope of economic pressure gradually replacing military force as the compelling sanction. Economic pressure might be that first felt if the outstanding feature of the arrangement were that any constituent State resorting to hostilities as the result of a difference with another,

184

not previously submitted to an international court of enquiry, by that fact caused boycott or non-intercourse to be proclaimed and maintained against it by the whole group. This would not prevent certain members of the group from carrying on military operations, as well, against it. Some of the group would go to war in the military sense—all in the economic sense; the respective rôles would be so distributed as to secure the most effective action. From the moment of the offending nation's defiance of the international agreement to which it had been a party, its ships could enter no civilized ports outside its own, nor leave them. Payment of debts to it would be withheld; the commercial paper of its citizens would not be discounted; its citizens could not travel in any civilized country in the world, their passports being no longer recognized.

Thus, the outlaw nation could neither receive from nor send to the outside world material or communication of any kind—neither food nor raw material of manufacture, nor letters, nor cables. Money due to him throughout the world would be sequestrated for disposal finally as the international court's judgment should direct; and that rule would apply to royalties on patents and publications, and would, of course, involve precautionary seizure or sequestration of all property—ships, goods, bank balances, business—held by that nation's citizens abroad.

It is doubtful whether at the present stage of international understanding this arrangement could be carried beyond the point of using it as a means to secure delay for enquiry in international disputes. Its use as a sanction for the judgments of international tribunals will probably require a wider agreement as to the foundations of international law than at present exists. But a union of Christendom on the basis of common action against aggression would be a very great step to the more ambitious plans.

It has, however, been suggested (by the Fabian Society) to use this method as a sanction for the judgment of an international court in the following terms:

In the event of non-compliance with any decision or decree or injunction of the International High Court, or of non-payment of the damages, compensation, or fine within the time specified for such payment, the Court may decree execution and may call upon the Constituent States or upon some or any of them, to put in operation, after duly published notice, for such period and under such conditions as may be arranged, the following sanctions:

(a) To prohibit all postal, telegraphic, telephonic, and wireless communication with the recalcitrant State;

(b) To prohibit all passenger traffic (other than the exit of foreigners), whether by ship, railway, canal, or road, to or from the recalcitrant State;

(c) To prohibit the entrance into any port of the Constituent States of any of the ships registered as belonging to the recalcitrant State, except so far as may be necessary for any of them to seek safety, in which case such ship or ships shall be interned;

(d) To prohibit the payment of any debts due to the citizens, companies, or subordinate administrations of the recalcitrant State, or to its national Government; and, if thought fit, to direct that payment of such debts shall be made only to one or other of the Constituent Governments, which shall give a good and legally valid discharge for the same, and shall account for the net proceeds thereof to the International High Court;

(e) To lay an embargo on any or all ships within the jurisdiction of such Constituent State or States registered as belonging to the recalcitrant State;

186

(f) To prohibit any lending of capital or other moneys to the citizens, companies, or subordinate administrations of the recalcitrant State, or to its national Government; Co-operation must be organized as part of international law.

(g) To prohibit the issue or dealing in or quotation on the Stock Exchange or in the press of any new loans, debentures, shares, notes, or securities of any kind by any of the citizens, companies or subordinate administrations of the recalcitrant State, or of its national Government;

(h) To prohibit all imports, or certain specified imports, coming from the recalcitrant State, or originating within it;

(i) To prohibit all exports, or certain specified exports consigned directly to the recalcitrant State, or destined for it.

It should be noted that if the future European coalition means business at all in giving permanent effect to its settlement provisions, the chief Powers would be committed, during any period of war, by virtue of their military obligations, to everything contained in the plan just outlined. All that the project under discussion involves in addition is that (1) certain States interested in the observance of public right, but which, by their circumstances, are not suited to military cooperation, should give economic aid by taking part in the embargo arrangements. They should not be neutral, but should refuse intercourse with the recalcitrant State while according it to the others. (2) That such cooperation should be duly organized beforehand by public arrangement and be recognized as part of the normal measures of international public safety and, being duly recognized in this way, should become part of international law—an amended law in so far as the rules of neutrality are concerned. (3) That the arrangements should in-

187

Boycott
would
threaten
offending
nation after
the war.

clude provisions for prolonging embargo or discrimination against an offending State after the period of military operations had ceased.

The first point that occurs to one, of course, in considering such a plan is that it has proven ineffective in the present war since this condition of non-intercourse is exactly that in which Germany now finds herself, and it is not at all effective.

To which I reply:

1. That Germany, as already pointed out, is not yet subject to a condition of complete non-intercourse, since from the beginning of the war she has been receiving her mail and cables and maintaining communication with the outside world, morally an immensely important factor. Nor is it entirely moral. Large supplies have, despite the naval blockade, come to her through Scandinavia and Holland.

2. That, though of slow operation, it is the economic factor which in the end will be the decisive one in the operations against Germany; as the ring tightens and a necessary raw material like cotton is absolutely excluded, the time will come when this fact will tell most heavily. If the non-intercourse had been world-organized the effect would have operated from the first. Incidentally, of course, America and England, between them, control the cotton of the world.

3. The effect of the suggested embargo, boycott or economic pressure would be most decisive as a deterrent to aggression, not so much by what it might be able to accomplish during a war as by what its prolongation would mean to the aggressor afterwards.

Norman Angell, "The World's Highway," pp. 318–324.

188

WORLD-ORGANIZATION AND PEACE

The end of armed conflict is conceivable as the result Types of social organization. of either of two achievements. Permanent peace may come either upon the establishment of successful means for the settlement of disputes or upon the elimination of the causes which produce disputes. This paper is limited to discussion of the second of these alternatives. . . .

In large-scale organizations purposefully created because of their utility, history discloses few in which that utility, in its broader aspect, has been appreciated by all of the cooperating members. Only in organizations approaching a pure democracy has an approximation to such conditions been attained. In other forms of organization, force or reward has been employed to gain the cooperation of persons outside a limited number of organizers, who alone have appreciated the full utility of organization. Even in democracies, however, when population is too large for all to participate in government, it is possible only for the majority of the members of the organization to exercise control over general policies; executive functions are of necessity delegated. Thus three sub-forms of the utility type of organization are to be distinguished. They may be termed respectively the organizer-force, the organizer-reward, and the democratic-control-expert-executive forms.

Brief analysis and appeal to history will serve to indicate the relative stability of these forms, both with re-

189

spect to each other and to the sympathy type of organization.

Of the organizer-force form the slavery system and the militaristic empire are examples. Neither of these systems, however, has inherent stability. Both run the danger of revolt. The militaristic empire breaks down sooner or later because unlikeness of peripheral regions causes local patriotism to assert itself whenever there is possibility of success. Slavery does not survive the growth of intelligence. Governments of the organizer-force form, moreover, have to face the constant threat of revolution. If Germany be cited as a possible exception, the reply is, that special conditions have stimulated the loyalty of the Germans to their sovereign. Germany was unified but recently and then only by war. Her people have not yet wholly overcome the distrust of one another engendered by long-standing local differences. Germany has thus required a strong hand to create and to preserve her unity. In addition, the Germans, not altogether without reason, have believed themselves surrounded by hostile nations. These conditions sufficiently account for the exception. It must not be overlooked, however, that even in Germany there has been a growing dissatisfaction with the form of organization of her government. Thus the briefest examination of the organizer-force form of organization discloses the futility of expecting permanent international peace to result from an extension of this form throughout the world. Even in its local manifestations this form exhibits inherent instability and lack of harmony.

The organizer-reward form of organization also appears to have its own peculiar tendency towards instability. This was true of the feudal systems of the past, and is true of the great business corporations of to-day, both of which are examples of the organizer-reward form. In the feudal system the reward offered by the organizers in return for service was protection; in modern industry the reward is a money wage. In both cases, however, when subordinate members of the organization have been ignorant, there has been some tendency towards the exploitation as well as the utilization of such members. To the extent, however, that intelligence has developed, there has been less and less voluntary continuance of organizations whose utility has been thought by the subordinate members to be limited to one class in the organization. Force has been met by force. Since intelligence is increasing, it is not fortuitous that the great internal problem of advanced nations is the control of such exploitive industry as exists, while the great political problem of less advanced nations is the struggle for democracy. In both cases the struggle is to prevent the organizer-reward form from becoming the organizer-force form and to replace the instability and the lack of harmony of these forms by the greater stability and greater harmony of the democratic-control-expert-executive form. Far more than is the case in the other utility forms, the democratic form directs its policies with a view to the welfare of all its members. Minorities are represented on the executive staff. All members of the organization participate in control. The danger of dissatisfaction on the part of non-executive members is reduced to a minimum.

The most striking fact, however, with respect to the question of the relative stability and harmony of the various forms of organization is that the largest and the most permanent relatively harmonious organizations that have appeared among men are those great modern nations whose inhabitants live in a unified area of characterization and are essentially alike in language, race, customs, traditions and religion. Homogeneity in all

191

these respects, it is true, does not as yet exist even on a
national scale and there is certainly no prospect of such
homogeneity on a world scale in the near future. These
considerations must not blind us to the fact, however,
that England, France, Spain, Germany, Russia, Italy,
the Scandinavian nations, the United States, Japan and
China—the largest and internally the most harmonious
organizations yet known to man—are each composed of
individuals the vast majority of whom are relatively
alike in language, customs and traditions, and for the
most part in race and religion. Nations that are
markedly heterogeneous in the characteristics mentioned,
such as the Austro-Hungarian Empire, the Balkan
States and European Turkey, are notoriously unstable.
Furthermore, the stability possessed by the various util-
ity-form organizations that exist within or among the
stable nations of the world is, in large part, the result
of the stability and permanence of the nations themselves. The stability of all three of the utility forms
thus rests upon the inherent stability of the sympathy
type of organization.

If the foregoing analysis be correct, certain propositions of great importance for the problem of international peace may now be stated. First, nationality on
the basis of sympathy is likely to persist for an indefinite
period. Second, because of the ignorance of the inhabitants of a number of important nations, the organizer-
force and the organizer-reward forms of government and
of business organization are also likely to persist, for
a considerable period, in various parts of the globe.
Third, where the organizer-force or organizer-reward
form of organization is superimposed on nationality,
readiness to maintain harmony with other national
groups can exist only when such international harmony
is to the interest of the organizer class in each of such

192

nations. Where the democratic-control-expert-executive form prevails, readiness to maintain harmony with other national groups can exist only when such international harmony is to the interest of each nation so organized, taken as a whole.

Peace will follow increasing like-mindedness among the nations.

These propositions mean that, under present conditions, permanent world peace can be produced only if in the organizer-force and in the organizer-reward nations the organizer is less interested in personal fame than in the welfare of the whole organization, if the organizing class does not seek aggrandizement or if the organizing class is willing to permit a peaceful transition within the nation to the democratic-control-expert-executive form of organization rather than to seek perpetuation of its own control through foreign war. They mean also that such peace can be maintained only if democratic nations can be kept free from that trooping of emotion which sometimes suddenly sweeps vast bodies of men into unreasoning demand for aggressive action, and if the interests of such nations lead them to desire international peace. . . .

Let there be produced sufficient likeness among the peoples of the world, and harmonious organization based on sympathy will follow of itself. If there be created a sufficient likeness among all peoples in ideals of progress, in the desire for the betterment of the entire human race, and in other equally important mental and moral respects, then world harmony, based on sympathy, will ultimately develop in the same way that the present harmony within homogeneous nations has resulted, in large part, from a sympathy spontaneously created by resemblance in race, language, religion and customs.

That final permanent international peace can come, however, only on the basis of world-wide like-mindedness is the chief contention of this essay. If this con-

Action

be taken
towards
securing
this like-
mindedness.

tention is correct, advocates of international peace must not only adopt policies calculated to produce like-mindedness, but must not shrink from the endeavor to produce the central executive organization—the natural result of like-mindedness, and in itself, if established, a creator of like-mindedness.

From the standpoint of producting like-mindedness it is of comparatively small moment what one of a number of possible projects is used for the initial attempt. It is of supreme importance only that the project chosen should be the one most likely to succeed in evolving common response and cooperation.

The practical suggestions which follow, therefore, are based on these two notions: first, the desirability of creating like-mindedness among the peoples of the world on a plane above race, religion, language and customs; and second, the desirability of creating a central executive organization, so far as possible responsible to the peoples behind each national government, rather than responsible to constituent governments. They suggest action on the basis of combining the two most stable forms of harmonious organization, namely, the sympathy form growing out of like-mindedness, and the democratic-control-expert-executive form of the utility type.

The first suggestion under the principles thus outlined is that there be established a world consular staff, to assume some at least of the functions of the present national consular services. The first duty undertaken by a world consular service would be to systematize, for the benefit of business the world over, such investigations as are now carried on in a somewhat haphazard way by each national consular service. By centralization, much duplication of effort would be eliminated and a much more comprehensive plan of investigation car-

194

ried out. The results, as now, would be available for all business men of all nationalities. From the beginning, so far as possible, the chief executives of such a consular staff should be elected by the people of each nation, rather than appointed by governments—the purpose of this being to create in each voter the world over, some sense of participation in a world-undertaking, and to some extent a sympathy with other voters the world over. The cost both of the consular service and of the election of the executive officers of the service should be met, not by appropriations from national governments, but by a fixed percentage of the revenues of each nation. The usefulness of the service itself to all the people of the world would be, eventually, the guarantee that the contribution of this percentage would be maintained. Proposed changes in the percentage would ultimately have to be submitted to the voters of all peoples.

The suggestion as thus outlined is an ideal not likely to be soon realized, but it is possible that some beginning toward a world consular service could be provided for by the peace treaty to be signed at the close of the present war. Such a beginning might well be a provisional world-chamber of commerce, organized on the basis of constituent national chambers, the character and organization of which should be provided for in the treaty. The subject will hardly receive notice during the peace negotiations, however, unless, as the result of previous publicity and discussion, the possibilities of world organization latent in the proposition are fully realized.

The second suggestion for the production of world-wide like-mindedness is that there be undertaken a world investigation into the natural resources of the earth, and that a central world-conservation investigation commission be created. At the present time the conservation movement is organized on national rather than on world-wide lines, and the natural result is to strengthen local rather than international sympathy. The principle of scientific management would become much more effective if adopted from a world standpoint. Moreover, there is no reason why the results of a world-wide conservation investigation should not produce recommendations that, through appeals to the peoples back of the national governments, the governments themselves would be forced to heed. The machinery for the conservation investigation might develop out of the world consular service or become a part of the work of that service.

The third suggestion for the production of world-wide like-mindedness is that there be established a central bureau of advice and information on all "human betterment" projects. Thus far we have not advanced beyond the point of developing national bureaus of commerce and labor, hygiene, child welfare and other similar interests, and of holding "international congresses." A permanent world bureau would be far more systematic in the dissemination of knowledge of successful experiments. It would also tend to create world sympathy. With increasing prestige the bureau would naturally extend its functions to those of recommendation and advice to national and local governments.

The fourth suggestion is that there be established a permanent world commission on international migration. At the present time problems of migration, such, for example, as those of the Japanese and Chinese to the United States, are settled by the nations primarily interested, without recognition of the fact that migration is essentially a world problem in which all humanity has an interest. The local problems of migration

196

that arise from time to time are but a part of an age- long movement of population which is gradually producing an equilibrium between density of population and natural resources in every part of the world. Movements between two nations, however, will never be settled on reasons other than local. A world commission would at least work toward a world-policy in this possibly the most important of world-problems.

The fifth suggestion is that these and all other projects for the creation of the world-mind and centralized organization be furthered by utilizing all the modern methods of the commercial "accelerator of public opinion," the publicity agent and the advertiser versed in psychologically efficient methods. There should be an adequate world-publicity service, the task of which should be to develop like responses to the proposed projects in the populations back of governments, and by publicity methods to develop that like-mindedness which is essential for world-wide organization on the sympathy basis.

The development of many other projects similar to those outlined above, it is apparent, would inevitably tend toward the production of centralized organization with many departments. Separate world organizations for different purposes could not long exist without integration. The central organization would inevitably assume the duties of the international postal union; it would create a world monetary system; and it would assume the functions of an international court. With increasing prestige, such an organization would gain greater and greater moral power. Resting on like-mindedness in the populations back of national governments, it would ultimately develop a world-loyalty and find its recommendations enforced by the moral sense

197

Peace
proposals
should
inaugurate
like-
mindedness.
of the world. Force, except for local police purposes, would not be needed.

The final suggestion based on the preceding analysis is that the principle underlying these projects be adopted as at least one of the fundamental propositions for the guidance of peace negotiators at the close of the present war. Peace should be established not upon the basis of the interests of victorious nations alone, nor even upon the combined interests of victors and vanquished, but upon the basis of the future welfare of all peoples. The inauguration of policies for the production of like-mindedness might well be provided for in the peace treaty itself. National boundaries should not be set on a basis which will intensify national self-sufficiency and aloofness, but on a basis which will encourage inter-communication and the development of like-mindedness throughout the world. Moreover, the choice of national representatives for the peace negotiations should include men capable of taking the world-view rather than the exclusively nationalistic view. Representatives of the neutral nations should be admitted to the proceedings. A popular demand that these representatives be of the world-mind type should be created immediately by publicity methods. So far as possible, practical projects for the creation of the world-mind and world-organization should be provided for in the treaty of peace, and as a guarantee of good faith no indemnity other than a pro-rata contribution for the maintenance of these projects should be exacted. Provision should be made also for permanently meeting the cost of such projects, by agreement that a definite precentage of national taxes be set aside for the use of the world organizations created by the treaty. In short, an authoritative and intelligent beginning toward world-or-

198

ganization should be made at the close of the present war.

A. A. Tenney, "Theories of Social Organization, and the Problems of International Peace," Political Science Quarterly, March, 1915.

PART III

TOWARDS THE FUTURE

THE NEW OUTLOOK

No one dare predict just what the end of this world The war, a Katharsis for humanity. war will be, or when that end will come. It is possible, of course, that this cataclysm marks the end of centuries of progress, and it is possible that man in 1914 crossed over the watershed of civilization and is now to descend on the other side towards steadily growing barbarism and the steadily extending rule of force. That I say is possible; but I for one am an unconquerable optimist. I prefer to read history differently and to see in this appalling catastrophe what the Greek called a *katharsis*, a cleansing of the spirit. I prefer to think of it as history's way of teaching beyond peradventure or dispute the fallacy and the folly of the old ways and the old policies. Surely that struggle for the balance of power which the historian Stubbs described as the principle which gives unity to the plot of modern history,—surely that struggle has proved its futility. Surely we can see the vanity of Ententes and Alliances and of a division of the world into heavily armed camps each waiting for an opportunity or for an excuse to pounce upon the other. Surely the international politics of a Palmerston, or a Disraeli, or a Bismarck, striking and splendid as they were in their own way,—surely those policies are put behind us and are outgrown forever.

A democratic federated people can teach the world democracy and the use of the federative principle. A

203

people devoted to civil liberty and to international honor,
no less lightly held than the honor of an individual—
that people can teach the world the foundations upon
which to rebuild the shattered fabric of international law
and of broken treaties.

The outlook before the people of the United States
has changed. When Joseph Chamberlain returned
from South Africa his message to the people of Great
Britain was: "You must learn to think imperially."
The message which any American alive to the world's
situation to-day must bring to his fellow citizens is, you
must learn to think internationally! Domestic policies
and problems are perhaps no less important than they
have been in the past, but by their side and for the immediate future surpassing them in interest and in importance are the international problems and the international policies of the people of the United States.
For those problems and for those policies we must prepare—prepare thoughtfully, seriously, speedily; for
when the war shall be ended, we may truly say, as Gam-
betta said to the French people forty-five years ago,
"Now that the danger is past, the difficulties begin."

*Nicholas Murray Butler, Address at 147th Annual
Banquet of Chamber of Commerce of the State of
New York, Nov. 18, 1915.*

ABOVE THE BATTLE

O young men that shed your blood with so generous The tragedy and heroism of self-sacrificing youth! a joy for the starving earth! O heroism of the world! What a harvest for destruction to reap under this splendid summer sun! Young men of all nations, brought into conflict by a common ideal, making enemies of those who should be brothers; all of you, marching to your death, are dear to me. Slavs, hastening to the aid of your race; Englishmen fighting for honor and right; intrepid Belgians who dared to oppose the Teutonic colossus, and defend against him the Thermopylæ of the West; Germans fighting to defend the philosophy and the birthplace of Kant against the Cossack avalanche; and you, above all, my young compatriots, in whom the generation of heroes of the Revolution lives again; you, who for years have confided your dreams to me, and now, on the verge of battle, bid me a sublime farewell. . . .

O my friends, may nothing mar your joy! Whatever fate has in store, you have risen to the pinnacle of earthly life, and borne your country with you. And you will be victorious: Your self-sacrifice, your courage, your whole-hearted faith in your sacred cause, and the unshaken certainty that, in defending your invaded country, you are defending the liberty of the world— all this assures me of your victory, young armies of the Marne and Meuse, whose names are graven henceforth in history by the side of your elders of the Great Republic. Yet even had misfortune decreed that you should be vanquished, and with you France itself, no people could have aspired to a more noble death. It would have crowned the life of that great people of the Crusades—it would have been their supreme victory. Conquerors or conquered, living or dead, rejoice! As one of you said to me, embracing me on the terrible threshold: "A splendid thing it is to fight with clean hands and a pure heart, and to dispense divine justice with one's life."

You are doing your duty, but have others done theirs? Let us be bold and proclaim the truth to the elders of these young men, to their moral guides, to their religious and secular leaders, to the Churches, the great thinkers, the leaders of socialism; these living riches, these treasures of heroism you held in your hands; for what are you squandering them? What ideal have you held up to the devotion of these youths so eager to sacrifice themselves? Their mutual slaughter! A European war! A sacrilegious conflict which shows a maddened Europe ascending its funeral pyre, and, like Hercules, destroying itself with its own hands!

And thus the three greatest nations of the West, the guardians of civilization, rush headlong to their ruin, calling in to their aid Cossacks, Turks, Japanese, Cingalese, Soudanese, Senegalese, Moroccans, Egyptians, Sikhs and Sepoys—barbarians from the poles and those from the equator, souls and bodies of all colors. It is as if the four quarters of the Roman Empire at the time of the Tetrarchy had called upon the barbarians of the whole universe to devour each other.

Is our civilization so solid that you do not fear to shake the pillars on which it rests? Can you not see that all falls in upon you if one column be shattered? Could you not have learned if not to love one another, at least to tolerate the great virtues and the great vices of each other? Was it not your duty to attempt—you have never attempted it in sincerity—to settle amicably the questions which divided you, the problem of peoples annexed against their will, the equitable division of pro-ductive labor and the riches of the world? Must the stronger forever darken the others with the shadow of his pride, and the others forever unite to dissipate it? Is there no end to this bloody and puerile sport, in which the partners change about from century to century—no end, until the whole of humanity is exhausted thereby?

The rulers who are the criminal authors of these wars dare not accept the responsibility for them. Each one by underhand means seeks to lay the blame at the door of his adversary. The peoples who obey them submis-sively resign themselves with the thought that a power higher than mankind has ordered it thus. Again the venerable refrain is heard: ''The fatality of war is stronger than our wills.'' The old refrain of the herd that makes a god of its feebleness and bows down before him. Man has invented fate, that he may make it re-sponsible for the disorders of the universe, those disor-ders which it was his duty to regulate. There is no fatal-ity! The only fatality is what we desire; and more often, too, what we do not desire enough. Let each now repeat his *mea culpa*. The leaders of thought, the Church, the Labor Parties did not desire war . . . That may be . . . What then did they do to prevent it? What are they doing to put an end to it? They are stirring up the bonfire, each one bringing his fagot.

The most striking feature in this monstrous epic, the fact without precedent, is the unanimity for war in each of the nations engaged. An epidemic of homicidal fury, which started in Tokio ten years ago, has spread like a wave and overflowed the whole world. None has re-

sisted it; no high thought has succeeded in keeping out
of the reach of this scourge. A sort of demoniacal
irony broods over this conflict of the nations, from which,
whatever its result, only a mutilated Europe can emerge.
For it is not racial passion alone which is hurling millions of men blindly one against another, so that not even
neutral countries remain free of the dangerous thrill,
but all the forces of the spirit, of reason, of faith, of
poetry, and of science, all have placed themselves at the
disposal of the armies in every State. There is not one
amongst the leaders of thought in each country who
does not proclaim with conviction that the cause of his
people is the cause of God, the cause of liberty and of
human progress. And I, too, proclaim it.

Strange combats are being waged between metaphy-
sicians, poets, historians—Eucken against Bergson;
Hauptmann against Maeterlinck; Rolland against
Hauptmann; Wells against Bernard Shaw. Kipling
and D'Annunzio, Dehmel and de Régnier sing war
hymns, Barrès and Maeterlinck chant pæans of hatred.
Between a fugue of Bach and the organ which thunders
Deutschland über Alles, Wundt, the aged philosopher of
eighty-two, calls with his quavering voice the students
of Leipzig to the holy war. And each nation hurls at
the other the name "Barbarians. . . ."

Come, friends! Let us make a stand! Can we not
resist this contagion, whatever its nature and virulence
be—whether moral epidemic or cosmic force? Do we
not fight against the plague, and strive even to repair
the disaster caused by an earthquake? Or must we bow
ourselves before it, agreeing with Luzzatti in his famous
article that *"In the universal disaster, the nations
triumph"?* Shall we say with him that it is good and
reasonable that "the demon of international war, which
mows down thousands of beings, should be let loose,"

so that the great and simple truth, "love of our coun- try," be understood? It would seem, then, that love of our country can flourish only through the hatred of other countries and the massacre of those who sacrifice themselves in the defense of them. There is in this theory a ferocious absurdity, a Neronian dilettantism which repels me to the very depths of my being. No! Love of my country does not demand that I shall hate and slay those noble and faithful souls who also love theirs, but rather that I should honor them and seek to unite with them for our common good. . . .

There was no reason for war between the Western nations; French, English, and German, we are all brothers and do not hate one another. The war-preaching press is envenomed by a minority, a minority vitally interested in maintaining these hatreds; but our peoples, I know, ask for peace and liberty and that alone. The real tragedy, to one situated in the midst of the conflict and able to look down from the high plateaus of Switzerland into all the hostile camps, is the patent fact that actually each of the nations is being menaced in its dearest possessions—in its honor, its independence, its life. Who has brought these plagues upon them? Brought them to the desperate alternative of overwhelming their adversary or dying? None other than their governments, and above all, in my opinion, the three great culprits, the three rapacious eagles, the three empires, the tortuous policy of the house of Austria, the ravenous greed of Czarism, the brutality of Prussia. The worst enemy of each nation is not without, but within its frontiers, and none has the courage to fight against it. It is the monster of a hundred heads, the monster named Imperialism, the will to pride and domination, which seeks to absorb all, or subdue all, or break all, and will suffer no greatness except itself. For the

Western nations Prussian imperialism is the most dangerous. Its hand uplifted in menace against Europe
has forced us to join in arms against this outcome of a
military and feudal caste, which is the curse not only
of the rest of the world but also of Germany itself,
whose thought it has subtly poisoned. We must destroy
this first: but not this alone; the Russian autocracy too
will have its turn. Every nation to a greater or less
extent has an imperialism of its own, and whether it be
military, financial, feudal, republican, social, or intellectual, it is always the octopus sucking the best blood
of Europe. Let the free men of all the countries of
Europe when this war is over take up again the motto
of Voltaire: *"Ecrasons l'infâme!"*

When the war is over! The evil is done now, the torrent let loose and we cannot force it back into its channel unaided. Moreover crimes have been committed
against right, attacks on the liberties of peoples and on
the sacred treasuries of thought, which must and will
be expiated. Europe cannot pass over unheeded the violence done to the noble Belgian people, the devastation
of Malines and Louvain, sacked by modern Tillys. . . .
But in the name of heaven let not these crimes be expiated by similar crimes! Let not the hideous words
"vengeance" and "retaliation" be heard; for a great
nation does not revenge itself, it re-establishes justice.
But let those in whose hands lies the execution of justice
show themselves worthy of her to the end.

It is our duty to keep this before them; nor will we
be passive and wait for the fury of this conflict to spend
itself. Such conduct would be unworthy of us who
have such a task before us. . . .

The neutral countries are too much effaced. Confronted by unbridled force they are inclined to believe
that opinion is defeated in advance, and the majority

of thinkers in all countries share their pessimism. There Take risks for the honor of humanity! is a lack of courage here as well as of clear thinking. For just at this time the power of opinion is immense. The most despotic of governments, even though marching to victory, trembles before public opinion and seeks to court it. Nothing shows this more clearly than the efforts of both parties engaged in war, of their ministers, chancellors, sovereigns, of the Kaiser himself turned journalist, to justify their own crimes, and denounce the crimes of their adversary at the invisible tribunal of humanity. Let this invisible tribunal be seen at last, let us venture to constitute it. Ye know not your moral power, O ye of little faith! If there be a risk, will you not take it for the honor of humanity? What is the value of life when you have saved it at the price of all that is worth living for? . . .

Et propter vitam, vivendi perdere causas. . . .

But for us, the artists and poets, priests and thinkers of all countries, remains another task. Even in time of war it remains a crime for finer spirits to compromise the integrity of their thought; it is shameful to see it serving the passion of a puerile, monstrous policy of race, a policy scientifically absurd—since no country possesses a race wholly pure. Such a policy, as Renan points out in his beautiful letter to Strauss, *"can only lead to zoological wars, wars of extermination, similar to those in which various species of rodents and carnivorous beasts fight for their existence. This would be the end of that fertile admixture called humanity, composed as it is of such various necessary elements."* Humanity is a symphony of great collective souls; and he who understands and loves it only by destroying a part of those elements, proves himself a barbarian and shows his idea of harmony to be no better than the idea of order another held in Warsaw.

211

We are build-
ers of the City
of God! For the finer spirits of Europe there are two dwelling-
places: our earthly fatherland, and that other City of
God. Of the one we are the guests, of the other the
builders. To the one let us give our lives and our faithful hearts; but neither family, friend, nor fatherland,
nor aught that we love has power over the spirit. The
spirit is the light. It is our duty to lift it above tem-
pests, and thrust aside the clouds which threaten to obscure it; to build higher and stronger, dominating the
injustice and hatred of nations, the walls of that city
wherein the souls of the whole world may assemble.

I feel here how the generous heart of Switzerland
is thrilled, divided between sympathies for the various
nations, and lamenting that it cannot choose freely between them, nor even express them. I understand its
torment; but I know that this is salutary. I hope it will
rise thence to that superior joy of a harmony of races,
which may be a noble example for the rest of Europe.
It is the duty of Switzerland now to stand in the midst
of the tempest, like an island of justice and of peace,
where, as in the great monasteries of the early Middle
Ages, the spirit may find a refuge from unbridled force;
where the fainting swimmers of all nations, those who
are weary of hatred, may persist, in spite of all the
wrongs they have seen and suffered, in loving all men
as their brothers.

I know that such thoughts have little chance of being
heard to-day. Young Europe, burning with the fever of
battle, will smile with disdain and show its fangs like a
young wolf. But when the access of fever has spent itself, wounded and less proud of its voracious heroism,
it will come to itself again.

Moreover I do not speak to convince it. I speak but
to solace my conscience . . . and I know that at the

same time I shall solace the hearts of thousands of others who, in all countries, cannot or dare not speak themselves.

Romain Rolland, in Journal de Genève, September 15, 1914.

THE NEW IDEALISM

Germany
wishes
lasting
peace.

What wishes may we have for the future? What tasks and what prospects does the New Year unroll before us? Naturally, our first wish is for a decisive victory,—a victory which will bring us an honorable peace. A discussion of how the conditions of peace should be drawn up seems to us premature, in fact it runs counter to our feeling; for we are still too much under the tension and excitement of the fight to pursue such thoughts. However, it may be said that the German people unanimously desire a settlement which will guarantee a lasting peace and which will prevent further wars. Moreover, the wish is general that, when it is time for peace negotiations, not only professional diplomats, but also representatives of the various professions and industries shall be consulted. Just as war is an affair of the whole people, so, in its conclusion, the voice of the whole people should have due weight.

Closely bound up with the desire for an honorable peace is the hope that the mighty spiritual movement, which the war has called forth, may continue to influence German life after the war. This war must be the starting-point of a new epoch. The tremendous sacrifices which it entails will be justified only in case new life comes forth out of loss and death and the achievements of the moment are transformed into permanent gain. In this connection we think, first of all, of the wonderful consciousness of unity which the war has

214

awakened. The long history of the German people fur- nishes no counterpart of such a unity of sentiment as we enjoy to-day. We must now see to it that this unanimity of purpose is deeply implanted in German life. Since, through common effort, so much has been accomplished during the war, when peace has been re-established, no one should be prevented from cooperating in the solution of our common tasks. In the future there should be no discrimination on account of political partisanship, whether in the pursuit of a profession or in the holding of a public office.

But especially must we hope that the sense of belonging together, the sense of being dependent on each other, the sense of being under obligation to each other will persist beyond the war into peace. It is, however, not only for the feelings of the individuals, but also for our national life, that we should seek to win lasting gain from the storms of the present. All the earnestness and all the mighty force, which we have now exerted, must be used in an energetic fight against all that has threatened to lower our standards of life.

Such a reinvigoration of German idealism parallels a similar movement which has spread throughout the whole of humanity. Old forms of life have often been found too narrow; they have, moreover, frequently lost their basis in our minds. Therefore, the position of man in the universe has seemed obscure and the purpose of his life has become very uncertain. On the other hand, there now awakens a deep longing for the restrengthening, deepening and inner renewal of life.

As Germans, we must consider our attitude towards the world of as much importance as our attitude towards ourselves. We must not allow ourselves to indulge in a narrow national life. We must not, and shall not, have a false racial pride. On the contrary, we must

215

ceaselessly broaden our lives, steadily preserving our
inter-relations with all mankind. Our great nation cannot attain its proper level without keeping the whole of
humanity in mind. We wish to think highly enough of
ourselves to believe that we are capable of drawing to
ourselves everything great and good, that has arisen or
shall arise anywhere, so that we may use it in building
up the ethical civilization (Wesenkultur) which our
nature demands.

> *Rudolf Eucken, "German Thoughts and Wishes for
> the New Year, 1915."*

THE FUTURE OF PATRIOTISM

There is another way of looking at this matter which will appeal to those who are speculating upon the future of mankind. Any one who thinks about the possibility of a world state is stopped to-day by the fact that there is no world patriotism to support it. How are we to transfer allegiance from the national to the international State?

The answer depends upon an analysis of nationality. I have described it as a retreat to the authority and flavor of our earliest associations, as a defensive-offensive reaction to what seems to us secure. Our loyalty turns to what we associate with our protection and our ambitions. The reason we are not loyal to mankind in general or to The Hague or to internationalism is that these conceptions are cold and abstract beside the warmth of the country and place where we were born. Impressed by the fear of Russian invasion, the internationalism of German socialists vanished. Internationalism offered no protection. The German army did. To be a German was to be part of a tangible group with power; to be a citizen of the world was to be homeless everywhere.

And yet we find Canadians and Australians and New Zealanders fighting and dying for a thing called the British Empire, a vague, formless organization of one-quarter of the human race. What is it that has produced this super-national patriotism? Nothing less, it

217

seems to me, than a realization that the protection and growth of the Dominions is bound up with the strength of the Empire. Home is the place where you are safe; loyalty reaches back to the source of your security. That is why danger has welded the British Empire instead of disintegrating it.

Imagine the Empire shattered, its navy gone, and the Dominions left to fetch for themselves. What would Canada and Australia do? They would, it seems to me, develop a great loyalty to the United States. They would not face the world alone. They would have to find some larger political organization in which they could feel secure.

In other words, loyalty overflows the national State because in the world to-day the national State is no longer a sufficient protection. People have got to a point in their development where isolation terrifies them. They want to be members of a stronger group. In Europe they turned to a system of alliances because no nation dared to stand alone. We have turned in this country in part to an understanding with Great Britain, in part to the Latin-American States. All of which proves that patriotism is not a fixed quantity, that it is not attached to the map as it was drawn when we were at school, and that it is not only capable of expansion, but is crying for it.

Fear has almost always played a large part in welding States together. The fear of England was a great argument for federal union under our Constitution; the sense of weakness in the presence of unfriendly neighbors undoubtedly helped to break down the separatism of the little German principalities. Just as the appearance of an enemy tends to blot out political differences within a nation, so it will often unite a number of nations. The rise of Germany had that effect on

218

the Great Powers of Europe; the fear of her created a league almost coextensive with western civilization. It covered up the feud between France and England which comes down through the centuries; it jolted together an understanding with Russia, the great bogy of liberals.

Problem is to broaden the basis of loyalty.

It is not pleasant to think of fear as one of the most powerful forces that unify mankind. It would be more gratifying to think that cooperation was always spontaneous and free. But the facts will not justify this belief. The inner impulse to compose differences seems often to work most actively when there is pressure from without. Forced by danger to cooperate, men seem to discover the advantages of cooperation. The Germans are daily discovering good qualities in the Turks; the British are seeing deeper into the souls of Russians. . . .

The only way in which world organization can command a world patriotism is by proving its usefulness. If it affords a protection and produces a prosperity such as the national State cannot produce, it will begin to draw upon the emotions of men. If they are capable of loving anything so abstract and complicated as the British Empire, or even the United States, they are not incapable of attaching themselves to a still larger State. For the moment it was evident that patriotism could embrace something more extensive and abstract than a village which a man might know personally, world organization ceased to be an idle dream. If men could be citizens of an empire scattered over all the seas, there was no longer anything inconceivable about their becoming citizens of a State which covered modern civilization. The idea has ceased to be a psychological impossibility.

Our problem is to broaden the basis of loyalty. And for that task we have considerable experience to guide us. Within a hundred and twenty-five years we have

219

seen the welding together of the United States, Germany,
Italy, and Austria-Hungary. We have seen small rival
States converted into members of federal unions. We
have watched patriotism expand from the local unit to
the larger one. We have seen Massachusetts patriots
converted into American patriots, Bavarians into Germans, Venetians into Italians. In the last few years we
have been witnessing the growth of an imperial patriotism within the British Empire.

There is, so far as I can see, not the least ground
for supposing that the broadening of loyalty must stop
at the existing frontiers. The task of the great unifi-
ers, like Hamilton, Cavour, and Bismarck, looked just
as difficult in their day as ours does now. They had
States' rights, sovereignty, traditional jealousy, and
economic conflicts to overcome. They conquered them.
Who dares to say that we must fail? . . .

Loyalty is a fluctuating force, not attached by any
necessity to some one spot on the map or contained
within some precise frontier. Loyalty seeks an authority to which it can be loyal, and when it finds an authority which gives security and progress and opportunity it fastens itself there. The problem of world organization is to attach enough loyalty to the immature
World State to enable it to weather the inevitable attacks.

*Walter Lippmann, "The Stakes of Diplomacy," pp.
172–188.*

220

THE FUTURE OF CIVILIZATION

What hopes dare we cherish, in this hour of conflict, for the future of civilization?

Our task is to extend the sphere of Law.

The great, the supreme task of human politics and statesmanship is to extend the sphere of Law. Let others labor to make men cultured or virtuous or happy. These are the tasks of the teacher, the priest, and the common man. The statesman's task is simpler. It is to enfold them in a jurisdiction which will enable them to live the life of their soul's choice. The State, said the Greek philosophers, is the foundation of the good life; but its crown rises far above mere citizenship. "There where the State ends," cries Nietzsche, echoing Aristotle and the great tradition of civilized political thought, "there *men begin*. There, where the State ends, look thither, my brothers! Do you not see the rainbow and the bridge to the Overman?" Ever since organized society began, the standards of the individual, the ideals of priest and teacher, the doctrines of religion and morality, have outstripped the practise of statesmanship. For the polestar of the statesman has not been love, but law. His not the task of exhorting men to love one another, but the simpler duty of enforcing the law, "Thou shalt not kill." And in that simple, strenuous, necessary task statesmen and political thinkers have watched the slow extension of the power of Law, from the family to the tribe, from the tribe to the city, from the city to the nation, from the nation to the Commonwealth. When

221

will Law take its next extension? When will warfare, which is murder between individuals and "rebellion" between groups of citizens, be equally preventable between nations by the common law of the world?

The answer is simple. When the world has a common will, and has created a common government to express and enforce that will.

In the sphere of science and invention, of industry and economics, as Norman Angell and others have taught us, the world is already one Great Society. For the merchant, the banker, and the stockbroker political frontiers have been broken down. Trade and industry respond to the reactions of a single, world-wide, nervous system. Shocks and panics pass as freely as airmen over borders and custom-houses. And not "big business" only, but the humblest citizen, in his search for a livelihood, finds himself caught in the meshes of the same world-wide network. "The widow who takes in washing," says Graham Wallas, in his deep and searching analysis of our contemporary life, "fails or succeeds according to her skill in choosing starch or soda or a wringing machine under the influence of half a dozen competing world-schemes of advertisement. . . . The English factory girl who is urged to join her Union, the tired old Scotch gatekeeper with a few pounds to invest, the Galician peasant when the emigration agent calls, the artisan in a French provincial town whose industry is threatened by a new invention, all know that unless they find their way among world-wide facts, which only reach them through misleading words, they will be crushed." The Industrial Revolution of the past century, steam-power and electricity, the railway and the telegraph, have knit mankind together, and made the world one place.

But this new Great Society is as yet formless and in-

articulate. It is not only devoid of common leadership and a common government; it lacks even the beginnings of a common will, a common emotion, and a common consciousness. Of the Great Society, consciously or unconsciously, we must all perforce be members; but of the
Great State, the great World-Commonwealth, we do not
yet discern the rudiments. The economic organization
of the world has outstripped the development of its citizenship and government—the economic man, with his
far-sighted vision and scientific control of the resources
of the world, must sit by and see the work of his hands
laid in ashes by contending governments and peoples.
No man can say how many generations must pass before
the platitudes of the market and the exchange pass into
the current language of politics.

In the great work which lies before the statesmen and
peoples of the world for the extension of law and common citizenship and prevention of war there are two
parallel lines of advance.

One road lies through the development of what is
known as International, but should more properly be
called *Inter-State Law*, through the revival, on a firmer
and broader foundation, of the Concert of Europe conceived by the Congress of Vienna just a hundred years
ago—itself a revival, on a secular basis, of the great
medieval ideal of an international Christendom, held together by Christian Law and Christian ideals. That
ideal faded away forever at the Reformation, which
grouped Europe into independent sovereign States ruled
by men responsible to no one outside their own borders.
It will never be revived on an ecclesiastical basis. Can
we hope for its revival on a basis of modern democracy,
modern nationality, and modern educated public opinion? Can Inter-State Law, hitherto a mere shadow of
the majestic name it bears, almost a matter of conven-

tion and etiquette, with no permanent tribunal to interpret it, and no government to enforce it, be enthroned with the necessary powers to maintain justice between the peoples and governments of the world?

Such a Law the statesmen of Great Britain and Russia sought to impose on Europe in 1815, to maintain a state of affairs which history has shown to have been intolerable to the European peoples. There are those who hope that the task can be resumed, on a better basis, at the next Congress. "Shall we try again," writes Professor Gilbert Murray, "to achieve Castlereagh's and Alexander's ideal of a permanent Concert, pledged to make collective war upon the peace-breaker? Surely we must. We must, at all cost and in spite of all difficulties, because the alternative means such unspeakable failure. We must learn to agree, we civilized nations of Europe, or else we must perish. I believe that the chief counsel of wisdom here is to be sure to go far enough. We need a permanent Concert, perhaps a permanent Common Council, in which every awkward problem can be dealt with before it has time to grow dangerous, and in which outvoted minorities must accustom themselves to giving way."

Other utterances by public men, such as Mr. Roosevelt and our own Prime Minister, might be cited in the same sense; but Professor Murray's has been chosen because he has the courage to grasp the nettle. In his words the true position is quite clearly set forth. If Inter-State Law is to become a reality we must "be sure to go far enough." There is no half-way house between Law and no Law, between Government and no Government, between Responsibility and no Responsibility. If the new Concert is to be effective it must be able to compel the submission of all "awkward problems" and causes of quarrel to its permanent Tribunal at The Hague or elsewhere; and it must be able to enforce the decision of its tribunal, employing for the purpose, if necessary, the armed forces of the signatory Powers as an international police. "Outvoted minorities must accustom themselves to giving way." It is a bland and easy phrase; but it involves the whole question of world-government. "Men must accustom themselves not to demand an eye for an eye and a tooth for a tooth," the earliest law-givers might have said, when the State first intervened between individuals to make itself responsible for public order. Peace between the Powers, as between individuals, is, no doubt, a habit to which cantankerous Powers "must accustom themselves." But they will be sure to do so if there is a Law, armed with the force to be their schoolmaster towards peaceable habits. In other words, they will do so because they have surrendered one of the most vital elements in the independent life of a State—the right of conducting its own policy—to the jurisdiction of a higher Power. An Inter-State Concert, with a Judiciary of its own and an army and navy under its own orders, is, in fact, not an Inter-State Concert at all; it is a new State: it is, in fact, the World-State. There is no middle course between Law and no Law: and the essence of Statehood, as we have seen, is a Common Law. . . .

In discussing proposals for a European Council, then, we must be quite sure to face all that it means. But let us not reject Professor Murray's suggestion off-hand because of its inherent difficulties: for that men should be discussing such schemes at all marks a significant advance in our political thought. Only let us be quite clear as to what they presuppose. They presuppose the supremacy, in the collective mind of civilized mankind, of Law over Force, a definite supremacy of what may be called the civilian as against the military ideal, not in a

225

We must
work for
"The Prin-
ciple of the
Common-
wealth."
majority of States, but in every State powerful enough
to defy coercion. They presuppose a world map definitely settled on lines satisfactory to the national aspirations of the peoples. They presuppose a *status quo*
which is not simply maintained, like that after 1815,
because it is a legal fact and its disturbance would be
inconvenient to the existing rulers, but because it is in-
herently equitable. They presuppose a similar democratic basis of citizenship and representation among the
component States. They presuppose, lastly, an educated
public opinion incomparably less selfish, less ignorant,
less unsteady, less materialistic, and less narrowly national than has been prevalent hitherto. Let us work
and hope for these things: let us use our best efforts to
remove misunderstandings and promote a sense of common responsibilities and common trusteeship for civilization between the peoples of all the various sovereign
States; but meanwhile let us work also, with better hopes
of immediate if less ambitious successes, along the other
parallel road of advance.

The other road may seem, in this hour of dreams and
disaster, of extremes of hope and disillusionment, a long
and tedious track: it is the old slow high road of civilization, not the short cut across the fields. It looks forward
to abiding results, not through the mechanical cooperation of governments, but through the growth of an organic citizenship, through the education of the nations
themselves to a sense of common duty and a common
life. It looks forward, not to the definite establishment,
in our day, of the World-State, but only to the definite
refutation of the wicked theory of the mutual incom-
patibility of nations. It looks forward to the expression
in the outward order of the world's government of what
we may call "the Principle of the Commonwealth," of
Lord Acton's great principle of the State composed of

free nations, of the State as a living body which lives This is a world-principle. through the organic union and free activity of its several national members.. And it finds its immediate field of action in the deepening and extension of the obligations of citizenship among the peoples of the great, free, just, peace-loving, supra-national Commonwealths whose patriotism has been built up, not by precept and doctrine, but on a firm foundation of older loyalties.

The principle of the Commonwealth is not a European principle: it is a world-principle. It does not proceed upon the expectation of a United States of Europe; for all the Great Powers of Europe except Austria-Hungary (and some of the smaller, such as Holland, Belgium, and Portugal) are extra-European Powers also. Indeed if we contract our view, with Gladstone and Bismarck and the statesmen of the last generation, to European issues alone, we shall be ignoring the chief political problem of our age—the contact of races and nations with wide varieties of social experience and at different levels of civilization. It is this great and insistent problem (call it the problem of East and West, or the problem of the color-line) in all its difficult ramifications, political, social, and, above all, economic, which makes the development of the principle of the Commonwealth the most pressing political need of our age. For the problems arising out of the contact of races and nations can never be adjusted either by the wise action of individuals or by conflict and warfare; they can only be solved by fair and deliberate statesmanship within the bosom of a single State, through the recognition by both parties of. a higher claim than their own sectional interest—the claim of a common citizenship and the interest of civilization. It is here, in the union and collaboration of diverse races and peoples, that the principle of the Commonwealth finds its peculiar field of operation. Without this prin-

227

ciple, and without its expression, however imperfect, in the British Empire, the world would be in chaos to-day.

We cannot predict the political development of the various Great Powers who between them control the destinies of civilization. We cannot estimate the degree or the manner in which France, freed at last from nearer preoccupations, will seek to embody in her vast dominion the great civilizing principles for which her republic stands. We cannot foretell the issue of the conflict of ideas which has swayed to and fro in Russia between the British and the Prussian method of dealing with the problem of nationality. Germany, Italy, Japan—here, too, we are faced by enigmas. One other great Commonwealth remains besides the British. Upon the United States already lies the responsibility, voluntarily assumed and, except during a time of internal crisis, successfully discharged, of securing peace from external foes for scores of millions of inhabitants of the American continent. Yet with the progress of events her responsibilities must yearly enlarge: for both the immigrant nationalities within and the world-problems without her borders seem to summon her to a deeper education and to wider obligations.

But upon the vast, ramifying, and inchoate Commonwealth of Great Britain lies the heaviest responsibility. It is a task unequally shared between those of her citizens who are capable of discharging it. Her task within the Commonwealth is to maintain the common character and ideals and to adjust the mutual relations of one quarter of the human race. Her task without is to throw her weight into the scales of peace, and to uphold and develop the standard and validity of inter-State agreements. It is a task which requires, even at this time of crisis, when, by the common sentiment of her citizens, the real nature and purpose of the Common-

228

wealth have become clear to us, the active thoughts of all to bring home to all the meaning of Law.
political students. For to bring home to all within her
borders who bear rule and responsibility, from the village headman in India and Nigeria, the Basutu chief and
the South Sea potentate, to the public opinion of Great
Britain and the self-governing Dominions, the nature
of the British Commonwealth, and the character of its
citizenship and ideals, and to study how those ideals may
be better expressed in its working institutions and executive government—that is a task to which the present
crisis beckons the minds of British citizens, a task which
Britain owes not only to herself but to mankind.

*Alfred E. Zimmern, "The War and Democracy," pp.
371–382.*

229

TOWARDS THE PEACE THAT SHALL LAST

War must
pass away
like human
sacrifice.

At every stage of warfare in the past, men and women in all nations have endeavored to abate and lessen it. Their repeated endeavors have been answered by repeated wars, until the present war in Europe completes the works of death, desolation, and tyranny.

In spite of this, these protests against war are destined to succeed; as once before in the history of the race, the sentiment of pity, of respect for human life, called a halt to senseless slaughter.

There came a time in the history of the Greek and Jewish people when a few set their faces against *human sacrifice as a religious rite* of their highest faith,—bound up, like our wars, with old fealties and solemn customs and with their most desperate fears. Humble men and women, out of sheer affection for their kind, revolted. In face of persecution and ridicule, they warned their countrymen that in pouring human blood upon altars to the gods, they wrought upon their kind more irreparable wrong than any evil against which they sought to forefend. Finally, there came to be enough people with courage and pity sufficient to carry a generation with them; and human sacrifice became a thing of the past.

It took the human race many centuries to rid itself of human sacrifice; during many centuries more it relapsed again and again in periods of national despair. So have

230

we fallen back into warfare, and perhaps will fall back again and again, until in self-pity, in self-defense, in self-assertion of the right of life, not as hitherto, a few, but the *whole people of the world,* will brook this thing no longer.

OUR RIGHT TO PROTEST

By that opportunity, now ours as never before, to weigh the case against war and to draw the counts from burning words spoken by those who protest and who are of all peoples—*we make single judgment and complete indictment.*

By that good fortune which has placed us outside the conflict; by that ill fortune by which the belligerent and his rights have heretofore bestrode the world; by mine-strewn channels, and by international codes which offer scant redress—*we speak as people of a neutral nation.*

By the unemployed of our water-fronts, and the augmented misery of our cities; by the financial depression which has curtailed our school building and crippled our works of good-will; by the sluicing of human impulse among us from channels of social development to the back-eddies of salvage and relief—*we have a right to speak.*

By the hot anger and civil strife that we have known; by our pride, vain-glory, and covetousness; by the struggles we have made for national integrity and defense of our hearthstones; by our consciousness that every instinct and motive and ideal at work in this war, however lofty or however base, has had some counterpart in our national history and our current life—*we can speak a common language.*

By that comradeship among nations which has made for mutual understanding; by those inventions which have bound us in communication and put the horrors of

231

war at our doors; by the mechanical contrivances which
multiply and intensify those horrors; by the quickening
human sympathies which have made us sensitive to the
hurts of others—*we can speak as fellow-victims of this
great oppression.*

By our heritage from each embattled nation; by our
debt to them for languages and faiths and social institutions; for science, scholarship and invention; by the
broken and desolated hearts that will come to us when
the war ends; by our kinships and our unfeigned friendships—*we can speak as brothers.*

By all these things, we hold the present opportunity
for conscience-searching and constructive action to be
an especial charge upon us; upon the newcomers among
us from the fatherlands; and upon the joint youth of
all the peoples of the two Americas.

WHAT WAR HAS DONE AND IS DOING

Its Blights

War has brought low our conception of the *precious-
ness of human life* as slavery brought low our conception of human liberty.

It has benumbed our growing sense of the *nurture of
life;* and at a time when we were challenging Reichstag, Parliament, and Congress with the needlessness of
infant mortality and child labor, it entrenches a million
youths with cold and fever and impending death.

It has thwarted the chance of our times toward the
fulfilment of life, and scattered like burst shrapnel the
hands of the sculptors and the violinists, the limbs of
the hurdlers and swimmers, the sensitive muscles of the
mechanics and the weavers, the throats of the singers
and the interpreters, the eyes of the astronomers and
the melters—every skilled and prescient part of the hu-

man body, every type of craft and competence of the human mind. It has violated humanity.

It has set back our promptings toward the *conservation of life;* and in a decade when England and France and Russia, Germany and Austria and Belgium, have been working out social insurance against the hazards of peace, it throws back upon the world an unnumbered company of the widowed and the fatherless, and of aged parents left bereft and destitute.

It has blocked our way toward *the ascent of life,* and in a century which has seen the beginnings of effort to upbuild the common stock, has cut off from parenthood the strong, the courageous and the high-spirited.

Its Injuries

It has in its development of armaments, pitted human flesh against machinery.

It has wrested the power of self-defense from the hands of free-men who wielded lance and sword and scythe, and has set them as machine-tenders to do the bidding of their masters.

It has brought strange men to the door-sills of peaceful people; men like their own men, bearing no grudges one against another; men snatched away from their fields and villages where their fathers lie buried, to kill and burn and destroy till this other people are driven from their homes of a thousand years or sit abject and broken.

It has stripped farms and ruined self-sustaining communities, and poured into a bewildered march for succor, the crippled and aged and bedridden, the little children and the women great with child unborn.

It has razed the flowing lines in which the art and aspiration of earlier generations expressed themselves, and has thus waged war upon the dead.

It has tortured and twisted the whole social fabric of the living.

It has burdened our children and our children's children with a staggering load of debt.

It has inundated the lowlands of the world's economy with penury and suffering unreckonable, hopelessly depressing standards of living already much too low.

It has rent and trampled upon the net-work of world cooperation in trade and craftsmanship which had made all men fellow-workers.

It has whetted a lust among neutral nations to profit by furnishing the means to prolong its struggles.

It has blasted our new internationalism in the protection of working women and children.

It has distracted our minds with the business of destruction and stayed the forward reach of the builders among men.

It has conscripted physician and surgeon, summoning them from research and the prolongation of life to the patchwork of its wreckage.

It has sucked into its blood and mire our most recent conquests over the elements—over electricity, and air and the depths of ocean; and has prostituted our prowess in engineering, chemistry and technology, to the service of terror and injury.

It has bent our achievements in transportation into runways, so that neither volcanoes nor earthquakes, nor the rat-holes of famine, but only the plagues can match war in unbounded disaster.

Its Wrongs

It has in its compulsory service made patriotism a shell, empty of liberty.

It has set up the military independent of and superior to the civil power.

234

It has turned effort into destruction.

It has substituted arbitrary authority and the morals of foot-loose men who escape identity in the common uniform, for the play of individual conscience, and that social pressure which in household and village, in neighborhood and State, makes for individual responsibility, for decency, and fair play.

It has battened on apathy, unintelligence and helplessness such as surrender the judgment and volition of nations into a few hands; and has nullified rights and securities, such as are of inestimable value to the people and formidable to tyrants only.

It has threatened the results of a hundred martyrdoms and revolutions, and put in jeopardy those free governments which make possible still newer social conquests.

It has crushed under iron heels the uprisings of civilization itself.

Its Evils

It has turned the towers of art and science into new Babels, so that our philosophers, and men of letters, our physicists and geographers, our economists and biologists and dramatists, speak in strange tongues, and to hate each other has become a holy thing among them.

It has made were-wolves of neighboring peoples, in the imaginations of each other.

It has put its stamp upon growing boys and girls, and taught them to hate other children who have chanced to be born on the other side of some man-made boundary.

It has massed and exploded the causes of strife, fostering religious antagonisms and racial hates, inbreeding with the ugliest strains of commercialism, perverting to its purposes the increase of over-dense populations and their natural yearning for new opportunities for enterprise and livelihood.

235

It has not only shattered men's breasts, but loosened the black fury of their hearts; so that in rape, and cruelty, and rage, we have ancient brutishness trailing at the heels of all armies.

It has found a world of friends and neighbors, and substituted a world of outlanders and aliens and enemies.

It has lessened the number of those who feel the joys and sorrows of all peoples as of their own.

It has strangled truth and paralyzed the power and wish to face it, and has set up monstrous and irreconcilable myths of self-justification.

It has mutilated the human spirit.

It has become a thing which passeth all understanding.

STRIKING HANDS

We have heard the call from overseas of those who have appealed to men and women of good-will in all nations to join with them in throwing off this tyranny upon life.

We must go further; we must throw open a peace which shall be other than a shadow of old wars and a prelude to new. We do more than plead with men to stay their hands from killing. We hail living men. As peace-lovers, we are charged with the sanctity of human life; as democrats and freemen we are charged with its sovereignty.

By the eight million natives of the warring States living among us without malice or assault one upon another, let us leave the occasions of fighting no longer for idle war boards to decide.

By the blow our forebears struck at barbarism when they took vengeance out of private hands, let us wrest the manufacture of armaments and deadly weapons from the gun-mongers and powder-makers who gain by it.

By those electric currents that have cut the ground
236

from under the old service of diplomacy, and spread the new intelligence, let us put the ban upon intrigue and secret treaties.

For we hold that not soldiers, nor profit-takers, nor diplomats, but the people who suffer and bear the brunt of war should determine whether war must be; that with ample time for investigation and publicity of its every cause and meaning, with recourse to every avenue for mediation and settlement abroad, war should come only by the slow process of self-willing among men and women who solemnly publish and declare it to be a last and sole resort.

With our treated borderland, 3000 miles in length without fort or trench from the Atlantic to the Pacific, which has helped weld us for a century of unbroken peace with our neighbors to the north, we would spread faith not in entrenched camps but in open boundaries.

With the pacts of our written constitutions before us which bind our own sovereign States in amity, we are convinced that treaty-making may be lifted to a new and inviolable estate, and lay the foundations for that world organization which for all time shall make for peace upon earth and good-will among men.

With our experience in lesser conflicts in industrial life, which have none the less embraced groups as large as armies, have torn passions and rasped endurance to the uttermost, we can bear testimony that at the end of such strife as cleaves to the heart of things, men are disposed to lay the framework of their relations in larger molds than those which broke beneath them.

With our ninety million people drawn from Alpine and Mediterranean, Danubean, Baltic, and Slavic stocks; with a culture blended from these different affluents, we hold that progress lies in the predominance of none; and that the civilization of each nation needs to be re-

237

We must
lead through
our own
ideals in
the war
on war.

freshed by that cross-breeding with the genius and the
type of other human groups, that blending which began
on the coast lands and islands of the Ægean Sea where
European civilization first drew its sources from the
Euphrates and the Nile.

With memories of the tyranny which provoked our
Revolution, with the travail still upon us by which we in
our turn have paid for the enslavement of a people, with
the bitterness only now assuaged which marked our period of mistrust and reconstruction, we bear witness that
boundaries should be set where not force, but justice and
consanguinity direct; and that, however boundaries fall,
liberty and the flowering-out of native cultures should
be secure.

With our fair challenge to the spirit of the East and
to the chivalry of the West in standing for the open door
in China when that Empire, now turned Republic, was
threatened by dismemberment, we call for the freeing of
the ports of every ocean from special privilege based on
territorial claims, throwing them open with equal chance
to all who by their ability and energy can serve new
regions to their mutual benefit.

With the faith we have kept with Cuba, the regard
we have shown for the integrity of Mexico and our
preparations for the independence of the Philippine Islands, we urge the framing of a common colonial policy
which shall put down that predatory exploitation which
has embroiled the West and oppressed the East and shall
stand for an opportunity for each latent and backward
race to build up according to its own genius.

By our full century of ruthless waste of forest, ore
and fuel; by the vision which has come to us in these
latter days of conserving to the permanent uses of the
people, the water power and natural wealth of our public

238

domain, we propose the laying down of a planetary policy of conservation.

By that tedium and monotony of life and labor for vast companies of people, which when war drums sound, goads the field worker to forsake his harvest and the wage-earner to leap from his bench, we hold that the ways of peace should be so cast as to make stirring appeal to the heroic qualities in men, and give common utterance to the rhythm and beauty of national feeling.

By the joy of our people in the conquest of a continent; by the rousing of all Europe, when the great navigators threw open the new Indies and the New World, we stand for such a scheming-out of our joint existence that the achieving instincts among men, not as one nation against another, nor as one class against another, but as one generation after another, shall have freedom to come into their own.

Jane Addams,
Lillian Wald,
Paul U. Kellogg.

APPENDIX

PEACE PROPOSALS AND PROGRAMS

PEACE PROPOSALS AND PROGRAMS

1. INTERNATIONAL

NEUTRAL CONFERENCE FOR CONTINUOUS MEDIATION, STOCKHOLM

To the Governments, Parliaments and Peoples of the Warring Nations:

A conference composed of delegates from six neutral countries—Denmark, Holland, Norway, Sweden, Switzerland and the United States—has been convened at Stockholm upon the initiative of Henry Ford to work for the achievement of an early and lasting peace, based upon principles of justice and humanity. This conference represents no government. It has no official sanction. It represents the good will of millions throughout the civilized world who cannot stand idly by while the deadly combat rages unchecked. It does not attempt to impose its judgment upon the belligerents, but its members, as private individuals, unhampered by considerations which restrain governments, have resolved to do everything within their power to promote such discussion as may tend to bring the belligerents together on just and reasonable terms.

Through a thousand channels utterances have already reached the conference pleading that a long continuance of the struggle will mean ruin for all, but as both sides believe that only complete victory can decide the issue,

243

Ford Neutral Conference at Stockholm.

ever new sacrifices of blood and treasure are made, exhausting the present and impoverishing the future. Still, we are convinced that an agreement between the warring nations might even now be reached were certain universal principles to be accepted as a basis of discussion; principles which cannot be violated with impunity, whatever the military results of the war.

The first duty of a neutral conference, then, is to call attention to those universal principles and concrete proposals upon which agreement seems possible, and upon which there may be founded a peace that will not only satisfy the legitimate demands of the warring nations themselves, but also advance the welfare of humanity at large. The neutral conference does not propose to discuss all the issues at stake. Nor does it desire to set forth a plan for the construction of a perfect world. But it emphasizes the universal demand that peace, when it comes, shall be real, insuring mankind against the recurrence of a world war. Humanity demands a lasting peace.

In presenting this appeal to governments, parliaments and peoples for discussion and comment the neutral conference hopes that no formal objection may prevent its sympathetic consideration both by those in authority and by the people whom they represent.

(A) *Right of Nations to Decide Their Own Fate.*— History demonstrates that dispositions contrary to the wishes of the peoples concerned bring with them the danger of future wars of liberation. Hence the acceptance of these principles appears generally to be regarded as an essential prerequisite to the satisfactory settlement of this war; namely, that no transfer of territory should take place without the consent of the population involved, and that nations should have the right to decide their own fate.

It follows that the restoration of Belgium must first be agreed upon before there can be an understanding between the belligerent powers. Furthermore, the occupied French territory should be returned. A reconsideration of the difficult Alsace-Lorraine question is also an absolute necessity. The independence of Serbia and Montenegro should be assured.

In its wider interpretation, the principle of the right of nations to decide their own fate postulates the solution of a problem like the Polish question by guaranteeing the union of the Polish nation as an independent people. Further applications would be the adjustment of the frontiers between Austria and Italy, as far as possible, according to the principle of nationality; autonomy for Armenia under international guarantee, and the solution of various national questions in the Balkans and in Asiatic Turkey by international agreement.

(*B*) *Economic Guarantees.*—Economic competition is generally admitted to be one of the causes of the present war. Hence the demand becomes more and more insistent that the economic activity of all peoples should be afforded development on equal terms. The recognition of the principle of the open door in the colonies, protectorates, and spheres of influence would be an important step in this direction, as would also the internationalization of certain waterways, e. g., the Dardanelles and the Bosphorus. The German colonies ought to be returned, the exchange of colonies made possible by satisfactory compensation, and Germany's access to the Near East guaranteed.

(*C*) *Freedom of the Seas.*—The principle of the freedom of the seas should be recognized.

(*D*) *Parliamentary Control of Foreign Policy.*—Effective parliamentary control of foreign policy should be established, so that secret treaties and secret diplomacy may no longer endanger the most vital interests of the nation.

(*E*) *International Organization.*—Far more important, however, for the welfare of humanity than the solutions thus far suggested is the creation of an international organization, founded, upon law and justice, which would include an agreement to submit all disputes between States for peaceful settlement. Hence the almost universal opinion that in the coming treaty of peace the principle of such an international order of justice must be accepted.

(*F*) *Disarmament.*—Equally important with the insistence upon an international organization is the demand that disarmament be brought about by international agreement.

(*G*) *A World Congress.*—In order to bring about the creation of an international order of justice it will be necessary to secure the adherence thereto of both belligerents and neutrals. The difficulties that result from the present catastrophe do not affect the warring nations alone. They affect the whole world. In their settlement the whole world should participate. A world congress should therefore be called together. Such a congress should concern itself with more than the immediate questions arising out of this war. Problems like that of guaranteeing political and spiritual freedom to special nationalities united with other peoples, though not direct issues of this war, are nevertheless of vital importance to the future maintenance of peace.

In the foregoing an attempt has been made to suggest a possible approach to the task of uniting again the international bonds that have been torn asunder in this fratricide war. Whatever may be the ultimate solution, there is abundant evidence of the growing conviction among belligerents and neutrals alike that the hope of the world lies in the substitution of law and order for international anarchy. The neutral conference, therefore, feels justified in hoping that the end of this war will witness the institution of an international order of justice which shall make possible an enduring peace for all mankind.

Easter, 1916.

————•————

CENTRAL ORGANIZATION FOR A DURABLE PEACE

The Hague.

An important international gathering was held at The Hague from the seventh to the tenth of April, 1915. The meeting, for which arrangements had been made by the "Dutch Anti-War Council," who sent invitations to a limited number of persons, was composed of more than thirty people, belonging to the following countries: United States of America, Austria, Belgium, Germany, Great Britain, Holland, Hungary, Norway, Sweden and Switzerland. Letters of sympathy were also received from Denmark, France, Italy, Russia and Spain.

The object of the meeting was not to suggest steps to bring the war to an end, but to consider by what principles the future peace of the world could be best guaranteed. After full discussion a minimum program was unanimously adopted.

MINIMUM-PROGRAM

1. No annexation or transfer of territory shall be made contrary to the interests and wishes of the population concerned. Where possible their consent shall be obtained by plebiscite or otherwise.

The States shall guarantee to the various nationalities,

247

included in their boundaries, equality before the law, religious liberty and the free use of their native languages.

2. The States shall agree to introduce in their colonies, protectorates and spheres of influence, liberty of commerce, or at least equal treatment for all nations.

3. The work of the Hague Conferences with a view to the peaceful organization of the Society of Nations shall be developed.

The Hague Conference shall be given a permanent organization and meet at regular intervals.

The States shall agree to submit all their disputes to peaceful settlement. For this purpose there shall be created, in addition to the existent Hague Court of Arbitration (a) a permanent Court of International Justice; (b) a permanent international Council of Investigation and Conciliation. The States shall bind themselves to take concerted action, diplomatic, economic or military, in case any State should resort to military measures instead of submitting the dispute to judicial decision or to the mediation of the Council of Investigation and Conciliation.

4. The States shall agree to reduce their armaments. In order to facilitate the reduction of naval armaments, the right of capture shall be abolished and the freedom of the seas assured.

5. Foreign policy shall be under the effective control of the Parliaments of the respective nations.

Secret treaties shall be void.

———————•———————

UNION OF INTERNATIONAL ASSOCIATIONS: BRUSSELS

Secretary-General: Paul Otlet.

Project of World-Charter ("Charte Mondiale"), by M. Paul Otlet.

1. Court of arbitration and court of justice.

2. Council of inquiry and conciliation.

3. Council of States, taking in concert diplomatic, economic and military measures. International armed force consisting of national contingents under an international general staff.

4. International Parliament with two houses—the lower composed of delegates from the various Parliaments; upper, of delegates from the international associations representing the fundamental social forces.

5. No annexation and no right of conquest. Guarantee of rights of minorities. Freedom of nationalities.

6. Democratic control of foreign policy. Suppression of alliances and of secret treaties.

7. Considerable reduction of armies, and application of war budgets to education, etc.

8. Freedom of commerce, at least in colonies.

9. Woman suffrage. Reform of education and of the press.

INTERNATIONAL BUREAU OF PEACE (BUREAU INTERNATIONAL DE LA PAIX)

President: H. La Fontaine.

1. Neutral States should be called to participate in the peace negotiations, because a permanent peace ought to be guaranteed by the signature of all the powers of the world.

2. No annexations must take place without the consent of the populations concerned. In all the States of diverse nationalities the rights of minorities must be guaranteed.

3. There should be established an international organization of States, with permanent bodies and espe-

International Bureau of Peace.

cially an international tribunal before which will be brought international disputes.

4. Armaments must be reduced according to general agreement and placed under an international control. All industrial establishments occupied with the manufacture of munitions must be expropriated.

5. Diplomacy in all the nations must be put under the control of parliaments and public opinion. All treaties and agreements which are not made public and have the ratification of the representative bodies of the nation are to be considered null and void.

6. All alliances, offensive or defensive, are to be prohibited.

7. To all colonies without distinction must be applied the principle of the "open door." No State shall be able to impose a tariff system on another. The development of free trade through international agreements must be furthered.

8. The public institutions and the honor of each nation are to be protected against foreign insult by penal regulations internationally devised and guaranteed by an international judicial body.

9. A new peace conference is to be called with the object of establishing the permanent character of the institution and ensuring its automatic reunion.

INTERNATIONAL CONGRESS OF WOMEN

The Hague, Holland, April 28th, 29th, 30th, 1915

International Congress of Women.

In a preparatory meeting of English, German, Belgian and Dutch women, held at Amsterdam (February, 1915), the following resolutions were drawn up to be put before the International Congress:

I. *Plea for definition of terms of peace.*

Considering that the people in each of the countries now at war believe themselves to be fighting, not as aggressors but in self-defense and for their national existence, this International Congress of Women urges the Governments of the belligerent countries, publicly to define the terms on which they are willing to make peace 'and for this purpose immediately to call a truce.

II. *Arbitration and conciliation.*

This International Congress of Women, believing that war is the negation of all progress and civilization, declares its conviction that future international disputes should be referred to arbitration or conciliation; and demands that in future these methods shall be adopted by the governments of all nations.

III. *International pressure.*

This International Congress of Women urges the Powers to come to an agreement to unite in bringing pressure to bear upon any country which resorts to arms without having referred its case to arbitration or conciliation.

IV. *Democratic control of foreign policy.*

War is brought about not by the peoples of the world, who do not desire it, but by groups of individuals representing particular interests. This International Congress of Women demands therefore that Foreign Politics shall be subject to Democratic Control; and at the same time declares that it can only recognize as democratic a system which includes the equal representation of men and women.

V. *Transference of territory.*

This International Congress of women affirms that

251

there should be no transference of territory without the consent of the men and women in it.

VI. *Women's responsibility.*

This International Women's Congress is convinced that one of the strongest forces for the prevention of war will be the combined influence of the women of all countries and that therefore upon women as well as men rests the responsibility for the outbreak of future wars. But as women can only make their influence effective if they have equal political rights with men, this Congress declares that it is the duty of all women to work with all their force for their political enfranchisement.

VII. *Women delegates in the conference of the powers.*

Believing that it is essential for the future peace of the world that representatives of the people should take part in the Conference of the Powers after the war, this International Women's Congress urges, that among the representatives women delegates should be included.

VIII. *Woman suffrage resolution.*

This International Women's Congress urges, that in the interests of civilization the Conference of the Powers after the war should pass a resolution affirming the need in all countries of extending the parliamentary franchise to women.

IX. *Promotion of good feeling between nations.*

This International Congress of Women, which in itself is evidence of the serious desire of women to bring together mankind in the work of building up our common civilization, considers that every means should be used for promoting mutual understanding and good will between the nations and for resisting any tendency to hatred and revenge.

———•———

RESOLUTIONS OF WOMEN'S INTERNATIONAL PEACE CONGRESS AT THE HAGUE

I.—WOMEN AND WAR

1. *Protest.*

We women, in International Congress assembled, protest against the madness and the horror of war, involving as it does a reckless sacrifice of human life and the destruction of so much that humanity has labored through centuries to build up.

2. *Women's Sufferings in War.*

This International Congress of Women opposes the assumption that women can be protected under the conditions of modern warfare. It protests vehemently against the odious wrongs of which women are the victims in time of war, and especially against the horrible violation of women which attends all war.

II.—ACTION TOWARD PEACE

3. *The Peace Settlement.*

This International Congress of Women of different nations, classes, creeds and parties is united in expressing sympathy with the suffering of all, whatever their nationality, who are fighting for their country or laboring under the burden of war.

Since the mass of the people in each of the countries now at war believe themselves to be fighting, not as aggressors but in self-defense and for their national existence, there can be no irreconcilable difference between them, and their common ideals afford a basis upon which a magnanimous and honorable peace might be estab-

253

lished. The congress therefore urges the governments of the world to put an end to this bloodshed and to begin peace negotiations. It demands that the peace which follows shall be permanent, and therefore based on principles of justice, including those laid down in the resolutions adopted by this congress—namely:

That no territory should be transferred without the consent of the men and women in it, and that the right of conquest should not be recognized.

That autonomy and a democratic parliament should not be refused to any people.

That the governments of all nations should come to an agreement to refer future international disputes to arbitration or conciliation, and to bring social, moral and economic pressure to bear upon any country which resorts to arms.

That foreign politics should be subject to democratic control.

That women should be granted equal political rights with men.

4. *Continuous Mediation.*

This International Congress of Women resolves to ask the neutral countries to take immediate steps to create a conference of neutral nations which shall without delay offer continuous mediation. The congress shall invite suggestions for settlement from each of the belligerent nations, and in any case shall submit to all of them, simultaneously, reasonable proposals as a basis of peace.

III.—PRINCIPLES OF A PERMANENT PEACE

5. *Respect for Nationality.*

This International Congress of Women, recognizing the right of the people to self-government, affirms that there should be no transference of territory without the consent of the men and women residing therein, and urges that autonomy and a democratic parliament should not be refused to any people.

6. *Arbitration and Conciliation.*

This International Congress of Women, believing that war is the negation of progress and civilization, urges the governments of all nations to come to an agreement to refer future international disputes to arbitration and conciliation.

7. *International Pressure.*

This International Congress of Women urges the governments of all nations to come to an agreement to unite in bringing social, moral and economic pressure to bear upon any country which resorts to arms instead of referring its case to arbitration or conciliation.

8. *Democratic Control of Foreign Policy.*

Since war is commonly brought about not by the mass of the people, who do not desire it, but by groups representing particular interests, this International Congress of Women urges that foreign politics shall be subject to democratic control, and declares that it can only recognize as democratic a system which includes the equal representation of men and women.

9. *The Enfranchisement of Women.*

Since the combined influence of the women of all countries is one of the strongest forces for the prevention of war, and since women can only have full responsibility and effective influence when they have equal political rights with men, this International Congress of Women demands their political enfranchisement.

255

10. *Third Hague Conference.*

This International Congress of Women urges that a third Hague Conference be convened immediately after the war.

11. *International Organization.*

This International Women's Congress urges that the organization of the Society of Nations should be further developed on the basis of a constructive peace, and that it should include:

(a) As a development of The Hague Court of Arbitration, a permanent International Court of Justice to settle questions or differences of a justiciable character, such as arise on the interpretation of treaty rights or of the law of nations.

(b) As a development of the constructive work of The Hague Conference, a permanent international conference holding regular meetings, in which women should take part, to deal not with the rules of warfare but with practical proposals for further international cooperation among the States. This conference should be so constituted that it could formulate and enforce those principles of justice, equity and good-will in accordance with which the struggles of subject communities could be more fully recognized and the interests and rights not only of the great Powers and small nations, but also those of weaker countries and primitive peoples, gradually adjusted under an enlightened international public opinion.

The International Conference shall appoint: A permanent council of conciliation and investigation for the settlement of international differences arising from economic competition, expanding commerce, increasing population and changes in social and political standards.

12. *General Disarmament.*

This International Congress of Women, advocating universal disarmament and realizing that it can only be secured by international agreement, urges as a step to this end that all countries should, by such an international agreement, take over the manufacture of arms and munitions of war and should control all international traffic in the same. It sees in the private profits accruing from the great armament factories a powerful hindrance to the abolition of war.

13. *Commerce and Investments.*

The Congress urges that in all countries there shall be liberty of commerce, that the seas shall be free and the trade routes open on equal terms to the shipping of all nations.

Inasmuch as the investment by capitalists of one country in the resources of another and the claims arising therefrom are a fertile source of international complications, this congress urges the widest possible acceptance of the principle that such investments shall be made at the risk of the investor, without claim to the official protection of his government.

14. *National Foreign Policy.*

This International Congress of Women demands that all secret treaties shall be void, and that for the ratification of future treaties the participation of at least the legislature of every government shall be necessary.

This International Congress of Women recommends that national commissions be created and international conferences convened for the scientific study and elaboration of the principles and conditions of permanent peace which might contribute to the development of an international federation. These commissions and conferences should be recognized by the governments and should include women in their deliberations.

15. *Women in National and International Politics.*

This International Congress of Women declares it to be essential, both nationally and internationally, to put into practise the principle that women should share all civil and political rights and responsibilities on the same terms as men.

V.—THE EDUCATION OF CHILDREN

16. This International Congress of Women urges the necessity of so directing the education of children that their thoughts and desires may be directed toward the ideal of constructive peace.

VI.—WOMEN AND THE PEACE SETTLEMENT CONFERENCE

17. This International Congress of Women urges that in the interests of lasting peace and civilization the conference which shall frame the peace settlement after the war should pass a resolution affirming the need in all countries of extending the parliamentary franchise to women.

18. This International Congress of Women urges that representatives of the people should take part in the conference that shall frame the peace settlement after the war, and claims that among them women should be included.

VII.—ACTION TO BE TAKEN

19. *Envoys to the Governments.*

In order to urge the governments of the world to put an end to this bloodshed and to establish a just and last-.

ing peace, this International Congress of Women delegates envoys to carry the message expressed in the congress resolutions to the rulers of the belligerent and neutral nations of Europe and to the President of the United States.

These envoys shall be women of both neutral and belligerent nations, appointed by the international committee of this congress. They shall report the result of their missions to the International Women's Committee for Constructive Peace as a basis for further action.

20. *Women's Voice in the Peace Settlement.*

This International Congress of Women resolves that an international meeting of women shall be held in the same place and at the same time as the conference of the Powers which shall frame the terms of the peace settlement after the war, for the purpose of presenting practical proposals to that conference.

———•———

CONFERENCE OF SOCIALISTS OF THE ALLIED NATIONS

London, Feb. 14, 1915.

I

This conference cannot ignore the profound general causes of the European conflict, itself a monstrous product of the antagonisms which tear asunder capitalist society and of the policy of colonial dependencies and aggressive imperialism, against which international Socialism has never ceased to fight, and in which every government has its share of responsibility.

The invasion of Belgium and France by the German armies threatens the very existence of independent nationalities, and strikes a blow at all faith in treaties. In these circumstances a victory for German imperialism

Socialists of Allied Nations.

259

would be the defeat and the destruction of democracy and liberty in Europe. The Socialists of Great Britain, Belgium, France, and Russia do not pursue the political and economic crushing of Germany; they are not at war with the people of Germany and Austria, but only with the governments of those countries by which they are oppressed. They demand that Belgium shall be liberated and compensated. They desire that the question of Poland shall be settled in accordance with the wishes of the Polish people, either in the sense of autonomy in the midst of another State, or in that of complete independence. They wish that throughout all Europe, from Alsace-Lorraine to the Balkans, those populations that have been annexed by force shall receive the right freely to dispose of themselves.

While inflexibly resolved to fight until victory is achieved to accomplish this task of liberation, the Socialists are none the less resolved to resist any attempt to transform this defensive war into a war of conquest, which would only prepare fresh conflicts, create new grievances, and subject various peoples more than ever to the double plague of armaments and war.

Satisfied that they are remaining true to the principles of the International, the members of the Conference express the hope that the working class of all the different countries will before long find themselves united again in their struggle against militarism and capitalist imperialism. The victory of the Allied Powers must be a victory for popular liberty, for unity, independence, and autonomy of the nations in the peaceful federation of the United States of Europe and the world.

II

On the conclusion of the war the working classes of all the industrial countries must unite in the International in order to suppress secret diplomacy, put an end to the interests of militarism and those of the armament makers and establish some international authority to settle points of difference among the nations by compulsory conciliation and arbitration, and to compel all nations to maintain peace.

III

The Conference protests against the arrest of the deputies of the Duma, against the suppression of Russian Socialist papers and the condemnation of their editors, as well as against the oppression of Finns, Jews, and Russian and German Poles.

--------●--------

Conference of Socialists from Sweden, Norway, Denmark and Holland, Held at Copenhagen

The Conference states that Capitalism, in its imperialistic form, expressed by the constantly increasing armaments, and by arrogant politics of aggrandizement, supported by the secret and irresponsible diplomacy of the Great Powers, have now led the world to the catastrophe predicted and always warned against by the Social Democracy.

In this moment, when the world is struck with terror at the horrible devastation this war has caused, the Conference desires to give expression to the firm and strong will to peace, existing within the nations represented at the Conference.

The delegates are of opinion that the chief aim of the conference is to be the strengthening and uniting of that public will which, undoubtedly, in all countries, demands the end of the war in such a way that a permanent peace may be secured. To realize this aim, the conference addresses itself to the democratic workmen, particularly to those of the belligerent countries, pointing at the same time to those principles of international solidarity and proletarian conception of justice which have been sanctioned, at all our international congresses. These principles were expressed by the Congress of Copenhagen, 1910, in the following way:

The parliamentary representatives of the Social Democracy are bound to work in order to realize the following aims:

1. International compulsory arbitration.

2. Restriction of the preparations for war ending in final disarmament.

3. Abolition of secret diplomacy with full parliamentary responsibility as to foreign politics.

4. Recognition of the right of self-determination of nations, of resistance to oppression and war-intrigues.

The Conference considers it the duty of all socialistic parties to be active in order to render possible an early conclusion of peace, and to work energetically in favor of such conditions of peace as may form a basis of international disarmament and of the democratization of foreign politics.

The Conference protests against the infringement of international right in the case of Belgium and expresses a hope that the Social Democracy in all belligerent countries will in the strongest way possible oppose every violent annexation at variance with the right of self-determination of the peoples.

The Conference, thus, reiterates the principles of peace of the International, and summons the International Bureau to convoke the social democratic parties to joint deliberation, if not earlier, at least at the beginning of the negotiations of peace, in order to examine the conditions of peace, because the Conference considers it absolutely necessary that the conditions of peace be not stipulated without the collaboration of the working men and women, or against their will, and summons the working class in all countries to concentrate their efforts in order to realize a permanent peace throughout the world. This war, with all its horrors, has only been possible, because the Capitalist class of the different countries still holds the power in its hands. The Conference hence summons the Socialists to work with the greatest energy in order to conquer the political power, so that Imperialism may be ruined, and that the International Social Democracy may fulfil its great mission of emancipating the people.

Copenhagen, Jan. 17–18, 1915.

PEACE PROPOSALS AND PROGRAMS

2. UNITED STATES

LEAGUE TO ENFORCE PEACE

OBJECTS

League to enforce Peace.

1. An International Court to try all justiciable questions.

2. A Council of Conciliation for consideration of non-justiciable questions.

3. Use of joint economic pressure and military force against signatory beginning hostilities contrary to terms of alliance.

4. Formulation and adoption of a code of international law.

The League's proposal is that economic pressure and military force shall be used to compel signatory Powers to take their international differences to the court for adjudication rather than to the battlefield. It frankly hopes to promote peace and aid its establishment by using economic and military force.

NATIONAL PEACE CONVENTION,

HELD UNDER THE AUSPICES OF THE EMERGENCY PEACE FEDERATION, CHICAGO,

February 27 and 28, 1915.

National Peace Convention.

1. Foreign policies of nations should not be aimed at creating alliances for the purpose of maintaining the

264

"balance of power," but should be directed to the establishment of a "Concert of Nations," with

(a) An international court for the settlement of all disputes between nations;
(b) An international congress, with legislative and administrative powers over international affairs, and with permanent committees in place of present secret diplomacy;
(c) An international police force;
(d) The embodiment in international law of the principle of non-intercourse, as the sanction and enforcement of international obligations.

2. The gradual reduction and final abolition of national armaments should be accomplished upon the adoption of this peace program by a sufficient number of nations, or by nations of sufficient power to ensure protection to those disarmed; such reduction should be graduated in each nation according to the degree of disarmament elected in other nations, and should be progressive until complete abolition is finally attained.

3. The manufacture of armaments for private profit should be prohibited, and the export of munitions of war from one country to another should be directly under governmental control.

4. The protection of private property at sea, of neutral commerce and of communications should be secured by the neutralization of the seas, and of such maritime trade routes as the Dardanelles and the Panama and Suez Canals.

5. National and international action should be aimed at the removal of inequitable trade barriers and other more fundamental economic causes of war.

6. The democracies of the world should be extended

and reinforced by general application of the principles of self-government and of universal adult suffrage.

7. No province should be transferred from one government to another without the consent of the population of such province.

8. No treaty, alliance, or other arrangement should be entered upon by any nation, unless ratified by the representatives of the people; treaties for securing delay before commencing hostilities, and adequate machinery for insuring democratic control of foreign politics should be created.

---•---

WORLD PEACE FOUNDATION

Boston, Mass.

1. No territory should be transferred from one nation to another in disregard of the inhabitants, nor any readjustment be made of which the effect would necessarily be to sow the seeds of future war.

2. As the alliances and ententes of Europe have proved their incapacity to safeguard the welfare of the people, the nations of that continent should establish and maintain a representative council in order to insure mutual conference and concerted action.

3. Competition in armaments should end. The nations should agree to abandon compulsory military service and to limit military force to purposes of police and international defense.

4. All manufactures of arms, armaments and munitions for use in war should hereafter be national property. No private citizen or corporation should be permitted to engage in such manufacture. The export of such goods for use in armies and fleets should be prohibited.

266

5. No neutral nation should permit its citizens to make loans to belligerents for war purposes. As our own State Department has said: "Loans by American bankers to any foreign nation which is at war are inconsistent with the true spirit of neutrality."

———•———

AMERICAN SCHOOL PEACE LEAGUE

1. *A Concert of Europe.* The surest method of establishing permanent peace is to bring about a Concert of Europe, based upon the knowledge that, with nations as with individuals, cooperation and not conflict is the law of progress. In order to insure mutual conference and concerted action, there should be organized a representative Council whose deliberations and decisions would be public. This would mark the end of offensive alliances and ententes which have proved their inability to safeguard the real and permanent interests of the people.

2. *Nationality Must be Respected.* No territory should be transferred from one nation to another against the will of the inhabitants, nor should any readjustments be made which might breed fresh wars. National boundaries should coincide as far as possible with national sentiment. No terms of settlement should be regarded as satisfactory if they impose upon any nation such harsh and humiliating terms of peace as would be inconsistent with its independence, self-respect, or well-being. All idea of revenge should, of course, be rooted out.

3. *Limitation of Armaments.* Since the policy of huge national armaments has lamentably failed to preserve peace, competition in armaments should end. The nations should agree to have no military forces other than those maintained for international police duty. Militarism should be abandoned by all nations, because

267

they recognize the absolute futility of force as a means of advancing the moral or material well-being of any country. To facilitate the elimination of militarism, the conditions of peace should stipulate that all manufactories of arms, armaments, and munitions for use in war shall hereafter be national property. No private citizen or corporation should be permitted to engage in such manufacture.

PROGRAM OF WOMEN'S PEACE PARTY

Organized in Washington, January 10, 1915.

Women's
Peace
Party.

1. The immediate calling of a convention of neutral nations in the interest of early peace.

2. Limitation of armaments, and the nationalization of their manufacture.

3. Organized opposition to militarism in our own country.

4. Democratic control of foreign policies.

5. The further humanizing of governments by the extension of the franchise to women.

6. "Concert of Nations" to supersede balance of power.

7. Action toward the gradual organization of the world to substitute law for war.

8. The substitution of an international police for rival armies and navies.

9. Removal of the economic causes of war.

10. The appointment of our Government of a commission of men and women, with an adequate appropriation, to promote international peace.

Washington, January, 1916.

1. That no increased appropriations for war preparations be voted during the present session.

2. That a joint committee be appointed to conduct a thorough investigation with public hearings, and report within the next six months upon the following matters:

a. The condition of our military and naval defenses with special reference to the expenditures of past appropriations;

b. The probability of aggressive action by other nations against the United States by reason of antagonism with respect to race, trade, national expansion, property holding in foreign lands and other causes of war;

c. The possibility of lessening by legislative or diplomatic action the sources of friction between this country and other nations.

3. That action be taken to secure by our Government the immediate calling of a conference of neutral nations in the interest of a just and early peace. (To that end we endorse the principles embodied in House Joint Resolution 38.)

4. That action be taken to provide for the elimination of all private profit from the manufacture of armaments.

5. That action be taken which shall provide Federal control over unnaturalized residents.

6. That action be taken to bring about the creation of a joint commission of experts representing Japan, China, and the United States to study the complex and

important question at issue between the Orient and the United States and make recommendations to the various governments involved.

7. That action be taken to convene the Third Hague Conference at the earliest possible moment and that all voting American delegates shall be civilians who represent various important elements in the country, including if possible the business, educational and labor interests and women, and that the delegates from the United States be instructed to advocate world organization and a peaceful settlement of all international difficulties.

One change was made in the platform adopted by the party a year ago. Economic pressure, instead of an international police, was urged as a substitute for rival armies and navies.

———•———

NEW YORK PEACE SOCIETY

In the platform of the New York Peace Society appear these five "conditions of a permanent peace":

1. A union of a sufficient number of Powers to guarantee permanent peace by the maintenance of military force which can be used at need as a police against any Power which threatens hostilities.

2. A treaty which shall not only arrange the boundaries of the States and their colonies, but also guarantee the territories so established against attack either from within or without the league.

3. The removal of enmities. (a) By making peace in a generous spirit at the close of the present war, and before the forces on either side shall have been completely crushed. (b) By respecting racial affiliations in the adjustments of territory made in the treaty of peace.

4. A renewal of the conferences at The Hague, the

meetings to be held so frequently as to constitute a Standing Committee of the nations for promoting measures of common interest, and for removing in their incipient stages causes of contention.

5. A treaty agreement to refer all differences within the league for adjudication either to arbitration or to a permanent court.

"The present war," says the platform in part, " has made it clear that the arming of all nations menaces the peace of all. A common reduction of armaments under an international agreement seems to present itself as the sole condition of tolerable security and welfare of all. Such a consummation would give to humanity its own possible compensation for the unparalleled tragedy of the war."

————————•————————

SOCIALIST PARTY OF AMERICA

I. *Terms of peace at close of present war* must be such as to protect the nations from future wars and conserve the identity of the smaller nations. Socialist Party of America.

1. No indemnities.

2. No transfer of territory, except upon consent and by vote of the people within the territory.

II. *International Federation—United States of the World.*

1. Court or courts for the settlement of all disputes between nations.

2. International congress, with legislative and administrative powers over international affairs, and with permanent committees in place of present secret diplomacy.

3. International police force.

III. *National disarmament.*

1. National disarmament shall be effected immediately

271

upon the adoption of the peace program by a sufficient number of nations, or by nations of sufficient power so that the international police force developed by the terms of the program shall be adequate to insure the protection of the disarmed.

2. No increase in existing armaments under any circumstances.

3. Pending complete disarmament the abolition of the manufacture of armaments and munitions of war for private profit.

4. International ownership and control of strategic waterways, such as the Dardanelles, Straits of Gibraltar, and the Suez, Panama and Kiel Canals.

5. Neutralization of the seas.

IV. *Extension of democracy.*

1. Political democracy.

　(*a*) The declaration of offensive war to be made only by direct vote of the people.

　(*b*) Abolition of secret diplomacy and the democratic control of foreign policies.

　(*c*) Universal suffrage, including woman suffrage.

2. Industrial democracy.

Radical social changes in all countries to eliminate the economic causes of war, such as,

　(*a*) Federation of the working classes of the world in a league of peace.

　(*b*) Socialization of the national resources, public utilities and fundamental equipment of industry of the nations.

　(*c*) Elimination of all unearned income.

　(*d*) Immediate and progressive amelioration of the conditions of labor.

V. *Immediate action.*

1. Efforts to be made in every nation to secure the official adoption of the above program, by the governing bodies at the earliest possible date. The adoption of the program (contingent upon its acceptance by a sufficient number of the nations to ensure its success) to be immediately announced to the world as a standing offer of federation.

2. The federation of all the possible peace forces that can be united in behalf of the above program for active propaganda among all nations.

3. Efforts through the international and the national organizations of the Socialist party of all nations to secure universal cooperation of all socialist and labor organizations in the above program.

———•———

DAVID STARR JORDAN'S RESOLUTIONS AS TO RATIONAL TERMS OF PEACE

WHEREAS, The Great War in Europe is working havoc without parallel among the best racial elements in all nations concerned, thereby exhausting the near future and bringing subsequent impoverishment to the race;

David Starr Jordan.

WHEREAS, An intolerable burden of sorrow and misery is thrown on the women and children of Europe, those who had no part in bringing on the war and no possible interests to be served by it;

WHEREAS, No possible gain, economic or political (the restoration of Belgium being secured), can compensate any nation for the loss, distress and misery involved in this war and aggravated by each day of its continuance;

WHEREAS, No probability appears that military operations in any quarter can of themselves bring the war to its end;

273

WHEREAS, A sweeping victory tends to leave an increasing legacy of hate, with seeds of future wars;

RESOLVED, That the rational interests of the civilized world demand that the war be brought to a speedy close; and

RESOLVED, That a way to honorable and lasting peace may be possible along the following lines:

1. Recognition of the fact that no nation can establish rule or dominion over any other civilized nation, large or small, that peace cannot be maintained by the overruling power of any one nation, but rather by international agreements of those nations which reject aggressive war.

2. Guaranteed security to the small States of Europe, with relief of peoples held in unnatural allegiance.

3. The freedom, under international guarantees, of the High Seas and of the channels of trade, with immunity of commerce from belligerent attack.

4. The removal of hampering tariff restrictions.

5. Compensation to Belgium, as determined by impartial arbitration.

6. The neutralization of Constantinople, with adequate safeguarding of the rights of Christian and Jewish peoples within the Ottoman Empire.

7. An international conference to secure terms of peace; with reduction of national armament, the establishment of a supreme international tribunal, the maintenance of an international police force, accompanied by recognition of the stability of International Law.

May 13, 1915.

SIX LESSONS OF THE WAR

First.—That the various Hague Conventions, sol- Nicholas Murray Butler. emnly entered into in 1899 and in 1907, have been vio- lated frequently since the outbreak of hostilities, and that, obviously, some greater and more secure sanction for such Conventions must be provided in the future.

Second.—That in not a few instances the rules and usages of international law have been thrown to the winds, to the discredit of the belligerents themselves and to the grave distress, physically and commercially, of neutral powers.

Of course every one understands that international law is merely a series of conventions without other than moral sanction. If, however, the world has gone back to the point where a nation's plighted faith is not moral sanction enough, then that fact and its implications ought to be clearly understood and appropriate punitive action provided for.

Third.—That any attempt to submerge nationalities in nations other than their own is certain to result in friction and conflict in the not distant future. Any at- tempt to create new nations, or to enlarge or diminish the area of nations, without having regard to nationality, is simply to organize a future war.

Fourth.—That the transfer of sovereignty over any given district or people without their consent, is certainly an unwise, and probably an unjust, action for any government to take, having regard for the peace and happiness of the world.

Fifth.—That the international organizations which had been carried so far in such fields as maritime law, postal service, railway service, and international arbitration, should be taken up anew and pursued more vigorously, but upon a sounder and a broader foundation, and made a certain means of protecting the smaller and the weaker nations.

Sixth.—That competitive armaments, instead of being an assurance against war, are a sure cause of war and an equally certain preventive of those policies of social reform and advance that enlightened peoples everywhere are eager to pursue.

Nicholas Murray Butler, quoted in N. Y. Times, May 16, 1915.

———————•———————

CHAMBER OF COMMERCE OF THE UNITED STATES

Chamber of Commerce of the U. S.

1. A more comprehensive and better-defined sea-law.

2. An international court.

3. A council of Conciliation.

4. International conferences for the better establishment and progressive amendment of international law.

5. Power to enforce agreement: The organization of a system of commercial and financial non-intercourse, to be followed by military force if necessary, to be applied to those nations entering into the foregoing arrangements and then going to war without first submitting their differences to an agreed-upon tribunal.

276

PEACE PROPOSALS AND PROGRAMS

3. GREAT BRITAIN

Union of Democratic Control

1. No Province shall be transferred from one Government to another without the consent by plebiscite or otherwise of the population of such Province.

2. No Treaty, Arrangement, or Undertaking shall be entered upon in the name of Great Britain without the sanction of Parliament. Adequate machinery for ensuring democratic control of foreign policy shall be created.

3. The Foreign Policy of Great Britain shall not be aimed at creating Alliances for the purpose of maintaining the Balance of Power; but shall be directed to concerted action between the Powers, and the setting up of an International Council, whose deliberations and decisions shall be public, with such machinery for securing international agreement as shall be the guarantee of an abiding peace.

4. Great Britain shall propose as part of the Peace settlement a plan for the drastic reduction by consent of the armaments of all the belligerent Powers, and to facilitate that policy shall attempt to secure the general nationalization of the manufacture of armaments, and the control of the export of armaments by one country to another.

Union of Democratic Control.

London, July 17, 1915.

PROPOSED ARTICLES OF SETTLEMENT

The signatory States, desirous of preventing any future outbreak of war, improving international relations, arriving by agreement at an authoritative codification of international law and facilitating the development of such joint action as is exemplified by the International Postal Union, hereby agree and consent to the following Articles:

THE ESTABLISHMENT OF A SUPERNATIONAL AUTHORITY

1. There shall be established as soon as possible within the period of one year from the date hereof (*a*) an International High Court for the decision of justiciable issues between independent Sovereign States; (*b*) an International Council with the double function of securing, by common agreement, such international legislation as may be practicable, and of promoting the settlement of non-justiciable issues between independent Sovereign States; and (*c*) an International Secretariat.

The Constituent States

2. The independent Sovereign States to be admitted as Constituent States, and hereinafter so described, shall be:

(*a*) The belligerents in the present war;

(*b*) The United States of America;

(*c*) Such other independent Sovereign States as have been represented at either of the Peace Coferences at The Hague, and as shall apply for admission within six months from the date of these Articles; and (*d*) Such other independent Sovereign States as may hereafter be admitted by the International Council.

Covenant Against Aggression

3. It is a fundamental principle of these Articles that the Constituent States severally disclaim all desire or intention of aggression on any other independent Sovereign State or States, and that they agree and bind themselves, under all circumstances, and without any evasion or qualification whatever, never to pursue, beyond the stage of courteous representation, any claim or complaint that any of them may have against any other Constituent State, without first submitting such claim or complaint, either to the International High Court for adjudication and decision, or to the International Council for examination and report, with a view to arriving at a settlement acceptable to both parties.

Covenant Against War Except as a Final Resource

4. The Constituent States expressly bind themselves severally under no circumstances to address to any Constituent State an ultimatum, or a threat of military or naval operations in the nature of war, or of any act of aggression; and under no circumstances to declare war, or begin military or naval operations of the nature of war, or violate the territory or attack the ships of another State, otherwise than by way of repelling and defeating a forcible attack actually made by military or naval force, until the matter in dispute has been submitted as aforesaid to the International High Court or to the International Council, and until after the expiration of one year from the date of such submission.

On the other hand, no Constituent State shall, after

submission of the matter at issue to the International Council and after the expiration of the specified time, be precluded from taking any action, even to the point of going to war, in defense of its own honor or interests, as regards any issues which are not justiciable within the definition laid down by these Articles, and which affect either its independent sovereignty or its territorial integrity, or require any change in its internal laws, and with regard to which no settlement acceptable to itself has been arrived at.

THE INTERNATIONAL COUNCIL

5. The International Council shall be a continuously existing deliberative and legislative body composed of representatives of the Constituent States, to be appointed in such manner, for such periods and under such conditions as may in each case from time to time be determined by the several States.

Each of the eight Great Powers—viz., Austria-Hungary, the British Empire, France, Germany, Italy, Japan, Russia and the United States of America—may appoint five representatives. Each of the other Constituent States may appoint two representatives.

Different Sittings of the Council

6. The International Council shall sit either as a Council of all the Constituent States, hereinafter called the Council sitting as a whole, or as the Council of the eight Great Powers, or as the Council of the States other than the eight Great Powers, or as the Council for America, or as the Council for Europe, each such sitting being restricted to the representatives of the States thus indicated.

There shall stand referred to the Council of the eight Great Powers any question arising between any two or more of such Powers, and also any other question in which any of such Powers formally claims to be concerned, and requests to have so referred.

There shall also stand referred to the Council of the eight Great Powers, for consideration and ratification, or for reference back in order that they may be reconsidered, the proceedings of the Council for America, the Council for Europe, and the Council of the States other than the eight Great Powers.

There shall stand referred to the Council for Europe any question arising between two or more independent Sovereign States of Europe, and not directly affecting any independent Sovereign States not represented in that Council, provided that none of the Independent Sovereign States not so represented formally claims to be concerned in such question, and provided that none of the eight Great Powers formally claims to have it referred to the Council of the eight great Powers or to the Council sitting as a whole.

There shall stand referred to the Council for America any question arising between two or more independent Sovereign States of America, not directly affecting any independent Sovereign State not represented in that Council, provided that none of the independent Sovereign States not so represented formally claims to be concerned in such question, and provided that none of the eight Great Powers formally claims to have it referred to the Council of the eight Great Powers or to the Council sitting as a whole.

There shall stand referred to the Council for the States other than the eight Great Powers any question between two or more of such States, not directly affecting any of the eight Great Powers and which none of the eight Great Powers formally claims to have referred to the Council sitting as a whole.

The Council shall sit as a whole for—

(a) General legislation and any question not standing referred to the Council of the eight 'Great Powers, the Council of the States other than the eight Great Powers, the Council for Europe or the Council for America respectively;

(b) The appointment and all questions relating to the conditions of office, functions and powers of the International Secretariat, and of the President and other officers of the International Council;

(c) The settlement of Standing Orders, and all questions relating to procedure and verification of powers;

(d) The financial affairs of the International Council and International High Court, the allocation of the cost among the Constituent States, and the issue of precepts upon the several Constituent States for the shares due from them;

(e) The admission of independent Sovereign States as Constituent States; and

(f) Any proposal to alter any of these Articles, and the making of such an alteration.

Membership of the Council and Voting

7. All the Constituent States shall have equal rights to participation in the deliberations of the International Council. Any Constituent State may submit to the International Council sitting as a whole any proposal for any alteration of International Law, or for making an enactment of new law; and also (subject to the provisions of these Articles with regard to the submission of justiciable issues to the International High Court) may bring before the Council any question, dispute or difference arising between it and any other Constituent State.

When the International Council is sitting as the Council of the eight Great Powers or as the Council of the States other than the eight Great Powers each of the States represented therein shall have one vote only.

When the International Council is sitting as a whole or as the Council for Europe or as the Council for America, the number of votes to be given on behalf of each State shall be as follows:

As agreed to by the Hague Conference, the relative position of the States works out into the following scale of votes:

Austria-Hungary, the British Empire, France, Germany, Italy, Japan, Russia, the United States of America	20 votes each	
Spain	12 "	
The Netherlands	9 "	
Belgium, Denmark, Greece, Norway, Portugal, Sweden, China, Roumania, Turkey	6 "	"
Argentina, Brazil, Chile, Mexico	4 "	"
Switzerland, Bulgaria, Persia	3 "	"
Colombia, Peru, Uruguay, Venezuela, Serbia, Siam	2 "	"
The other Constitutent States	1 vote	"

Legislation Subject to Ratification

8. It shall be within the competence of the International Council to codify and declare the International Law existing between the several independent Sovereign States of the world; and any such codifying enactment, when and in so far as ratified by the Constituent States, shall be applied and enforced by the International High Court.

It shall also be within the competence of the International Council from time to time, by specific enactment, to amend International Law, whether or not this has been codified; and any such enactment when and in so far as ratified by the several Constituent States shall

283

be applied and enforced by the International High Court.

Whenever any Constituent State notifies its refusal to ratify as a whole any enactment made by the International Council, it shall at the same time notify its ratification of such part or parts of such enactment as it will consent to be bound by; and the International Council shall thereupon reenact the parts so ratified by all the Constituent States, and declare such enactment to have been so ratified, and such enactment shall thereupon be applied and enforced by the International High Court.

When any enactment of the International Council making any new general rule of law has been ratified wholly or in part by any two or more Constituent States, but not by all the Constituent States, it shall, so far as ratified, be deemed to be binding on the ratifying State or States, but only in respect of the relations of such State or States with any other ratifying State or States; and it shall be applied and enforced accordingly by the International High Court.

Non-Justiciable Issues

9. When any question, difference or dispute arising between two or more Constituent States is not justiciable as defined in these Articles, and is not promptly brought to an amicable settlement, and is of such a character that it might ultimately endanger friendly relations between such States, it shall be the duty of each party to the matter at issue, irrespective of any action taken or not taken by any other party, to submit the question, difference or dispute to the International Council with a view to a satisfactory settlement being arrived at. The Council may itself invite the parties to lay any such question, difference or dispute before the Council, or

the Council may itself take any such matter at issue into its own consideration.

The Constituent States hereby severally agree and bind themselves under no circumstances to address to any other Constituent State an ultimatum or anything in the nature of a threat of forcible reprisals or naval or military operations, or actually to commence hostilities against such State, or to violate its territory, or to attack its ships, otherwise than by way of repelling and defeating a forcible attack actually made by naval or military force, before a matter in dispute, if not of a justiciable character as defined in these Articles, has been submitted to or taken into consideration by the International Council as aforesaid for investigation, modification and report, and during a period of one year from the date of such submission or consideration.

The International Council may appoint a Permanent Board of Conciliators for dealing with all such questions, differences or disputes as they arise, and may constitute the Board either on the nomination of the several Constituent States or otherwise, in such manner, upon such conditions and for such term or terms as the Council may decide.

When any question, difference or dispute, not of a justiciable character as defined in these Articles, is submitted to or taken into consideration by the International Council as aforesaid, the Council shall, with the least possible delay, take action, either (1) by referring the matter at issue to the Permanent Board of Conciliators, or (2) by appointing a Special Committee, whether exclusively of the Council or otherwise, to enquire into the matter and report, or (3) by appointing a Commission of Enquiry to investigate the matter and report, or (4) by itself taking the matter into consideration.

The Constituent States hereby agree and bind themselves, whether or not they are parties to any such matter at issue, to give all possible facilities to the International Council, to the Permanent Board of Conciliators, to any Committee or Commission of Enquiry appointed by either of them, and to any duly accredited officer of any of these bodies, for the successful discharge of their duties.

When any matter at issue is referred to the Board of Conciliation, or to a Special Committee, or to a Commission of Enquiry, such Board, Committee or Commission shall, if at any time during its proceedings it succeeds in bringing about an agreement between the parties upon the matter at issue, immediately report such agreement to the International Council; but, if no such agreement be reached, such Board, Committee or Commission shall, so soon as it has finished its enquiries, and in any case within six months, make a report to the International Council, stating the facts of the case and making any recommendations for a decision that are deemed expedient.

When a report is made to the International Council by any such Board, Committee or Commission that an agreement has been arrived at between the parties, the Council shall embody such agreement, with a recital of its terms, in a resolution of the Council.

When any other report is made to the Council by any such Board, Committee or Commission, or when the Council itself has taken the matter at issue into consideration, the Council shall, after taking all the facts into consideration, and within a period of three months, come to a decision on the subject, and shall embody such decision in a resolution of the Council. Such resolution shall, if necessary, be arrived at by voting, and shall be published, together with any report on the subject, in the Official Gazette.

A resolution of the Council embodying a decision settling a matter at issue between Constituent States shall be obligatory and binding on all the Constituent States, including all the parties to the matter at issue, if either it is passed unanimously by all the members of the Council present and voting; or where the proposed enactment does not affect the independent sovereignty or the territorial integrity, nor require any change in the internal laws of any State, and where such enactment shall have been assented to by a three-fourths majority of the votes given by the representatives present and voting.

The International Secretariat

10. There shall be an International Secretariat, with an office permanently open for business, with such a staff as the International Council may from time to time determine.

It shall be the duty of the International Secretariat to make all necessary communications on behalf of the International Council to States or individuals; to place before the President to bring before the Council any matter of which it should have cognizance; to organize and conduct any enquiries or investigations ordered by the Council; to maintain an accurate record of the proceedings of the Council; to make authentic translations of the resolutions and enactments of the Council, the report of the proceedings, and other documents, and to communicate them officially to all the Constituent States; and to publish for sale an *Official Gazette* and such other works as the Council may from time to time direct.

Subject to any regulations that may be made by the International Council, the International Secretariat shall take charge of and be responsible for (*a*) the funds belonging to or in the custody of the International Council and the International High Court; (*b*) the collection of all receipts due to either of them; and (c) the making of all authorized payments.

11. The International High Court shall be a permanent judicial tribunal, consisting of fifteen Judges, to be appointed as hereinafter provided. Subject to these Articles it shall, by a majority of Judges sitting and voting, control its own proceedings, determine its sessions and place of meeting, settle its own procedure, and appoint its own officers. It may, if thought fit, elect one of its members to be President of the Court for such term and with such functions as it may decide. Its members shall receive an annual stipend of ———, whilst if a President is elected he shall receive an additional sum of ———. The Court shall hear and decide with absolute independence the issues brought before it in conformity with these Articles; and shall in each case pronounce, by a majority of votes, a single judgment of the Court as a whole, which shall be expressed in separate reasoned statements by each of the Judges sitting and acting in the case. The sessions of the Court shall be held, if so ordered, notwithstanding the existence of a vacancy or of vacancies among the Judges; and the proceedings of the Court shall be valid, and the decision of a majority of the Judges sitting and acting shall be of full force, notwithstanding the existence of any vacancy or vacancies or of the absence of any Judge or Judges.

The Judges of the Court

12. The Judges of the International High Court shall be appointed for a term of five years by the International Council sitting as a whole, in accordance with the fol-

lowing scheme: Each of the Constituent States shall be formally invited to nominate one candidate, who need not necessarily be a citizen or a resident of the State by which he is nominated. The eight candidates severally nominated by the eight Great Powers shall thereupon be appointed Judges by the International Council sitting as the Council of the eight Great Powers. The remaining seven Judges shall be appointed by the International Council sitting as a whole, after selection by exhaustive ballot from among the candidates nominated by the Constituent States other than the eight Great Powers. On the occurrence of a vacancy among the Judges nominated by the eight Great Powers, the State which had nominated the Judge whose seat has become vacant shall be invited to nominate his successor, and the candidate so nominated shall thereupon be appointed by the International Council sitting as the Council of the eight Great Powers. On the occurrence of a vacancy among the other Judges, each of the Constituent States other than the eight Great Powers shall be invited to nominate a candidate to fill the vacancy; and the International Council sitting as a whole shall, by exhaustive ballot, choose from among the candidates so nominated the person to be appointed.

A Judge of the International High Court shall not be liable to any legal proceedings in any tribunal in any State, and shall not be subjected to any disciplinary action by any Government, in respect of anything said or done by him in his capacity as Judge; and shall not during his term of office be deprived of any part of the emoluments or privileges of his office. A Judge of the International High Court may be removed from office by a resolution of the International Council sitting as a whole, carried by a three-fourths majority.

The Court Open Only to State Governments

13. The International High Court shall deal only with justiciable questions, as defined in these Articles, at issue between the national Governments of independent Sovereign Sates, and shall not entertain any application from or on behalf of an individual person, or any group or organization of persons, or any company, or any subordinate administration, or any State not independent and Sovereign. The International High Court may, if it thinks fit, deal with a suit brought by a Constituent State against an independent Sovereign State which is not a Constituent State; or with a suit between two or more such States.

Justiciable Issues

14. The justiciable questions with which the International High Court shall be competent to deal shall be exclusively those falling within one or other of the following classes, viz.:

(*a*) Any question of fact which, if established, would be a cause of action within the competence of the Court;

(*b*) Any question as to the interpretation or application of any international treaty or agreement duly registered as provided in these Articles, or of International Law, or of any enactment of the International Council; together with any alleged breach or contravention thereof;

(*c*) Any question as to the responsibility or blame attaching to any independent Sovereign State for any of the acts, negligences or defaults of its national or local Government officers, agents or representatives, occasioning loss or damage to a State other than their own, whether to any of the citizens, companies or subordinate administrations of such State, or to its national Government; and as to the reparation to be made, and the compensation to be paid, for such loss or damage;

(*d*) Any question as to the title, by agreement, prescription, or occupation, to the sovereignty of any place or district;

(*e*) Any question as to the demarcation of any part of any national boundary;

(*f*) Any question as to the reparation to be made, or the amount of compensation to be paid, in cases in which the principle of indemnity has been recognized or admitted by all the parties;

(*g*) Any question as to the recovery of contract debts claimed from the Government of an independent Sovereign State by the Government of another independent Sovereign State, as being due to any of its citizens, companies or subordinate administrations, or to itself;

(*h*) Any question which may be submitted to the Court by express agreement between all the parties to the case.

The question of whether or not an issue is justiciable within the meaning of these Articles shall be determined solely by the International High Court, which may determine such a question whether or not formal objection is taken by any of the litigants.

If any State, being a party to any action in the International High Court, objects that any point at issue is not a justiciable question as herein defined, the objection shall be considered by the Court; and the Court shall, whether or not the objecting State enters an appearance, or argues the matter, pronounce upon the objection, and either set it aside or declare it well founded.

It shall be within the competence of the International High Court, with regard to any justiciable question in respect of which it may be invoked by one or more of the parties, summarily to enjoin any State, whether or not a party to the case, to refrain from taking any specified positive action or to discontinue any specified positive action already begun, or to cause to be discontinued any specified positive action begun by any person, company or subordinate administration within or belonging to such State, which in the judgment of the Court is designed or intended, or may reasonably be expected to change the *status quo* with regard to the question at issue before the Court, or seriously to injure any of the parties to the case. Any such injunction of the International High Court shall be binding, and shall be enforceable, in the same way as a judgment of the Court, in the manner hereinafter described.

Immediate Publicity for All Treaties, Existing and Future

15. No treaty or agreement between two or more independent Sovereign States shall be deemed to confer any right to invoke the International High Court, or shall be treated as valid, or be in any way recognized by the International Council or the International High Court, or shall be held to confer any rights, to impose any obligations, or to change the status or legal rights of any person, company, subordinate administration, district or State, unless a duly authenticated copy of such Treaty or Agreement has been deposited by one or all of the States that are parties to it, in the Registry of the International High Court, within twelve months from the date of these Articles, in accordance with any rules that may from time to time be made by the Court for this purpose; or in the case of a Treaty or Agreement hereafter made, within three months from the date of such Treaty or Agreement.

It shall be the duty of the officer in charge of the Registry immediately after deposit to allow the duly accredited representative of any Constituent State to inspect and copy any Treaty or Agreement so deposited; and promptly to communicate a copy to the International Secretariat for publication in the *Official Gazette*.

Undertaking to Submit All Justiciable Questions to the International High Court

16. The Constituent States severally undertake and agree to submit to the International High Court for trial and judgment every question, difference or dispute coming within the definition of a justiciable question as laid down by these Articles that may arise between themselves and any other independent Sovereign State or States; and at all times to abstain, in respect of such questions, from anything in the nature of an ultimatum; from any threat to take unfriendly or aggressive action of any kind with a view to redressing the alleged grievance or punishing the alleged wrongdoing; and from any violation of the territory of any other State or attack on the ships of such State or other military or naval operations, or other action leading or likely to lead to war.

Enforcement of the Decrees of the Court

17. When in any case upon which judgment is given by the International High Court, the Court finds that any of the parties to the case has, by act, negligence, or default, committed any breach of international obligation, whether arising by Treaty or Agreement, or by International Law, or by enactment of the International Council in accordance with these Articles, the Court may simply declare that one or other litigant State is in default, and leave such State voluntarily to make reparation; or the Court may, in the alternative, itself direct reparation to be made or compensation to be paid for

such wrong, and may assess damages or compensation, and may, either by way of addition to damages or compensation, or as an alternative, impose a pecuniary fine upon the State declared in default, hereinafter called the recalcitrant State; and may require compliance with its decree within a specified time under penalty of a pecuniary fine, and may prescribe the application of any such damages, compensation, or fine.

In the event of non-compliance with any decision or decree or injunction of the International High Court, or of non-payment of the damages, compensation, or fine within the time specified for such payment, the Court may decree execution, and may call upon the Constituent States, or upon some or any of them, to put in operation, after duly published notice, for such period and under such conditions as may be arranged, any or all of the following sanctions—viz.:

(*a*) To lay an embargo on any or all ships within the jurisdiction of such Constituent State or States registered as belonging to the recalcitrant State;

(*b*) To prohibit any lending of capital or other moneys to the citizens, companies, or subordinate administrations of the recalcitrant State, or to its national Government;

(*c*) To prohibit the issue or dealing in or quotation on the Stock Exchange or in the press of any new loans, debentures, shares, notes or securities of any kind by any of the citizens, companies or subordinate administrations of the recalcitrant State, or of its national Government;

(*d*) To prohibit all postal, telegraphic, telephonic and wireless communication with the recalcitrant State;

(*e*) To prohibit the payment of any debts due to the citizens, companies or subordinate administrations of the recalcitrant State, or to its national Government; and, if thought fit, to direct that payment of such debts shall be made only to one or other of the Constituent Governments, which shall give a good and legally valid discharge for the same, and shall account for the net proceeds thereof to the International High Court;

(*f*) To prohibit all imports, or certain specified imports, coming from the recalcitrant State, or originating within it;

(*g*) To prohibit all exports, or certain specified exports consigned directly to the recalcitrant State, or destined for it;

(*h*) To prohibit all passenger traffic (other than the exit of foreigners), whether by ship, railway, canal or road, to or from the recalcitrant State;

(*i*) To prohibit the entrance into any port of the Constituent States of any of the ships registered as belonging to the recalcitrant State, except so far as may be necessary for any of them to seek safety, in which case such ship or ships shall be interned;

(*j*) To declare and enforce a decree of complete nonintercourse with the recalcitrant State, including all the above-mentioned measures of partial non-intercourse;

(*k*) To levy a special export duty on all goods destined for the recalcitrant State, accounting for the net proceeds to the International High Court;

(*l*) To furnish a contingent of war-ships to maintain a combined blockade of one or more of the ports, or of the whole coastline of the recalcitrant State.

The International High Court shall arrange for all the expenses incurred in putting in force the above sanctions, including any compensation for loss thereby incurred by any citizens, companies, subordinate administrations or national Governments of any of the Constituent States other than the recalcitrant State, to be raised by a levy on all the Constituent States in such proportions as may be decided by the International Council; and for the eventual recovery of the total sum by way of additional penalty from the recalcitrant State.

When on any decree or decision or injunction of the International High Court execution is ordered, or when any sanction or other measure ordered by the Court is directed to be put in operation against any Constituent State, it shall be an offense against the comity of nations for the State against which such decree, decision, injunction or execution has been pronounced or ordered, or against which any sanction or other measure is directed to be enforced, to declare war, or to take any naval or military action, or to violate the territory or attack the ships of any other State or to commit any other act of aggression against any or all of the States so acting under the order of the Court; and all the other Constituent States shall be bound, and do hereby pledge themselves, to make common cause with the State or States so attacked, and to use naval and military force to protect such State or States, and to enforce the orders of the International High Court, by any warlike operations that may for the purpose be deemed necessary.

[See *New Statesman,* special supplement, July 17, 1915, for program, with notes and queries, here omitted.]

——————•——————

INDEPENDENT LABOR PARTY

Annual Conference, Norwich, April 5 and 6, 1915.

Drafted Resolutions:

Independent
Labor Party.

This Conference calls upon the workers to guard against allowing elements to enter the peace settlement which would be a pretext and excuse for future devastating wars; in order that the peace may be just and lasting, the Conference demands:

1. That the people concerned shall give consent before there is transfer of territory:

2. No future treaty, agreement or understanding be entered into without the knowledge of the people and the consent of Parliament, and machinery to be created for the democratic control of foreign policy:

3. Drastic all-round reduction of armaments, by international agreement, together with the nationalization of the manufacture of armaments, and the national control of the export of armaments, by one country to another:

4. British foreign policy to be directed in future toward establishing a federation of the nations, and the setting up of an International Council, whose decisions shall be public, together with the establishment of courts for the interpretation and enforcement of treaties and International Law.

5. This Conference is of opinion that an International Arbitration Court should be established, with power, as an alternative to war, to enforce its decisions by declaring a postal, commercial, transport and financial boycott against any dissenting nation.

6. This Conference is of opinion that no war should be declared without the consent of Parliament.

7. Recognizing that a permanent peace must be based upon mutual confidence and goodwill between the nations, which can only be shown effectively by the abandonment of all material preparations for war, this Conference urges the abolition of armaments, the disbanding of military and naval forces, and the prohibition of the manufacture and import or export of munitions of war.

National Peace Council: Federation of British Peace Societies

National
Peace
Council.

1. Establishment of an international peace commission such as those already established between the United States and certain other Powers.

2. Peace commission to extend its functions to include both those of a commission of inquiry and of a permanent Hague court of arbitration.

3. Formation of a permanent Congress of Nations composed of delegates appointed by the Parliaments, to settle important international affairs which might give rise to war; further elaboration by the Congress of the Hague Conventions regulating the conduct and methods of warfare.

4. No territorial change without consent of the population involved.

5. Foreign policies and treaties subject to parliamentary control.

6. Armament question to be put before Congress of Nations.

7. Congress to seek to remove obstacles to freedom of trade.

Women's Movement for Constructive Peace

London

Object: to organize public union and to bring its pressure to bear upon the Governments of the world to the furtherance of the following ends:

PROPOSITIONS

1. The reinforcement of the Democracies of the world by the inclusion of the mother-half of the human race into the ranks of articulate citizenship.

2. The creation of some constitutional machinery, where none at present exists, by which the Democracies may exercise some control over foreign policy.

3. That all treaties and alliances on the part of any Democratic nation shall be ratified by the representatives of the people.

4. That the manufacture of armaments shall be nationalized and that the export of ammunition from one country to another shall be vetoed.

5. That the allies shall be held to their slogan that this is a war to end war.

6. That at the conclusion of peace no province shall be transferred from one Government to another without the consent of the population concerned; that this consent shall be obtained by plebiscite and that women, who have suffered equally with men, shall be included in the plebiscite.

7. That women as well as men should be sent as representatives of their nation to the Hague Conference.

8. That the Democracies shall press for some kind of international agreement by which all the nations shall put themselves at the back of any one lawabiding nation that is aggressively attacked, or of any small country that is menaced by a stronger Power.

9. That the idea be brought to the front and the possibility discussed of the formation of an European Senate composed of representatives of every European nation. That this Senate exist for the discussion of international concerns and in this way a means may be constructed whereby nations can seek to obtain what is necessary to the development of their national life by bargain and by exchange, instead of by secret treachery or open slaughter and loot.

That the Hague Conference which regulates the rules of war is based upon a pernicious principle in that it treats as natural the existence of war, and only aims to prune off some features regarded as objectionable, instead of trying to render war impossible.

————•————

AUSTRALIAN PEACE ALLIANCE

Australian Peace Alliance.

1. The establishment of an effective and permanent international arbitration court elected on a democratic basis, including women delegates.

2. The setting up of adequate machinery for ensuring democratic control of foreign policy.

3. The general reduction of armaments and the nationalization of their manufacture.

4. The organization of the trades unions and workers' associations, with a definite view of ending war.

5. The termination of the present war at the earliest possible moment, and the following principles to govern the terms of peace:

> (I.) No Province or Territory in any part of the world shall be transferred from one Government to another without the consent by plebiscite of the population of such Province.
>
> (II.) No treaty, arrangement or undertaking shall be entered upon in the name of Great Britain without the sanction of Parliament. Adequate machinery for ensuring democratic control of foreign policy shall be created.
>
> (III.) The foreign policy of Great Britain shall not be aimed at creating Alliances for

300

the purpose of maintaining the "Balance of Power," but shall be directed to the establishment of a concert of Europe and the setting up of an international council, whose deliberations and decisions shall be public.

(IV.) Great Britain shall propose as part of the peace settlement a plan for the drastic reduction of armaments by the consent of all the belligerent Powers, and to facilitate that policy shall attempt to secure the general nationalization of the manufacture of armaments and the prohibition of the export of armaments by one country to another.

(V.) The universal abolition of conscription or compulsory military training.

--------●--------

MR. CHARLES RODEN BUXTON ON PEACE TERMS

1. Total evacuation by Germany of Belgium, France, Poland and Baltic provinces, and by Germany and Austria of Serbia. Charles Roden Buxton.

2. No indemnity, of course, from Great Britain, but compensation to Belgium by Germany for damage done.

3. The special demands of France against Germany, of Italy and Serbia against Austria, and of Russia against Turkey to be agreed upon with Great Britain by the States concerned. This country to use its influence to secure that such demands are in harmony with the principle of nationality.

4. Germany's right to a colonial empire to be recognized, though not necessarily to exactly the same territories as those previously possessed.

301

The following points might be referred to a conference representing neutral and belligerent States:

a. The repartition of Africa, with a view to more convenient frontiers and to the interests of the native population.

b. The question of equal economic opportunities, including the open door, in all colonial possessions.

c. The discussion and definition of immunity from capture of goods other than contraband and the modification of commercial blockade, whether by submarine warfare or otherwise.

d. As a condition of the preceding point the question of equal, comprehensive, and effective guarantees against future war on land as well as on sea; binding Germany as well as other nations, including ourselves.

BRAILSFORD ON A PEACE BY SATISFACTION

H. N.
Brails-
ford.

A peace in which neither side could dicate the settlement might aim either at general frustration or general satisfaction. A sullen peace, in which each side used up the remnants of its military strength to veto the claims of the adversary, would be of all peaces the worst, for it would leave standing all the old causes of unrest. This war came about because Europe had evolved in peace no machinery by which demands for large and necessary changes could be met without war. Each people postponed its larger ambitions until war should come, and the knowledge of each that only war offered a chance of satisfaction made our universal strife. The claims of the Entente Powers for certain satisfactions for the principle of nationality, are to us familiar and sympathetic. It must be realized that the German demand for economic expansion is deeply rooted, and in the modern world inevitable. For Manchuria, Morocco, Egypt and Tripoli, the Entente Powers made, or were ready to make war. The German craving for "a place in the sun" may be condemned by those of us who have opposed Imperialism at home, but the ruling classes cannot consistently censure it. For twenty years past, the unsolved problem for European statecraft was to find an outlet for these tremendous German energies, to cut a canal in which the broad river could flow without floods. The peace of Europe will never be secure until this passion for Imperial work overseas, which is to-day the strongest ambition in Germany, finds its useful satisfaction. The forges are there. If they cannot make rails, they will make cannon.

The formula of an enduring peace must be to remove all the causes of strife in Europe, and we shall succeed only if we can satisfy the enemy's legitimate claims while we secure justice for our friends. The general idea must be, win from him the largest recognition of the idea of nationality, while conceding to him the economic opportunities which he requires. The more, by the ordinary working of barter that we concede, the more shall we obtain. Let us attempt to sketch what the main lines of such an exchange might be.

(A)—ACTS OF RESTORATION

1.—Belgium must be restored, Serbia re-instated, and French territory evacuated.
2.—The German colonies must either be restored, or equivalent territories provided.

3.—The ideal solution for Poland, in a political sense,
would be independence. But could a land-locked
State, between three great military empires, ever
be secure? The Poles, themselves, are not averse
to the idea of their re-union as a State within the
Austrian Empire. If they had the same status as
Hungary, they would be internally independent.
But if Europe consented to allow this accession of
territory to Austria, conditions might be laid
down. It might be stipulated that a like status
should be given to Bohemia, and to the Serbo-Croats
of Croatia, Bosnia and Dalmatia. Thus Austria
would become a quintuple Federal Empire (Austria, Hungary, Bohemia, Poland, Jugoslavia), and
one of the main problems of the war, the liberation of the Western Slavs, would be satisfactorily
solved.

In return for this extension of territory Austria
might be required to cede the Eastern (Ruthenian)
part of Galicia to Russia, and the Trentino to Italy.

4.—The chief difficulty lies in Alsace-Lorraine. Let us
make the bold claim that it must be restored to
France (or such parts of it as desire this change).
What can we offer as a *quid pro quo?* The following economic concessions suggest themselves (5, 6,
and 7).

(C)—ECONOMIC CLAIMS

5.—That Germany be allowed to complete that closer
economic union with her Allies, and especially Austria, which seems to be her chief objective. We
cannot prevent the creation of ''Mid-Europe'' as an
economic unity, but we might reply to it by a boy-

cott. An amiable regulation of tariff questions is a necessity for peace.

6.—We might further agree not to oppose such economic expansion (railway and irrigation schemes) in Turkey as Germany can arrange. Turkey would become a German economic sphere, but there must be guarantees for the fair treatment of the trade in goods of other Powers.

7.—A general measure by which all Powers renounced differential tariffs in their tropical colonies would ease the struggle for territory. France would be reluctant to agree to this, but the condition is that she secures Alsace.

(D)—OTHER ISSUES

8.—The greater part of Macedonia, in accordance with the principle of nationality, must go to Bulgaria.

9.—Russia might acquire the Armenian provinces of Turkey. It lies with us to accord her an ice-free port on the Persian Gulf. A Russian protectorate over Persia might in the end be less fatal to Persian nationalism than the present partition and condominium.

10.—Finally, the whole bargain must rest upon Germany's assent to some scheme of permanent conciliation and the reduction of armaments, and upon our consent to consider a revision of certain usages of sea-warfare.

H. N. Brailsford.

PEACE PROPOSALS AND PROGRAMS

4. GERMANY

GERMAN AND AUSTRO-HUNGARIAN SOCIALISTS
Vienna, April 12–13, 1915.

1. Development of the international arbitration courts.

2. Recognition of the right of every people to determine its own destiny.

3. All treaties to be under democratic parliamentary control.

4. International agreement to limit armament with general disarmament as the ultimate goal.

BUND NEUES VATERLAND

1. Development of international organization.

2. Further development of international law by future Hague conferences.

3. No annexation.

4. No secret treaties.

5. Open door. Freedom of the seas.

MANIFESTO OF THE "DEUTSCHE FRIEDENSGESELLSCHAFT"

Notwithstanding the prohibition of the Government, demands for annexation are being more or less publicly advocated. Six large agricultural associations go especially far in these ideas; indeed for one petition signa-

306

tures are collected among those who because of "their rank and education consider themselves the spiritual leaders of public opinion." This movement has evidently the support of important circles. The worst of this is that those demands are known to the neutrals and to hostile countries, who make them the foundation of their accusations of German desires of conquest. Besides they kindle ill-feeling against Germany, as the Government and the whole German nation are held responsible for all this.

There is no doubt that the Imperial Government is unjustly accused in this respect, whatever may be her attitude towards other questions. Should such tendencies be publicly criticized, then the world would soon see that the greater part of the German nation is strongly opposed to them.

The prohibition to discuss the aims of the war, which is strictly maintained with respect to ourselves, prevents us from criticizing this question thoroughly; and from organizing our opposition to such tendencies.

So far we have gladly obeyed the order not to discuss these questions. After our experience, however, of the way in which this prohibition and the above-mentioned agitation are exploited abroad to the detriment of German interests, we think it our duty to appeal to the Government to grant "free speech to a free nation."

Until this has been granted, the German Peace Association can do no more than utter a general protest against the danger of such annexation ideas. When such ideas are considered the aim of war, the war will be prolonged indefinitely, for months, perhaps for years. Their realization would not strengthen, but weaken Germany, abroad as well as at home, in peace and in future wars. A new war would be inevitable shortly after such a peace.

307

The German Peace Association and all friends of the people desire that the military supremacy of the Central Powers, which we hope will decide the peace, shall be turned towards the consolidation of Germany's position in the world, towards the development of the economical and national forces of the German nation. But they hope also, that the coming peace may contain the elements of a durable peace and lay the foundation for a lasting community of justice and culture between the nations, which must be restored after the peace, howsoever bitter their hostility may be at present. The association is convinced that a sensible consideration of the vital interests of the German nation will prevail over empty phrases and private interests, when the conditions of peace shall be drawn up.

L. Quidde,
O. Umfrid,
Stuttgart.

———————•———————

MANIFESTO BY 88 GERMAN PROFESSORS AND STATESMEN

Mani-
festo of
Professors
and
States-
men.

Germany has not entered upon this war with the idea of conquering foreign territory, but in order to defend her existence, her internal unity, and her culture, which were threatened by a hostile coalition.

When peace shall be discussed, those objects alone should be Germany's care. Some petitions laid before Your Excellency go against them: so we consider it our duty energetically to resist such endeavors and to declare publicly that we think their realization a political error, which may produce dangerous consequences, and not a strengthening but an ominous weakening of the German Empire.

Practically we lay down the principle that annexation or conquest of nations, which so far have been politi-

cally independent, is not advisable. The German Empire is the result of the idea of national unity, of national kinship. Foreign elements have been amalgamated only slowly and incompletely; so we object to events, persons or tendencies which may be easily influenced one way or another, disturbing the leading principles of the creation of our Empire, and destroying the character of our national State.

Of course we cannot allow a territory which we should evacuate according to our conditions of the peace to become a stronghold for our enemies, we cannot allow the adversaries of Germany to settle there. There should not be any possibility of the hostile feelings of the inhabitants revealing themselves in hostile actions, which might threaten the peace and security of our border-provinces. Such dangers can be averted and we trust that suitable and effective measures will be chosen and applied to accomplish this. *But those measures should not after all lead to annexation in any form.*

With our whole nation we share the conviction that this war will end in a complete victory of Germany. All those heroic deeds, those endless sacrifices and labors, all this military glory and all the sorrow borne in mute heroism, entitle Germany to a price of victory corresponding—as far as that is possible—to what she has sacrificed.

The highest price will be the proudly acquired knowledge that Germany need not fear a world full of enemies, and the unprecedented display of strength she has shown before all the nations of the earth and the generations yet to come.

The German nation can only conclude a peace which assures the foundations of the strategical wants, of the political and economic interests of the country and the unimpeded development of its strength and its energy at home and on the free seas. We trust that with the help of the bodies indicated by the Constitution Your Excellency may succeed in obtaining such a peace resolutely, while we are in the zenith of our military successes.

PROPOSALS OF SOUTH GERMAN SOCIAL DEMOCRATS

1 a. Restitution of status quo ante, or

1 b. Plebiscite in disputed territories (Alsace-Lorraine, Schleswig, Poland, Baltic Provinces, Finland, Trentino). International possession of Bosphorus, Dardanelles, Suez Canal, Gibraltar, and Kiel Canal.

2. No indemnifications.

3. Confederacy of all European States.

4. Limitations of armies and navies. People's army for defense only.

5. Alliance of all against aggression.

6. International Parliaments and permanent international committees in place of diplomacy.

7. International police. International law-courts for minor international offenses.

8. Guarantees of democratic government: equality of electoral district, ten-year redistribution, proportional representation, payment of members.

PEACE AIMS OF GERMAN SOCIALISTS: CONFERENCE OF PARTY'S MEMBERS IN REICHSTAG WITH MEMBERS OF PARTY COMMITTEE.

(Reported in New York *Times,* August 26, 1915.)

1. Peace must be a permanent one, leading the nations to closer relations.

2. Germany's opponents must not be permitted to acquire any German territory.

310

3. "Most favored nation" clauses should be introduced into peace terms with all belligerents.

4. Tariff walls should be removed.

5. So far as possible, freedom of the seas should be established, the right of capture abolished, and the straits, important for the world's commerce, should be internationalized.

6. Austria and Turkey should not be weakened.

7. Annexations of foreign territories violate the rights of peoples to self-rule, and weaken internal strength and harmony in the German nation. Therefore, all plans of short-sighted politicians favoring conquest are opposed.

8. Finally, the party demands the establishment of an international court to which all future conflicts of nations shall be submitted.

———————•———————

The German Socialists' Peace Manifesto

The manifesto was published June 26, 1915, in the German Socialists. form of a full page advertisement in the Berlin *Vorwaerts*. The paper was promptly suspended but not until its message had crossed the German frontier. The New York *Times* publishes a translation in full as follows:

"For nearly a year the world has been devastated by the fury of war. Hundreds of thousands of human lives have been cut off in their prime, works of incalculable value to civilization have been destroyed, and there has been an appalling weakening of human forces. Millions of mothers, wives, and children are weeping for their lost sons, husbands and fathers. Want and harship heighten the misery now oppressing the nations. Must this terrible drama, which has no precedent in the history of the world, go on indefinitely?

311

"The Socialist Party foresaw this world catastrophe and predicted it. It has consistently fought, therefore, against the policies of imperial expansion and against the fatal competition in armaments, which in the last instance is the cause of this war. It has worked unceasingly for a good understanding among the nations, for the cause of our common civilization, and for the welfare of mankind. When last year threatening war clouds were gathering on the horizon the German Socialists up to the very last moment bent all their energies to preserving peace. But, to the misfortune of mankind, they were unable to avert the catastrophe.

"Then when the Czar's Cossacks came across the border, pillaging and burning, the Socialists made good the promise that had been given by their leaders—they put themselves at the service of the Fatherland and voted the means for its defense. They not only did their duty in defending Germany's national independence, but they worked with all their might to safeguard its internal interests in the matter of food supplies, in relieving the needy, and in protecting the working classes against avaricious tradesmen and narrow-minded bureaucrats.

"Faithfully observing the obligations which all Socialist parties are bound to respect, the German Socialist Party, from the very first days of this awful tragedy, has striven to further the cause of a speedy peace. When the first war loan was voted, in August, 1914, the Socialist group in the Reichstag, through its spokesman, Herr Haase, said: 'We demand that as soon as guarantees of national safety are secured and the enemy shows an inclination to make peace, the war be brought to an end on conditions admitting of friendly relations with neighboring nations.'

"This demand, which was accompanied by an expression disapproving any policy of conquest, was repeated

312

when the new war loan was voted on December 2. On
May 29, after Italy had intervened, the statement was
made in the Reichstag in behalf of the Socialist Party
that the desire for peace was increasing and that the Socialists wanted no policy of conquest. At a meeting in
Vienna on April 12 and 13 representatives of the German and Austro-Hungarian Socialist Parties again
adopted a resolution in favor of peace. But the German
Socialists have not been content with such measures. In
spite of opposition and suspicion, they have striven for a
renewal of international relations with the Social-Dem-
ocrats of all countries, and when the executive committee
of the international Socialist organization made a proposal to hold a meeting at The Hague to discuss the possibility of peace negotiations, the German Socialist leaders agreed, under condition that the French Socialist
Party participate. All efforts at an international agreement, however, were thwarted by the attitude of the
French Socialists.

"We recognize with satisfaction that in England, as
well as in France, there are Socialists who are working
for peace. That cannot blind us to the deplorable fact
that the majority of the Socialists, both in England and
France, favor continuing the war until Germany is completely conquered.

"The Socialists in the Reichstag and the official leaders of the Socialist Party have constantly and unitedly
fought against a policy of conquests and annexation.
We protest again with all possible emphasis against all
efforts looking to the annexation of foreign territory
and the oppression of other peoples—measures now demanded by the great business organizations and influential political leaders. The mere fact that such efforts
are being made tends to postpone the day of peace, which
the whole public is now so earnestly awaiting.

"The people want no conquest of land, they want peace. If the war is not to go on indefinitely until all the nations are completely exhausted, some one of the Powers involved must stretch out the hand of peace. Upon Germany, which has successfully defended itself against superior forces, and which has frustrated the plan to bring it to starvation, rests the duty of taking the first steps toward peace. In the name of humanity and civilization, and recognizing the favorable military position which our brave troops have won, we urge the Government to try to end the struggle. We expect of our fellow Socialists in other belligerent countries that they will make the same demand upon their own governments."

German Proposals for Peace

Letter of Dr. Bernhard Dernburg to American Newspapers, April 18, 1915.

Dr. Dernburg.

1. The peace must be of a permanent nature.

2. The world is one interlocking family of nations. World dominion is possible only with dominion on high seas. All the seas and narrows must be neutralized permanently by common and effective agreement guaranteed by all the Powers.

3. The free sea is useless without free cables. Cables must be jointly owned by the interested nations, with a world mail-system. Customs duties must be equal for all exports and imports, for whatever destination and from whatever source. Preferential tariffs with colonies are the basis of world-empire, and must not be permitted.

4. International law should be codified, with guarantees to save all neutrals from implication in wars in which they do not wish to take part.

314

5. A natural commercial relationship between Germany and Belgium must be established in workable form.

6. Germany should be permitted industrial expansion in such foreign parts as need or wish for development.

Dr. Dernburg's Speech at City Club, Cleveland, May 8, 1915.

1. Asks recognition of the truth that strong nations showing great vitality and large increase are entitled to enough soil, air and water to maintain and advance their growing population. The lack of such proper adjustment of the conditions of the European Powers during the last fifty years has been one of the primary causes for unrest in Europe, and one of the principal dangers to the peace of the world.

2. Since no readjustment of the kind can take place in Europe on national lines, it is necessary to seek the solution, first, by the apportioning of all uncivilized parts of the globe, that is, by a readjustment of colonial possessions, then by the creation of spheres of influence and non-interference with nations who are willing to take and to concede such spheres; further, by an open door and equal opportunity policy all over the globe; and finally, by the neutralization of all the seas and narrows, cables and overseas mails of the world. This readjustment must be sanctioned by a simple and codified international law, safeguarded so that it cannot be broken without putting the infractor outside the pale of international relationships, not only with the party attacked, but also with all the parties remaining neutral. England must give up her rule of the seas, which must be placed definitely in the hands of all the Powers of the world. World trade must be free and all colonies neutralized. The decision whether there is to be a free and

315

neutralized sea or a Chinese wall will also be decisive regarding the fate of Belgium. If the sea remains fortified, there can be no choice for Germany except to have her own sea fortresses as well, and since the only way of getting out into the high sea would be by way of Belgium, there would be no possibility of Germany's considering the return of Belgium to its former status.

———•———

PROF. DR. L. QUIDDE ON REAL GUARANTEES FOR A DURABLE PEACE

I. *The annexation of Belgium would prolong the war indefinitely.*

II. *The strength of the German Empire would decrease instead of increase by the annexation of Belgium, in times of peace as well as during the war.*

The annexation of Belgium would destroy every outlook of a better understanding between Germany and her present enemies, after the war. It would make almost the whole rest of the world remain our enemies and would call forth a coalition of all against one. Germany need not foster illusions in this respect, if she only considers the effect of the invasion into Belgium upon public opinion throughout the world, especially in those neutral countries who were originally Germany's friends.

He who wishes to annex Belgium must have the courage to face the fact that annexation will make the whole world our enemy for an indefinite space of time and will completely isolate Germany politically, so far as the feelings of the nations are to bring about such isolation.

III. *The annexation of Belgium is bound to bring about a new war.*

It is evident that neither England nor France can allow Belgium to be annexed by Germany as long as

316

they do not wish to be annihilated themselves. Especially England would have to prepare retaliation with all the force that she can display, and it would be easy enough for her to find allies to support her. One may differ vastly on the subject of annexation, its advantages and drawbacks, but one cannot deny that durable peace and annexation of Belgium are two things absolutely incompatible.

Finally Prof. Quidde asks how it will be possible to make a durable peace which at the same time guarantees the welfare of Germany. This will be first of all a general removal of the causes that have led to the war, followed by a thorough reorganization of Europe on lines offering a better security for peace.

The first essentials for that reorganization are the "open-door" and the "free sea," which will have to be guaranteed by international treaties.

One of the best grounded charges against International Law is, that International Law is in many cases so hopelessly rudimentary that the lack of precision forms a temptation to violate it. It is necessary that a strong agitation for the development, perfection and sanction of International Law should result from the experiences, the causes and the course of this war.

ED. BERNSTEIN ON PEACE TERMS

I

It is the vital interest of the majority of the German nation, that the present war should end by a peace treaty which, as to the rights and the relations of the nations, is in conformity with the principles laid down in the program of the German Social-Democrat Party and in the resolutions adopted by their party-meetings and by the International Social-Democratic Congresses.

Ed. Bernstein.

Only a peace based on these principles will result in renewing the friendly relations between Germany and the nations she is now at war with, as soon and as thoroughly as possible.

II

The supreme principle, insisted upon in the program and the resolutions of the Social-Democratic Party is the right of peoples to decide their own fate, within the limits of international law.

The German Socialists consider it their duty to defend this principle by all available means against any attack from any side whatsoever. No nation or part of a nation having so far enjoyed national independence, may be deprived of this right or see it impaired; no territory may be annexed, when the annexation would deprive the inhabitants of that right.

The Social-Democratic Party do not admit the right of conquest of one nation over any other.

III

In the case of countries of European civilization, which have lived under foreign rule, no territorial changes shall take place without a referendum being taken of the inhabitants. This referendum should be arranged and supervised by representatives of neutral States, so as to insure perfect freedom in voting. Any inhabitant, who is of age and has lived in the country for at least a year before the outbreak of the war, shall have the right to vote.

In the interests of peace, all peoples of European civilization living under foreign rule in sufficient numbers to form a community in the international Concert, shall obtain political independence.

When a sufficient number out of subject peoples in-

318

corporated by force in one State, desire to belong to another, they shall be given the right to decide by vote as to which State they will belong.

IV

Transfer of territory outside of Europe shall only take place under such conditions, as guarantee that the legal and material conditions of such native population shall not be injured.

V

Nations can only be safeguarded against a renewal of war or wars of retaliation by developing and strengthening international law.

In this respect the following means should be emphasized:

a. Development of the Hague Conference into a Permanent International Conference for the Codification of International Law and for International Arbitration. Concentration of the various Hague institutions into a permanent international court, suitably divided into branch courts.

b. All States to bring those differences they cannot themselves peaceably solve, before the Court of Justice to be instituted by the Hague Conference, where they will be settled either by mutual agreement, conciliation or abitration.

c. All signatory States to refrain from war or warlike measures till the Court of Justice has examined the cause of war and till all attempts to settle the difference in a peaceful manner, have proved useless. Any State or Union resorting to hostilities contrary to these rules to be treated as an enemy by all the others.

d. The Parliaments to decide about war and peace. Secret treaties to be abolished.

319

e. Development of International Law relating to the conduct of war and the protection of the civil population. Abolition of the right of capture at sea and of the right to levy war-contributions. No hostages to be taken. Abolition of the system of reprisals against inhabitants of an invaded country for acts of self-defense or defense of other non-combatants. Permanent committees to watch the actions of belligerents in occupied territories and the treatment of prisoners of war and of civil prisoners interned in the enemy's country.

f. Internationalization of transcontinental railways and of all waterways connecting seas or lakes surrounded by different countries, with the ocean.

g. Adoption of the principle of the Open Door for all Colonies, Protectorates and for every territory which lies in the sphere of influence of an European State.

h. These principles to be inserted into the constitutions of the Powers.

BELGIUM

Whereas, Art. 2 already excludes any forcible annexation of Belgian territory or any attack on the independence of Belgium by another State, Germany has moreover invaded Belgium, overpowered its army and occupied its territory without any provocation from the side of Belgium and as the Chancellor has himself admitted violating the neutrality of Belgium in defiance of the law of nations. Germany having thus made her way into Belgium to satisfy her own designs, beat down the resistance of the army and occupied the country by force, Germany is therefore bound in honor to evacuate Belgium immediately on the conclusion of peace, in accordance with the solemn delaration, made on August 4, 1914, by the German Ambassador, Prince

Lichnowsky, to the English Secretary of State, Sir Edward Grey, and to pay a full and ample indemnity to the people of Belgium for the material and moral injury which they have suffered.

PEACE PROPOSALS AND PROGRAMS

5. FRANCE

FRENCH GENERAL CONFEDERATION OF LABOR

C. G. T.

1. Federation of nations.
2. Compulsory arbitration of international disputes.
3. Independence of nationalities. Right of all peoples to dispose of themselves to be safeguarded.
4. Suppression of secret diplomacy.
5. End of competitive armament.
6. Conference of organized labor forces of the world at same time as conference of diplomats.

PEACE PROPOSALS AND PROGRAMS

6. SWITZERLAND

Resolutions of Swiss Peace Society
At Annual Meeting, May 17, 1915.

1. The avoidance of any annexation or territorial changes which are in opposition to the interests and wishes of a population; a guarantee of religious liberty, free speech and equality before the law, for the minority.

2. The creation of a permanent organization in which all European States shall be equally represented, for the purpose of safeguarding the order, peace and safety of our portion of the earth.

3. The development of an international law organization by continual Hague Conferences.

Swiss Peace Society.

Swiss Committee for the Study of the Principles of a Durable Treaty of Peace

President: Prof. Otto Nippold, Bern.

1. Participation of neutral nations in the settlement.

2. Prohibition of secret treaties and agreements between nations.

3. Participation of popular representative bodies in control of foreign policy.

4. No annexation except after plebiscite of populations concerned.

5. Limitation of armaments to point of mere protection.

Swiss Committee for Study of Peace.

6. Manufacture of armaments to become State monopoly.

7. The States which participate in the settlement are to mutually guarantee each other's territories.

8. Since the best guarantee for the preservation of world peace lies in the creation of international law and custom, arbitration must be substituted for war.

9. Disputed regions of the earth should be neutralized.

10. Free trade in all colonies.

PEACE PROPOSALS AND PROGRAMS

7. HOLLAND

Nederlandsche Anti-Oorlog Raad
The Hague
Founded on the 8th of October, 1914

The Council is of opinion that the following principles are indispensable to attain a lasting peace:

Dutch Anti-War Council.

1. Concert of the Powers instead of mutually opposed Alliances;

2. Limitation of armaments by international regulations;

3. Influence of the different Parliaments on the peace-treaty;

4. Avoidance of the dangers engendered by annexation or by transfer of territory against the will of the population;

5. Removal of the obstructions to commerce or at least of difference in treatment of the various nations in colonies and settlements, according to international regulations.

6. New endeavors to promote compulsory arbitration and compulsory inquiry of international differences.

DIFFERENTIAL NEUTRALITY FOR AMERICA

One would prefer to think otherwise, but the truth probably is that the future peace of the world, and the nature of international organization depends a good deal less upon definitely conceived plans like that of the League to Enforce Peace (however admirable and desirable it may be to promote definite projects of that kind) than upon the nature of the foreign policy which each nation individually pursues. Disagreements between nations arise generally in situations in which both sides honestly believe themselves to be in the right. Most nations are honestly in favor of peace in general, and would go to The Hague and assist in drawing up plans to maintain it; yet each may be persisting in a line of conduct which, in its own view entirely defensive and defensible, appears to another unwarrantably aggressive. And when that is the case paper arrangements for avoiding conflict are apt to break down.

So the most practical question for each of us for some time is likely to be this: what will be the effect of our own country's conduct in its relations with other countries, upon the future peace and international condition of the world? Or, to put the question in another form: What can our country *do*, irrespective of what others may do, to contribute to a more orderly international condition, saner world politics?

America is of course concerned in the present war whether she will or no. She may, by her material resources in supplies, ammunition, credit, be largely influencing its decision. As part of the problem of protecting her own rights, incidentally menaced by the operations of the war, she has taken very solemnly a certain position in international affairs. She has declared, for instance, that she stands irrevocably for the protection of innocent non-combatant life at sea in war time. She would undoubtedly stand as decisively for certain lesser rights

326

of trade and free communication on the seas as well (in the past she has gone to war in their defense) but for the fact that doing so against one belligerent would aid the cause of the other guilty of still greater offenses.

And if we look beneath diplomatically expressed claims into unofficial, but unmistakably expressed public opinion, we find America standing strongly for certain other rules of life between nations—the right of each nation to national existence for instance—like those violated in the invasion of Belgium.

Is America really serious in the stand thus made? Or is she going to avow by her future policy, if not in words, that she will take no real risk nor assume any real obligation in support of the principles she has been maintaining diplomatically and by her clearly expressed public opinion. Is she going to submit lamely, to the indignities and violation of right involved in the massacre of her innocent non-combatant citizens at sea?

I put the question in that form because it is generally a rhetorical prelude to the demand for warlike action. And yet the American who is moved by his country's dignity and right to have thought this thing out, as well as to have become angry about it, knows that warlike action is perhaps the very last thing—though it may be the last thing—which the situation calls for; and that warlike action alone would be a betrayal of his country's highest interests in the matter. If America is really serious she must prepare herself—in public opinion, in political education—for action of a different kind: for the abandonment of certain traditions about freedom from entangling alliances, for the assumption of risks and obligations which to most Americans is to ask a great deal more than the mere act of going to war.

Why will war of itself not suffice?

Suppose this country goes to war, over, for instance, the submarine issue; and is finally entirely successful, so far as defeating Germany is concerned. How do we then know that America has got what she has been fighting for? Our demands at the end of the war will be that American rights at sea shall be respected; that, most particularly, non-combatants shall not be drowned by attacks on merchantmen. Very good. Germany gives us her promise. She has given it before. How do we know that it will be kept—either by her or any other nation that in a future war may find a ruthless use of the submarine the only weapon left to it against a power commanding

327

the sea? Can we hope that if we show now that we are ready to fight "at the drop of the hat," in future a hard-pressed belligerent will be overawed by the great American navy? Then why is not the belligerent we now propose to deal with held in check by the combined navies of Great Britain, France, Russia, Italy, Japan and Portugal? Again, when we have that promise at the end of our victorious war how do we know that it will be kept, that we shall have got what we have been fighting for?

And what of the American case against the Allies? Is America now to surrender rights upon which she has insisted ever since she became an independent State and which she once fought a war and twice very nearly came to war to defend? Is America, in fighting Germany to make the British Order in Council the basis of future sea law, so that when say Japan goes to war with some other nation America will have to submit to Japanese control of her trade and communication with neutral States—even to mail and banking correspondence—as she now submits to British control?

It is quite obvious that American claims have this difference from those of the Allies: they, in so far as they are territorial can at the peace be satisfied on the spot. America's cannot. Hers depend absolutely upon the establishment, after the war, of a different and better international order; upon agreement as to what shall constitute international law and some method of ensuring its observance.

Now has it not become evident that the present German-American situation contains the elements of a great opportunity for America: not only of putting an end to a situation humiliating for herself but of creating a new state of world affairs out of which might grow—would almost inevitably grow—the restoration of general peace on conditions that civilization could accept?

But that result is certainly conditional on one thing: that American diplomacy is great enough to make precedent, to be dangerously honest to the point of dropping diplomatic make-believe and breaking with diplomatic usage.

Germany says in effect that she will make military sacrifices for the purpose of respecting American neutral right, if America on her side will reciprocally fulfil neutral obligation by insisting on the military sacrifice from *both* belligerents; so that American rights are not made a means of handicapping

328

one party as against the other; are not invoked in what Germany regards as so one-sided a fashion as to become an arm for the use of one belligerent against the other.

Now it is quite within precedent, right and usage, to reply, as in the past, to such a demand by diplomatic punctilio: "America cannot discuss the behavior of one belligerent with the other," and so forth and so forth. The American government could make excellent debating points and be diplomatically entirely correct.

But suppose, instead, it were undiplomatically honest and unprecedentedly bold and said bluntly what every one knows to be the truth: that because of the slowly acquired American conviction of the badness of the German cause—the danger to civilization and ourselves which this country has come to believe inherent in that cause—it is impossible for America to enforce the law—or what America holds to be the law—sharply against England, to take any action which would seriously add to the chances of German victory; to be, in other words, really neutral. Suppose America bold and honest enough to avow the quite simple obvious truth that we are not indifferent as to the outcome of the war and that in the long run our conduct won't be guided as though we were; that so long as we have reason to believe German policy a menace it will encounter in one form or another (not excluding necessarily even the military form) our active or latent opposition.

And then, suppose that on top of that impossibly bold and honest stand this country were further to announce that it can only act effectively for the sea law Germany desires, and otherwise withdraw its opposition, if Germany is prepared to reassure us as to her cause by stating definitely that the terms upon which she is prepared to discuss peace include such things as the evacuation of Belgium and France and indemnification for damage done; the acceptance of the international principles involved in the American claims; recognition of the absolute right to existence of all States great and small; readiness to enter, at least to the extent that others are ready, into European or world arrangements for the guarantee of that right and the mutual discussion and limitation of armaments; together with such minor details as agreement to the appointment of an international commission to enquire into the violation of the laws of war on land and sea and the punishment of the individuals convicted by that commission.

Once convinced that Germany stands for a policy such as peace on those terms would imply, America could on her side (so this impossibly honest diplomacy might make plain) stand effectively for the freedom of the sea as against England if needs be at least to the extent of upholding the Declaration of London; could assure Germany that this country would never be reckoned among her enemies, but on the contrary would co-operate with her in defense of that equality of commercial opportunity in the world of which Germany accuses her enemies of trying to deprive her.

Such a "Declaration of America's International Position" as that which I am here imagining would, in more precise terms, be about as follows:

1. Though America since the outbreak of the war has done everything possible to observe the form of neutrality which international practise had heretofore imposed upon States not actively participating in a war, the circumstances of the present conflict have shown that the future protection of her own particular interests are so identified with the maintenance of certain general rules of international intercourse that in all future wars she will differentiate in her treatment of the combatants. Thus in no case will American resources be available for the military purposes of a belligerent who had entered upon a war refusing to submit his case to enquiry and the necessary delay, and to adhere to certain rules necessary for the safeguarding of innocent non-combatant life.

The United States could not in consequence feel that her relations with Germany could be placed upon a really sound foundation of friendly cooperation until that country had

(a) accepted the international principles (as for instance the sanctity of non-combatant life) involved in the American claims and the further principle that their violation is an unfriendly act towards America whether American life and property are concerned or not;

(b) undertaken to evacuate Belgium, France and Serbia and indemnify Belgium for damage done;

(c) agreed to the appointment of an international commission of inquiry into the violation of the rights of non-combatants on land and sea, with authority to assess damages, and to payment of any damages in which Germany may be cast, and to punishment of individuals convicted of offenses against the laws of war.

On the acceptance of these terms by Germany, America would undertake:

330

A. Not to furnish military or naval aid to Germany's enemies in this war.

B. To become one of the guarantors of the integrity of Belgium.

C. In the event of the creation of new buffer States, to assist in the maintenance of their inviolability by refusing to allow American citizens to furnish their invader with supplies of any nature: by the application, that is, of the principle of differential neutrality above indicated.

D. To accord to German citizens in protectorates subject to American control, commercial access on equal terms with American citizens and to support by the differential neutrality already indicated the policy of the open door in all protectorates and non-self-governing territories. That is to say America would undertake not to furnish military or naval aid to any power or group of powers that refused to apply the principle of the open door in their protectorates, and to prohibit the export of supplies or munitions to such powers in their military operations.

E. To join, *pari passu*, with other powers in any arrangement for enforcing the submission of international disputes to enquiry.

Now whatever followed that announcement America and the world would gain. If Germany refused she would by that prove that she was still unchastened, not ready to surrender or modify her policy of world hegemony. America then knows that her fears are justified. She is definitely warned of a fact which sooner or later she will have to face if it is really a fact. And it is obviously far better that it should become patent to America (and the world) now, than later (after a possibly patched up peace). Indeed, on grounds simply of sheer national security America should attempt by some such means to establish now, when Germany is relatively helpless so far as damaging us is concerned, where she stands, what America faces. It would enable her to make her future policy definite and objective.

But suppose Germany, realizing at last that it is impossible to maintain a national policy which during the next generation or two will have to meet not only the opposition of the Western democracies of Europe and the potential forces of Russia, but all that North America might during the next generation develop into, accepts? What if the German government were pushed by the best elements of the German people to take the opportunity thus so publicly offered for putting themselves right with the world and starting afresh on a more workable basis?

331

If that happened—which after all is the most probable thing of all—America, without striking a blow, would have secured from Germany the main thing for which the Western democracies are now fighting. Not only would she have laid the foundation for the future protection of her own sea rights in the only way in which finally they can be protected—by an international law that is a reality because rooted in a real international order—but she would have helped win the battle of democracy by bringing about a discussion of terms before the democratic nations have bled themselves white.

Never in history had a nation such an opportunity. But to take it means breaking with routine, employing a new method, a new manner; great governmental boldness, great political honesty. And all that is, perhaps, too much to ask.

But that is no reason why we should not face the fact that on those conditions the opportunity is there. Nor why those most responsible for the direction of American public opinion should not help the nation to realize it.

NORMAN ANGELL.

INDEX

Algeciras, 30.

Alliances, 135 ff, 144, 166; prohibited, 94, 250, 266.

Alsace-Lorraine, autonomy of, 245, 260.

American School Peace League, program of, 267.

Angell, Norman, 33, 34, 82, 326.

Annexation, 76, 249, 306, 308, 311, 316, 322, 325.

Arbitration, 249, 251, 254, 262, 271, 306, 324; compulsory, 262, 322, 325.

Armaments, export of, 266; limitation of, 99, 124, 246, 248, 249, 250, 256, 262, 265, 266, 267, 271, 276, 277, 297, 300, 301, 306, 310, 322, 323, 325; national manufacture of, 102 ff, 250, 265, 266, 267, 268, 269, 271, 277, 299, 300, 301, 324.

Armed Peace, 121.

Australian Peace Alliance, program of, 300.

Autonomy, 249, 254, 262, 275, 306, 318, 322.

Backward peoples, 22.

Balance of Power, 94 ff, 124, 265, 277, 301.

Bauer, Otto, 35.

Belgium, restoration of, 245, 260, 262, 274, 301, 320; in-demnity, 321; and Germany, 58, 316, 320.

Berlin Conference of 1885, 29.

Bernstein, Ed., 317.

Bosphorus, neutralization of, 245.

Boycott, economic, 155, 174 ff, 186.

Brailsford, H. N., 302.

Bund Neues Vaterland, program of, 306.

Butler, Nicholas Murray, 275.

Buxton, Charles Roden, 301.

Capital, export of, 14, 21, 256.

Causes of war, 3, 5, 109, 265, 268.

Central "human betterment bureau," 196.

Central Organization for a Durable Peace, program of, 247.

Chamber of Commerce of U. S., program of, 276.

Charte Mondiale, 248.

Citizen Army, 310.

Coercion, international, 130, 133, 134, 155, 160, 174, 184, 251, 255, 264, 270, 276, 293.

Concert of nations, 98, 106, 267, 268, 322, 325.

Commercial privilege as cause of war, 5.

Commission on International Migration, World, 196.

265, 268, 276, 306, 314, 319, 320, 323.

International Parliament, 161, 249.

International Peace Commission, 298.

International organization, 29, 194, 276, 306.

International police force, 152, 181, 249, 264, 265, 268, 271, 310.

International Secretariat, 278, 287.

Justiciable issues, 290.

Kautsky, Karl, 40.

Language, guarantee of, 248.

League of Peace, 78, 79, 85, 120, 131, 135 ff, 143 ff, 165, 169, 270.

League to Enforce Peace, 148, 160, 264.

Like-mindedness, 193.

Loans for war, prohibition of, 186, 267.

Mediation, continuous, 243, 254.

Militarism, 123.

Military service, 109, 152, 266, 301.

Minorities, rights of, 61, 249, 275.

Monetary System, World, 197.

"Most favored nation," 311.

Nationality, 47, 192, 217; freedom of, 249, 254, 262, 275, 306, 318, 322; respect for, 254, 267.

National Peace Convention, program of, 264.

National Peace Council, program of, 298.

Naturalization, 269.

Neutral Conference for Continuous Mediation, program of, 243.

Neutralization of straits and canals, 10, 265, 271, 310, 311, 314, 315, 320; of disputed regions, 324; of Constantinople, 274; of colonies, 315.

Neutral States in peace negotiations, 249, 268, 269, 323.

Non-intercourse, 265.

"Open Door," the, 4, 250, 306, 320 (see Freedom of trade).

Patriotism, 217 ff.

Pacifism, 164.

Peaceful penetration, 23.

Permanent Credit Bureau, 20.

Persia, guarantees for, 60.

Philadelphia Conference of League to Enforce Peace, 170.

Plebiscite in transferred territory, 76, 87, 244, 247, 249, 251, 254, 266, 267, 271, 277, 297, 298, 299, 300, 310, 318, 323.

Preparedness, 269.

Poland, autonomy of, 245, 260.

Press, reform of, 74, 249.

"Principle of the Commonwealth," 227.

Private property at sea, 265.

Publicity organization, World, 197.

Quidde, Dr. L., 316.

Reform Club of New York, memorandum, 4, 10.

Religious liberty, 248.

Rights-of-way, economic, 60.

Scandinavia, guarantees for, 60.

Serbia, autonomy of, 245.

Slovene Unit, guarantees for, 60.